Why journalism?

Real news in the age of lies

Erik Fichtelius

ANIARA

Contents

To my daughters

Hedvig and Ebba

Introduction
What's the purpose of it all?

The question is demanding and concrete. What's the deal? What is the story? The answer facilitates both the gathering of facts and the presentation of news. Call it angle, refinement, simplification, news evaluation or whatever you want. But anyone who knows how to define the deal has found the holy grail of news journalism.

This book is about the purpose of it all. Why we have journalists and journalism. About the importance of real journalism to a democratic society. It is for journalists who want to reflect on and immerse themselves in their mission, and for news audiences who want to understand the reasonable demands placed on news journalism. To all those who want to understand what journalism is about. That journalists publish news because it is news and nothing else. But to understand that you need to know what a real news story is, and above all, what the "others" are. This requires us to clarify the concepts.

The title is inspired by Åsa Wikforss and Mårten Wikforss' book Therefore Democracy. Journalism is needed for democracy to work. I want to deepen and explain what kind of journalism is needed. Why Journalism is an adaptation and continuation of my book Real News. I have updated, shortened, added, and tried to refine my argument based on the challenging question in the introduction.

In doing so, I continue to knead the subject I have returned to in many books and lectures, namely the elusive and evasive concept of news. Although I have been a news journalist for over fifty years, I still struggle to understand what news is.

I am trying to define the concept of news, and with it the mission and responsibility of the news reporter. To do so, I have to grapple with concepts such as truth and relevance, objectivity, impartiality and unbiasedness. In doing so, I can rely on what others have written and researched, delve into the history of journalism, and draw on my own practical experience.

This book is based on Real News, but also on my earlier books What is News and News Journalism - Ten Golden Rules. It was a particularly exciting and enjoyable intellectual challenge to work hard on a revision of a book I had already written. It's fun to shorten, sharpen, and refine. A "finished" text gets a second chance.

The point is that real journalism should be independent and objective. It should not be thesis-driven, and the news reporter should be free of clients other than his or her own audience or readership and should refrain from pushing his or her own agenda.

A society needs journalists so that everyone can find out what happened as soon as possible. Preferably also when and where, who was involved, and how and why it happened. This touches on deep human needs. The questions of when, where, how, who, what and why are classic. The need for real news becomes shockingly clear when systematic lies become part of the public discourse. When anti-democratic forces seek to destroy the conditions and credibility of public institutions, part of the defense of democracy lies in reporting based on verifiable facts. Where journalists do not select news based on their own opinions or agendas. Journalism is needed to give everyone a common platform of facts and reality to have a conversation about what we should do and where we should go.

Humans need news to survive as a group or species. In the beginning of time, when people lived in small groups in caves or on the savannah, they had to stick together to survive. Cohesion required shared and reliable information. Everyone needed to know the location of prey or if there was a fire nearby. If an enemy or dangerous wild animal was approaching, the group needed to know so they could plan their defense.

Knowledge of social events and relationships was also important for the organization and management of the group. It was not necessarily the physically strongest who became tribal leader, but the one with the strongest social network. Those who could form alliances, who knew who was trustworthy and who was an enemy, could become leaders. Even gossip was important. The interest in and need for news is probably woven into the human genome.

Accidents, crimes, scandals, and sensations are the basic ingredients of news reporting in most cultures. The ancient Greeks, of course, were the first to systematize news reporting. When the Greeks defeated the Persians at the Battle of Marathon in 490 B.C., it was big news and important to get it to Athens quickly. The Greek soldier Pheidippides ran the 42 kilometers to the capital with the news of the victory. He was one of the first messengers. Incorrect or delayed information about who had won would have been devastating.

The Romans later figured out how to spread the news more widely. The news was published in special Acta Diurna, carved in stone or engraved on metal, which contained judgments and news from the Senate. The first Acta Diurna was placed on the wall of the Forum Romanum in 131 BC. It soon expanded to include reports of births and deaths, divorces, trials, military events, strange dogs, and sensations from the court. Fires, the crucifixion of slaves, and social gossip became the main news to attract an audience. The Acta Diurna had its own staff who gathered news in the first news service in history.

All the rules, ethics, laws and regulations, freedom of the press and expression, impartiality, objectivity, independence, and consequence neutrality that I write about are methods to make the system work. It all boils down to answering the question: What is the purpose of it all - why journalism, or what is the deal?

I have chosen to work with the concept of *consequence neutrality* to try to understand and analyze how journalism should work in the service of democracy. Consequence neutrality means that the news reporter should report what is true and relevant to the best of his or her ability, regardless of who or what benefits or suffers from the news. The reporter should be neutral about the consequences of the news and not pursue his or her own political agenda. But real news is about much more. Reporting real news has demands that must be met and conflicts of interest that must be resolved.

The fact that reporters and editors are becoming activists is perhaps one of the greatest threats to effective news reporting. When journalists and media companies fail to maintain impartiality and objectivity in news reporting, the foundations of public discourse are threatened and journalism fails in its important social role. Citizens deserve real news that is not cherry-picked or colored by the agenda of the broadcaster or the demands of the state.

It is a threat to democracy when those in power turn reporters into their enemies or enemies of the people. When these enemies of democracy try to turn real news into fake news, it becomes more important than ever for editors to defend their mission and for reporters to defend their professional identity.

To exercise power is to do something to achieve some effect. It is not a power that belongs to journalists. When reporters try to seize such power, the balance of society is threatened. Members of governments or parliaments and business leaders have executive power and can legitimately try to get their way. Editorial writers and opinion makers can, of course, try to influence power by writing and advocating policies or solutions. But the news reporter may not exercise such power. Reporters must not impose their views on others and impose their own solutions.

These simple requirements are not taken for granted today.

In 2017-2021, an authoritarian president in the United States has damaged democracy, in part by portraying free and fact-based media as "enemies of the people. At the same time, authoritarian regimes in the former Eastern Europe have resurrected the ghosts

of the communist era and acquired pro-regime media to control
the population. In Turkey, critics of the regime are systematically
imprisoned.

There are political leaders who want newspapers, radio and
television to report in favor of the government in power, even
in democratic countries. There are unthinking rulers, even in
Sweden, who want the news media to defend their "own" party,
company or society. It is bad enough when this development is
imposed from above. That is why it is important to be especially
vigilant when threats come from within, from media or employees
who are unable or unwilling to defend the classic virtues of
democratic news reporting. Various activist demand

Various activist demands that journalism defend or fight for
this or that supposedly good thing are completely misguided. This
is as true of the demands of the Maoist left in the early 1970s
as it is of the identity politics activists or right-wing nationalist
propagandists of the 2020s.

The liberal journalistic doctrine was well articulated in an 1852
editorial in The Times of London:

The first duty of the press is to obtain the earliest and most
correct intelligence of the events of the day and to make it
immediately, by revealing it, the property of the nation. The
politician collects information in secret and by secret methods,
he withholds even the loose information of the day with
unreasonable caution until the diplomacy of silence has lost the
battle against publicity. The press lives by disclosure: everything
that comes into its possession becomes part of the knowledge and

history of our time; it appeals daily and forever to the enlightened demands of public opinion.

What is the responsibility of the journalist? The Times continues:

The responsibility is more nearly akin to that of the economist or the lawyer, whose province is not to frame a system of convenient application to the exigencies of the day but to investigate truth and apply it on fixed principles to the affairs of the world. The duty of the journalist is the same as that of the historian - to seek the truth above all else and to present to his readers not what politics would like, but the truth as best he can find it.

The Times editorial captures the essence of a liberal press ideology. These ideas live on through the years in media policy documents around the world. They are more relevant and urgent today. But now we are inundated daily with propaganda, lies, fake news, and alternative facts. Media researchers talk about junk news, spread to confuse and influence. Democratic elections are threatened by troll factories and influence operations.6 Old-fashioned concepts like impartiality and objectivity, as well as the requirement for news providers to distinguish between news and views, are being challenged. Today, anyone can publish anything online, and the old gatekeeper function of newsrooms has been lost. News reporting is a way to verify facts, but with everything happening in real time, control and relevance assessment is weakened.

AI technology makes it increasingly easy to produce and falsify text, images and video. This increases the demands on journalistic institutions that are committed to not fabricating. What happens to journalism when news images are created directly from text, when the speeches of heads of state are fabricated, or when a chatbot can write texts that are completely in line with what living humans can achieve? It's food for thought when Chat GPT can define the concept of real news in a matter of seconds:

Real news refers to accurate, reliable, and verifiable information reported by credible sources. Unlike fake news, which is intentionally misleading or false, real news is intended to provide an accurate and objective account of events, facts and issues. Real news is an important part of a healthy and informed society, allowing people to stay informed and make informed decisions about the world around them.

A computer-generated text is different from a text set in lead, as it was when I started in the profession. I have come a long way in journalism and have faced many dilemmas as a reporter. I have lived with news from the time I wrote in the school column of *Upsala Nya Tidning* at the age of fourteen until today. For more than five decades I have worked as a journalist in various roles, mainly in public service, as a reporter, manager and publisher, but also as a teacher and author.

The philosopher Aristotle said, "Truth is to say of what is that it is, and of what is not that it is not". That goes a long way for a journalist. A spade should be called a spade, lies and hypocrisy should be exposed. I found my drive early on.

What made me so interested in Poland, which I write about in detail here, was probably the utterly shameless lies and hypocrisy in Eastern Europe. But similar lies and hypocrisy exist today and closer to home. I've heard self-righteous EU commissioners and Swedish politicians speak in platitudinous and solemn nonsense as if they were Polish party officials. When politics is at its worst, voters are faced with an elastic, plastic language that needs to be translated to be understood. That's when journalists are needed.

Hypocrisy and lies are particularly visible and tangible to a consumer reporter. From the "Falu sausage with beef in it" that lacks the detail of the beef cut, to the jar of "strawberry jam" that was never closer to a strawberry than the one rolled over the lid, to the large-scale and cynical food fraud. The Swedish agribusiness industry boasted of its pure, fine Swedish food, while its industries mixed rotting carcasses, slaughterhouse waste, dogs and cats into the "craft food" for the cannibalized cattle and livestock. Critics were silenced, problems were downplayed, and directors lied. The British Minister of Agriculture stood in front of the TV cameras in 1990 with his four-year-old daughter eating hamburgers to "prove" that there was nothing dangerous about British meat when mad cow disease broke out. That's how it used to be in Poland.

Journalists are needed to expose such things. They are also needed to report on the peace-loving Swedish foreign policy, which is based on huge arms exports, made profitable by large-scale smuggling and bribery. The journalist does not need to have an agenda, it is enough to tell it like it is. The reporter is neither a megalomaniac nor an enemy of the people.

Former US President Trump lied at least 15 times a day during his time in office, according to Washington Post calculations.

But President Kennedy also lied, and President Biden certainly tells untruths from time to time. It's a good thing that there are independent journalists who do their best to find the "best available version of the truth," as journalist Carl Bernstein put it. Journalists who do not let the president alone decide what is in the "national interest".

Sweden needs more local reporters and fewer municipal information officers. The local newspaper should not report in order to "put the municipality on the map", but to independently inform citizens about what is happening there. Society does not need more and louder shouting "alternative media", who accuse everyone else of fake news, while they themselves pump out hate and propaganda. The only alternative they offer is alternative facts. The media landscape doesn't need fake "news" sites that hide their propagandistic intentions behind a neutral facade.

With this book, I wanted to highlight experiences from practice, both my own and from history and research. The boundaries between the different roles make it all exciting. There is, and should be, a difference between being an opinion leader and a news reporter. During my time as a reporter, I had to give up some of my obvious civil liberties in Sweden to always say what I think. The difficulty of this and the attraction of being involved and influential is what makes the demand for objectivity so difficult and in some contexts even controversial. Ultimately, it is the responsibility of the editors to ensure that the rules and ethics are followed. This is also true when activists within a media company want to fight, for example, against nuclear power, racism and perceived injustice, or for generous immigration policies and a better climate. Of course, anyone who wants to can take action on an issue they care about. But this cannot be combined with news coverage and other programs on the same issue.

Anyone who wants to turn their own newsroom into a platform to fight for this or that cause is helping to weaken the credibility of the newsroom. The news reporter is not on anyone's side. In this sense, the news reporter is both faithless and ruthless.

The ongoing wars in the world make this so clear. The first casualty of war is the truth, but that shouldn't stop the reporter from trying to find the truth as best he can. Reporting from the Middle East has always been difficult, with constant attacks on reporters accused of being biased toward either Israel or the Palestinians. With the Hamas terrorist attack on October 7, 2023 and Israel's response, it is becoming increasingly difficult to report accurately and independently. Reporting is hampered by the reporter's inability to be on the ground, but also by manipulated images, false claims and outright propaganda. Stories and allegations are posted on social media to influence public opinion, not to give a true picture of what actually happened.

It is at times like these that the world needs real news. Russia's large-scale invasion is not a special operation against Nazis, but an attack on a sovereign state in violation of international law. But the Russian people have been caught in a web of lies.

These are not new challenges for reporters. When I began my journalism career in the late 1960s, the Vietnam War was at its worst. The United States was the aggressor. But then, as now, reporters were asked to take a stand for "good" against "evil. The US was waging a war in Southeast Asia that violated international law. Demonstrating against the U.S. war, for Vietnamese independence, was a matter of course.

Of course, for a citizen and a student in Uppsala in 1968. But for a reporter? Could you walk with a clenched left fist and a microphone in your right hand? What was the point of reporting? Why journalism? What was my mission as a reporter?

There were two ways to photograph a Vietnam demonstration in my hometown Uppsala, where the main road from the university library descended from a large hill down to the city center.

1 The photographer stands on the main square with a powerful telephoto lens on a tripod. He points the camera at the hill, several hundred meters away. Even a tiny trickle of people is squeezed into the telephoto lens. It turns into a powerful crowd, with banners and flags fluttering proudly in the wind. These are the people marching for peace and justice!

2 The photographer stands at the end of the hill, just where the steep road flattens out and ends at the corner of Nedre Slottsgatan. With a wide-angle lens, the picture is taken from the side, against some dull building facades. Even the most powerful demonstration here turns into a sparse line of confused hippies, and you can't even read what's on the banners because they're facing forward, not the photographer at the side.

I grew up with these two journalistic perspectives, especially in the days of the Vietnam demonstrations. The reporter and photographer of the communist newspaper *Gnistan (*The Spark) stood in the main square with a telephoto lens. *UNTs* dark blue editorial writer, who also doubled as a reporter, preferred to have the photographer stand at the corner at the bottom of the hill. Both portrayed the demonstration. Both were equally false, but for the same reason. The different teams were not reporting, they were playing their own politics. But the propagandistic intent was hidden behind a journalistic facade.

This is the experience I carry with me today when I hear calls for the media to report in support of Israel or Palestine, Russia or Ukraine. When I hear calls for the media to report to save us from the climate crisis, or to defend the rights of various groups, or some kind of identity politics. Journalism makes the world a better place, but not by telling us how, but by reporting what the world looks like.

Stockholm, March 2024

Erik Fichtelius

Mom, dinner and bribes

My mother was a textile artist in Uppsala. During a fancy dinner in the early summer of 1987 at the home of a well-established businessman in town, things suddenly got a bit tricky for her. Over coffee, the host began to rant about the terrible journalists:

- They are all communists. Tear down and destroy! Just think what they did to Bofors, the big Swedish arms manufacturer. Now the entire Swedish business community is infected with suspicions of bribery. It is becoming more and more difficult to do business abroad. The Indian government is threatened. Sweden's good relations with India are going down the drain. Bofors loses value. Journalists should think about what they are doing. They should take responsibility for the consequences! And the worst is Dagens Eko!

- Yes, but Erik is the boss there. My son...

The mood turned bad by the table. Mom had to leave soon, went home and called me the next morning. Her story raised a question in my mind.

Surely Ekot (the newsroom of national radio) should not take responsibility for the consequences for the arms manufacturer Bofors, for Swedish industry, for the memory of the assassinated

Prime Minister Olof Palme, for the relations between Sweden and India, for Prime Minister Rajiv Gandhi or for the Swedish government? The responsibility of the news organization must be to tell what has happened to the best of our ability if it is important for the audience to know. If this leads to Bofors becoming a dirty word in India or Olof Palme's peace work being associated with arms sales and bribes, it cannot be Ekot's fault. The reporter must remain neutral regarding these consequences. It occurred to me during my mother's conversation that a good word for this might be consequence neutrality.

In the winter of 1987, I was appointed head of the news department in Swedish Radio, the national public service radio company. In the spring, I launched a major project to investigate the Bofors affair as one of my first tasks. Bofors in Karlskoga was Sweden's largest arms manufacturer and had long been accused of shady dealings. In the fall of 1986 and spring of 1987 there were many reports and rumors about the company. Suspicions that Bofors had smuggled weapons to forbidden countries had been investigated by police and prosecutors since 1984. In the fall of 1986, Bofors managers were forced to admit that Robot 70 had ended up in Dubai and Bahrain on the Persian Gulf. The company managers claimed that the responsibility for this lay with the government and the Inspectorate of War Material.

The whistleblower Ingvar Bratt, a civil engineer at Bofors in Karlskoga, Sweden, had revealed how the major arms manufacturer had been smuggling parts of its production to countries in the Arab world that were forbidden to export.

How could the country's largest arms manufacturer allow part of its production to be illegally exported to prohibited buyers? This was the great mystery that surrounded the Bofors company. On one hand Sweden should have a strong defense and its own production of weapons, submarines, tanks and fighter planes was a cornerstone of Swedish neutrality and an important part of non-alignment. Simultaneously, Sweden is an important arms supplier to the rest of the world. Exports are profitable. Perhaps nothing to brag about, but a reality for Swedish employment and neutrality. Bofors' operations were reasonably transparent to military, police, civilian and other security services.

But on the other hand it should be practically and theoretically impossible that a large part of the production could take place in secret and be smuggled out. Not a single nut could be produced in Karlskoga without the knowledge of the Swedish government.

My idea that Bofors should be investigated was no more substantiated than a lot of questions. It smelled bad. There is something wrong with Bofors and it has been going on for years! It is not enough what the Swedish Peace and Arbitration Association says, Ekot must have its own facts on the matter. Now I had become the head of the country's most important newsroom with its own resources for independent investigative journalism. I muttered in the hallway that this should be investigated. I was laughed at by Titti Nylander, the foreign affairs reporter:

- Yeah, yeah, yeah, you guys are all talk. Do something!

As the new managing editor, I had room to maneuver and I set up a cross-editorial team that was not tied to the rolling schedule and was given a free hand.

- Find out everything you can about Bofors! There's something strange going on ...

A couple of weeks went by and nothing happened. A few weeks later, the team still had not found anything new. Soon things started to get tough for me as the new manager. Where are all the reporters? complained the producers that led the daily operations in the newsroom. Whenever the news desk needed a reporter, he or she seemed to be taken off schedule to pursue some fruitless, fuzzy idea that the managing editor had in his head.

- What the hell is Erik doing? We're supposed to be broadcasting news!

It was getting sweaty. I realized that the project didn't have much time left. In a way, the producers were right. Investigative projects could not be allowed to undermine the main mission of daily news broadcasting. I was also well aware that the key to success as head of news was to have the important and skilled producers on board. More than one of my predecessors had fallen by the wayside for lack of support from the editors of the shows. At that time, there was no organization in place for investigative journalism.

I almost threw in the towel just before the breakthrough came in early April. But then it was something completely different from what we had in mind at first. What we found was not about arms smuggling. Instead, Ekot found completely new and well-documented information about how Bofors paid many millions of kronor in suspected bribes to win a large order for field howitzers, heavy mobile artillery, for India. This was the largest single export deal by a Swedish company to date, worth SEK 8.4 billion. In 2024 it will be worth more than SEK 18 billion, or 2 billion US dollars. To win the contract in competition with, among others, a French arms manufacturer, Bofors apparently had to pay bribes. Initially, Ekot was able to document how Bofors paid over SEK 30 million to secret bank accounts at the Swiss Bank Corporation in Zurich in connection with the deal. Ekot broke the news on Maundy Thursday, April 16, 1987.

To be honest, no one in the newsroom understood how explosive this was. One of the staff members was completely opposed to running the story; it was not news that a large Swedish company was paying bribes, he thought.

But of course, it was news! The story was aired rather unplanned over the Easter weekend, when the producer in charge thought he didn't have much else to put on air. News is not always well planned. I myself was away from the newsroom for hernia surgery when the story went out. That's why Kerstin Brunnberg, the deputy managing editor, had to take the first hit. There was a big bang, but not the one we thought. The fact that large Swedish companies pay bribes or participate in international illegal cartels may be interesting, but it does not cause much outrage at home. This was big and important news, but Ekot had not realized it was world news. Nor did the news initially attract much attention in other Swedish media over the Easter weekend. Newspapers did not even come out on Good Friday. Bofors, for its part, denied any talk of bribery, but could not credibly explain the large payments. Ekot's reporters found strong documentation that withstood decades of Swedish and international scrutiny by police, prosecutors, and other investigators.

But it was only by chance that the revelation of Bofors' alleged bribery became world news. Coincidentally, at the end of 1986/87, just before I took over as head of news, the Swedish national news agency TT's monopoly on distributing the material of the London-based Reuters news agency in Sweden came to an end. The old Reuters distribution monopoly had long been a major source of irritation for Swedish radio. Reuters was the biggest and best international agency, but its telegrams reached Ekot with a delay of several hours. First, the *Tidningarnas Telegram Bureau*, TT, received the news, which was then evaluated, selected, translated and forwarded to the Swedish subscribers. Ekot had to make do with the American Associated press and the UPI news agency. I was interested in a separate agreement with Reuters, and they were interested in expanding their Scandinavian clientele. So an agreement was signed quite quickly. And in the spring of that year, Reuters and Ekot became good friends. Reuters even began to listen to and refer to Ekot when the program had something of interest to the world.

Therefore Reuters broadcast Ekot's news about Bofors all over the world. Swedish National Radio is a credible source, and in India it immediately went viral. The country's prime minister, Rajiv Gandhi, had promoted himself as "Mr. Clean," the man who would clean up corruption and shady deals. Now it was revealed that people close to him had been involved in receiving millions of dollars from the Swedish arms manufacturer Bofors for an arms contract. The scandal was a fact, and the Indian opposition immediately raised its voice in parliament. Gandhi, grandson of the country's independence hero and first prime minister, Jawaharlal Nehru, was exposed as a corrupt liar. Ekot had to rush its Asia correspondent, Rolf Porseryd, to India. As soon as he arrived, he began reporting on huge demonstrations, demands for an investigation and the resignation of the prime minister. Bofors became an Indian dirty word and would even become a verb in various Indian dialects: to do a Bofors, to pay a bribe.

Rolf Porseryd received a lot of attention in India. He himself had to hold press conferences on Ekot's revelation and was shadowed by security agents. Rajiv Gandhi hit back by accusing Swedish Radio of following the lead of the American intelligence agency CIA. Ekot was "part of a conspiracy and to have spread false allegations on behalf of the CIA in order to destabilize the Indian system and damage the regime", according to the Indian Prime Minister.

In the late 1980s, it was possible to make direct phone calls to people in power. Carl-Johan Åberg was Prime Minister Olof Palme's trade secretary and had traveled with him to India the previous year. Palme was in India as part of the Non-Aligned Movement's work on peace and freedom.

- Bofors could not have paid a bribe. Olof Palme promised when he met Rajiv Gandhi that there would be no intermediaries, Carl-Johan Åberg told us when Ekot's reporters called to check information in India about Palme's involvement. We had not recognized this connection from the beginning.

What Carl Johan Åberg effectively confirmed to the unsuspecting reporters was that Olof Palme and Rajiv Gandhi had discussed field howitzers and not just peace and non-alignment. The Swedish prime minister was involved in the affair. What was his responsibility for the fact that commissions had been paid anyway? The whole thing began to develop into a growing Swedish scandal that would tarnish Palme's memory as a peace broker.

Olof Palme was murdered in February 1986 and could not be held accountable. But the affair shook the Social Democrats and the Swedish government. Relations between Sweden and India deteriorated dramatically. Mama's dinner host was absolutely right, the reputation of the entire Swedish business community was damaged, not to mention the sinking of the Bofors brand.

In his memoirs, Ingvar Carlsson, Palme's deputy as prime minister, and successor precisely describes these damaging effects when he devotes a large section to the Bofors affair. Bofors, the Swedish export industry, Sweden's relations with India, Rajiv Gandhi's position, all were affected, according to Ingvar Carlsson. He also openly states that such a large export deal always requires government support. Efforts had been underway for several years, and Olof Palme had personally raised the matter with both Prime Minister Indira Gandhi and her representative, her son Rajiv Gandhi. The Swedish embassy in India urged the Swedish government to show its support, not least to counter Bofors' French competitors.

The Indians had complained several times in diplomatic contacts about "unauthorized" agents, and the Indian government had said it wanted to put an end to such intermediaries. The issue of middlemen had come up in talks between Carl Johan Åberg, Olof Palme and Rajiv Gandhi, both during the fortieth anniversary of the UN in New York in October 1985 and during Olof Palme's visit to India in January 1986. According to Ingvar Carlsson's account, Palme conveyed assurances from Bofors that there would be no intermediaries. This is what Åberg referred to when Ekot asked him about the first publication.

But Ekot had shown that huge payments had been made to secret bank accounts in Switzerland. Ekot's reporter Jan Mosander gives a vivid and dramatic description of Swedish hypocrisy and bribery in a chapter on the scandal in his book Among Spies, Communists and Arms Dealers. It soon became clear that the bribery was much more extensive than Ekot had thought. Within a few weeks, the reporters had documented payments of SEK 250 million. Investigations by the National Audit Office, police and prosecutors later revealed that Bofors had paid a total of SEK 310 million in what the company called first "commissions" and then "liquidation" costs.

Ekot's investigation got a dramatic breakthrough after a mysterious phone call to me as head of Ekot. I remember a dark, slightly mysterious voice that never introduced itself.

The call came just after lunch a few weeks after the first revelation. It was from a person who claimed to be well versed in

Bofors matters. The anonymous source provided a few new details about the payments, and I took notes as carefully as I could.

Excited and confused, I gathered Ekot's Bofors group. This must be checked out. What should we make of the anonymous person's claims? They couldn't be taken at face value, but the information meant that Ekot knew better where and what to look for. The mysterious source's information was accurate and could be verified. He refused to give his name and was never heard from again. One of the editors' most important sources remained anonymous, but still useful.

The Indian opposition rallied around Prime Minister Gandhi. The protests in India grew, and Rajiv Gandhi found it increasingly difficult to face the elections that would follow in 1989. Investigations and suspicions crept closer and closer to Gandhi and the Congress Party leadership, but his direct involvement could never be proven. Rajiv Gandhi lost power as head of government in the fall of 1989, and he publicly blamed much of the election loss on the Bofors affair.

- I think it was the Bofors issue that broke us," Gandhi said in an interview with the Associated Press after the defeat.

Ekot's news brought down the government of one of the world's largest countries. But the great mystery of how Sweden's largest war industry was able to smuggle so much of its production without government intervention was never really answered.

The news could have led to a war between India and Pakistan. Some reports circulated that Gandhi had planned an attack on the archenemy in the final stages of the election campaign. War with a neighbor always strengthens the government in power. But it never came to that.

But maybe I should have thought about the consequences?

25

Fichtelius' name must no longer appear in the paper!

In a small, rented flat in the city Nynäshamn south of Stockholm lives a long-haired and bearded guru-like genius. He is not unhappy, though he is poor and simple. If there were any justice in the world, however, we wouldn't meet Torgny Tholerus in a simple apartment, but in a luxury bungalow by the sea of at least 1,000 square meters, with a swimming pool, tennis court and a couple of Teslas in the garage. Torgny Tholerus single-handedly developed a Facebook-like network decades before Facebook founder Mark Zuckerberg. But that was in a different time and a different country, long before the time was right. Torgny Tholerus had very early ideas about how people could communicate with each other, and he had the opportunity to develop one of the world's first electronic messaging systems in Sweden. But he was too early.

I met Torgny Tholerus at the end of the sixties, and that led to a new direction in my life, because I was fired as a journalist before I even started. I was 19 years old and a freelancer at the newspaper in my hometown, Upsala Nya Tidning, UNT. When I was growing up, the paper had one page a week on school issues, and I started writing there when I was 14. I was allowed to write elsewhere in the paper, paid by the line or by the story, when I turned 17. That led to summer jobs, temporary jobs, and freelance work on a regular basis. When I started, the newspaper was based in an old building in the middle of the city, in the Old Square, down by the river Fyrisån. The paper was still set in led and printed in the basement. The times I managed to stay at the paper until the printing started at night, I could feel the whole house shaking as the presses rumbled and rolled away. It was a wonderful feeling to have the ink from the fresh morning paper on my fingers. My career choice was clear. In the fall of 1969, I was studying sociology at the university, writing news articles for the UNT and sometimes for Avdelning Alma, a student section in the paper every Thursday. The editor was a promising young journalist named Bertil Jobéus.

But I was fired. A budding career in journalism would be cut short before it had even begun.

It was October 1969. The student union newspaper, Ergo, had a somewhat amusing article about a group of anarchists who were planning to organize nudist meetings. "People need to get over their shyness and show each other what they really are," was the idea of one of the anarchists.

The managing editor of UNT thought this sounded like fun, so he asked the editor of Section Alma, Bertil Jobéus, to interview the anarchist in question. Bertil asked me, the obedient young freelancer. "Check Ergo, interview the chief anarchist about the planned nudist meetings," the managing editor ordered.

Yes, I said, and made an appointment with the long-haired student of philosophy Torgny Tholerus, who seemed as anachronistic as the anarchist leader. It was to be one of the most difficult interviews of my life. We met at Café Rosen, upstairs from the Karl Marx Bookstore. It was a spartanly decorated café with white-painted walls, posters of Marx, Mao, and Che Guevara on the walls, and, as I recall, rather bland tea.

Torgny Tholerus said almost nothing for an hour. He was obviously very shy. Would he be less shy with his clothes off? It was clear and cold in the fall, but he was still barefoot and had long, unkempt hair, almost Jesus-like. After an hour, Torgny began to thaw out and gently told me about the planned nudist meetings. They would be organized in a large apartment or in the bathhouse. No one could pretend anything by showing themselves to each other as God created us. Everyone could let go of prejudices and shyness.

I don't really know what the editor had in mind. Sex orgies and snake pits? That did not seem to be part of Torgny's cautious plans. They hadn't even found a suitable venue yet. And for the first meetings, Torgny only wanted to invite people who already knew each other, according to the article I wrote later. I still have the yellowed clip. Torgny describes how he wanted the meetings to take place in the nude:

- All participants undress first and then make contact in a kind of ritual embrace. The rest of the program is not fixed, but more serious discussions and games can be included.

He did not appear to be a particularly dangerous anarchist. Although the Anarchist Cooperation Group consisted of only ten members at the time, the idea was to build a miniature society that would grow to encompass all of humanity. There would be "maximum cooperation and flow of information, with maximum individual freedom. The tool was the open submission magazine *Anarkisten*, published by Torgny. The paper was stenciled and accepted all submissions at length.

To me, the magazine seemed more original and revolutionary than the nude dating scene. Anyone could write anything, in any length. Everyone had the right to be heard. That sounded rather anarchistic in an organizational sense. But how would it actually work? Torgny Tholerus had no answers, it was more of a liberal idea. Freedom, not censorship!

What could become of that in the UNT? The managing editor wanted to include the nudist meetings, I wanted to write more about the magazine with open submissions. The result was a rather modest three-column article in the following Thursday's Avdelning Alma under the headline "Difficult and blunt".

The article described the planned nudist meetings, the open-submission magazine, and Torgny's statement that he did not believe in a bloody, violent revolution. This did not prevent one or more readers from going berserk that Thursday morning and calling the editor-in-chief, i.e. the responsible publisher, not the managing editor who had come up with the idea in the first place.

- How can the liberal UNT promote anarchists? This is a scandal! was the chorus of complaints from some readers.

The editor-in-chief was furious. His editorial policy was that the paper should distinguish between news and views. The paper did not take a political line on the news pages; that was reserved for the editorial page. This is a position I share, but now the UNT was being criticized for writing positively about anarchists. The editor-in-chief felt that the representative interviewed had been addressed too intimately and sympathetically by his first name, Torgny. Not the candidate of philosophy, Tholerus.

The editor-in-chief's quick and spontaneous decision was to fire Bertil Jobéus, who had published the article in the Alma section. The managing editor remained silent, not even pretending that the article was his idea and order. Although this was a long time ago, in the sixties, at a time when workers' rights were not very strong, people could not be fired at will. Bertil Jobéus was a permanent editor and a member of the Swedish Journalists' Union.

The union intervened. At noon the hasty dismissal of Bertil Jobéus was withdrawn. But there must be a punishment for the terrible publicity given to the anarchists. Fichtelius was only a freelance student, paid by the article. He was not contracted to work and was too young to even be allowed to join the Union.

"Fichtelius' name must not appear in the paper again," was the editor-in-chief's decision. So, there I was. Without intending or wanting to "promote anarchism". I had no opinion about whether what Torgny Tholerus wanted to do was good or bad. I just told about his plans, what he thought and what he said. The editor and the managing editor thought it was news.

Bertil Jobéus kept me informed about the dramatic developments in the newsroom during the day. The managing editor did not get in touch with me but let Bertil Jobéus know that I could indeed continue writing in the paper, as long as I wrote unsigned and stayed out of sight from the editor-in-chief. The message was literally that my name could no longer appear. There was no explicit prohibition for me to continue writing.

How long could I stay away from the editor-in-chief? Would it be possible to hypocritically continue writing in the UNT behind his back? The situation was both absurd and untenable. Bertil Jobéus quickly came to the conclusion that he could not stay here. He applied for the Foreign Ministry's trainee program and was accepted by the end of the year. Bertil went on to have a brilliant diplomatic career, becoming head of the ministry's press office, consul general and ambassador.

For me, it was my first lesson in consequence neutrality and the beginning of my professional life.

At the same time, UNT had announced elsewhere that Swedish Radio was planning to open a local branch in Uppsala. The country's fourth-largest city, home to universities and important industries, had only UNT as its news provider, apart from the stenciled, open-submission newspaper. Gösta Knutsson, a prominent figure in Uppsala and the author of children's books about the cat *Pelle Svanslös*, had been the city's only radio representative. Now he was about to retire.

I called the Swedish Radio switchboard in Stockholm and asked to speak to the head of regional radio operations. His name was Olof Wahlund. He was very official and explained to me, the young freelance student in Uppsala, that they would certainly need contributors. But I should be patient and wait for the appointment of the head of Radio Uppland.

It took only a few weeks, and on the new station manager's first day at work, I called, introduced myself, and referred to my conversation with Olof Wahlund. The mere mention of Wahlund's name aroused respect, and I was immediately invited for an interview.

An interesting detail in this context is that this Wahlund, who was in charge of all regional operations of Swedish Radio, had a secret extra assignment. It was later revealed he worked for IB, the secret intelligence service of the Social Democrats to identify and fight communists. IB stood for Informations Byrån or Inhämtning Birger, after its head, Birger Elmér. Olof Wahlund was one of Elmér's closest men, and he was destined to be appointed to lead the whole operation. Things fell apart when the IB was exposed by the magazine *Folket i Bild Kulturfront* in May 1973. Olof Wahlund eventually got a new job at the Ministry of Defense. The commissions that later investigated the scandal were able to show that the IB had several agents at Sveriges Radio and TV, but also at other major newsrooms and newspapers.15 Despite all assurances of independence, autonomy and impartial reporting, there was a clear link between the state and Sveriges Radio, and opinion and political influence through spying on the press.

Of course, keeping an eye on all the regional offices of Sveriges Radio was a top job for an IB operator. But neither I nor the public knew anything about this in 1969. So, after I was fired from UNT, I ended up at a job interview at Swedish Radio with a reference to the secret IB chief. But he had no direct influence on my employment. I got the job because I managed to get the tape recorder to work. The newly appointed station manager explained to me at length how difficult it was to operate the Nagra, the expensive and heavy but portable Swiss tape recorder used by all radio companies in the world. Before he could start the exclusive tape recorder, the phone rang and I was left alone with the technical marvel. But a large knob clearly marked on/off, and I started recording while the boss was on the phone. When he hung up, the tape was already rolling. He was very impressed with my talent and announced that the permanent freelance job was mine. I managed to publish three unsigned articles in the UNT, but on December 5, 1969, my first news story from Uppsala was published in the national radio news.

My life took a new turn. And for Torgny Tholerus, too. It soon became clear to him that a stencil magazine that would publish everything was rather cumbersome. After ten issues, when it finally reached 600 copies, Torgny Tholerus gave up. His vision of a completely free flow of information would require something other than a stencil machine.

Tholerus must be considered a genius. He earned his bachelor's degree in mathematics and other subjects in a record 14 months. He then went on to study theoretical philosophy, but soon found another path. If everyone were to publish everything freely for everyone, it would require something that did not exist in 1969. This something existed only as a vision in Torgny Tholerus' mind. To devote himself to this task, he became a computer programmer and disappeared from my sight.

In the early 1980s, I wrote a lot about the new phenomenon of personal computers and became involved in the computerization of the news room in public service broadcasting.16 To research my stories, I used a new computerized information system at Stockholm University. It was the KOM system at the Stockholm computer center, QZ. At that time it was called an electronic graffiti board or a conference system for computer users.

In 1984, I was working on an article about "electronic conferencing systems" and was stunned when I suddenly realized who had developed KOM. It was a unique computerized messaging system, long before the Web and even before Arpanet, the US defense computer system that would later evolve into the Internet starting in 1969. Here it was possible for anyone to freely publish anything for anyone to read, just like the idea of the open newspaper. It was more primitive, slower, and not as neat and simple as today's social media platforms. But it existed in Sweden in the early eighties, and the man behind it was Torgny Tholerus. The chief anarchist and philosopher had become a super programmer. The talented mathematician and programmer had gotten a job at the Computer Science Laboratory at Uppsala University. In 1972 he met a kindred spirit: Jacob Palme, one of the heads of the Swedish defense research agency FOA, who was giving a lecture in Uppsala. Torgny handed over a paper summarizing his ideas for a public information system that would work with terminals in public libraries. This became a development project at FOA, and in 1974 Tholerus was hired by FOA to build an internal communication system. The project was supported by another Swedish Internet pioneer, Tomas Ohlin, who brought the FORUM system from the USA, the world's first electronic conferencing system. Tholerus was tasked with translating it into Swedish, but soon realized that the system had major limitations. When FOA moved, Tholerus was asked to develop FOA's own "teleconferencing system". He then developed KOM, and the Swedish Armed Forces got one of the world's first social computer networks. It was completed in 1978 and was initially used as an intranet by FOA employees. There were electronic conferencing and internal messaging. There were also general discussion forums that external users could join. In 1982 KOM was connected to the Arpanet in the USA. This allowed Swedish computer users to communicate with friends and colleagues, especially on the West Coast. On January 1, 1983, Arpanet switched to the TCP/IP protocol (which is still in use), and this date is considered the birth of the Internet.

The Swedish system was developed with Torgny Tholerus as programmer, and it grew. In 1987 the KOM system had over 2000 users, most of them outside FOA. I was one of them and used it to find sick cats and critical teleworkers for my radio reports. One of the groups on KOM was called Stubborn Cats - Exchange of Experiences. There I found owners of cats that had gotten sick from dry food. There I found Simson, a blue Persian who had a kidney problem. Cat food had become a profile topic for Konsumentekot (Consumer News) on the national radio where I worked, and Simson's owner was soon heard on the radio.

I also met critical technicians at Televerket (Swedish Telecom) who gave me information about the shortcomings of the call metering system. This provided important facts for a whole autumn of revelations about Televerket. To gain more knowledge and contacts, I started a discussion group on KOM called Telemonopoly for and against.

When I contacted Torgny Tholerus in 1984, he was developing a "Super KOM". His vision was that in 1995 there would be "home terminals" in every home, as common as telephones. The KOM system would cover the whole country, and everyone would be able to communicate with everyone else.

- For example, you could send a message to all the people in the same house you live in, and then either suggest organizing a farm party, or invite everyone in the house for a cup of coffee," Torgny Tholerus wrote to me.

Tholerus completed the PC version of Super-KOM in the fall of 1990. The computer system was to be moved from the central computer to the users' own personal computers. The work was partly funded by various EU grants. QZ was closed and Torgny Tholerus was employed at the Department of Computer and Systems Science (DSV) at Stockholm University. 1995 KOM95 was released, now with a graphical user interface. But by this time,

Torgny Tholerus' almost twenty year old system was outdated, and various web solutions were widely used instead.

Of course, the story could have taken a different turn, but in the fall of 2004, the EU grants for KOM development ran out and Torgny Tholerus became unemployed. He had the chance to develop his ideas as a developer and programmer, but what could have been a Swedish Internet and Facebook instead became an American success story.

This says a lot about the anarchist roots of the Internet and the Web, even globally. It was the idea that information should be free, anyone should be able to publish anything, no censorship, maximum freedom and general confusion. This was not just the idea of Torgny Tholérus. It was part of a global mindset. The online pioneers were freedom fighters. Everyone should have a voice. The first thing I read about the Net and personal computers was in a California hippie magazine called Whole Earth Review.

This image of the pioneers as digital revolutionaries and anarchists is one that today's Silicon Valley leaders like to cultivate. The sad development that followed instead is skillfully portrayed by journalists Martin Gelin and Karin Pettersson in their book Internet är trasigt.17 They quote author Fred Turner18 and his reflections on how it came to this:

Turner describes a small clique of idealistic and often very long-haired men who, rooted in the dreamy hippie utopias of the 1960s, built many of the institutions that would shape the young Web. Turner calls them "techno-utopians," and they provided an ideology for a new class of global tech elite. The book shows how a common thread runs from the rebellious and far-left ideas that characterized the godfathers of Silicon Valley to the technoarchism of the 1990s.

The pioneers were united by the idea that the state, government, and loosely defined "elites" should not interfere with the ongoing technological revolution. Instead, the tech moguls would be left to their own devices to create platforms that were shaped by the more vague ideas of the seventies about cosmic balance and all-human communities. Leaderless and rule-free collective living was a model for the systems that characterized the early days of the Internet, according to Turner.

When these libertarian ideals met the hungry entrepreneurs who flocked to Silicon Valley in the 1990s, with savvy entrepreneurs like Marc Andreessen and Peter Thiel, an unholy alliance emerged, where the hacker ideals of openness met the entrepreneurial ideals of profitability.19 The pioneers may have been idealistic hippies, but then cynical and profit-hungry capitalists took over. Gelin and Pettersson show how Facebook's algorithms favor hate and threats, disinformation and propaganda. In a deeply self-critical and sad interview with the New York Times in May 2017, Twitter founder Evan Williams says that "the internet is broken." He recounts how he built Twitter with the hope of strengthening democracy, tolerance, and openness, but instead found that the platform had become an unstoppable megaphone for extremists, hate and the pathologically dishonest propaganda of former US President Donald Trump.

But Torgny Tholerus remains optimistic. I catch up with him in the spring of 2020 for another interview, this time via Zoom. Torgny sits in his small apartment in Nynäshamn, I in Enskede, on the outskirts of Stockholm, both corona isolated.

- We were probably a bit too early because the Internet itself did not yet exist. The only thing you could do with the system was to have a central computer that people could call. That made it difficult to get a little more information," says Torgny.

- So why did someone else start Facebook?

- Well, then came the Internet. It was easier to do something bigger. I was all alone on the KOM system and had to redo the whole system seven times. I threw out all the code and started from scratch seven times.

- The point I'm trying to make is that the conditions were there. You could have been the father of both the Internet and Facebook. Why didn't your system win?

- It was the fact that the peripheral structure did not exist at that time. My knowledge was insufficient. I didn't know about database management and so on. The KOM system had limitations on the number of users. In the eighties, there were about 2,000 users at the most. Facebook has billions.

For Torgny Tholerus, life got pretty messy, by his own account. He never became a multi-billionaire, which was never his goal. Instead, it was about contributing to a better world. Is that still true? With all the hate posts, fake news and troll factories, can we really hold on to the beautiful vision of the sixties? Does it apply to the way the web is today?

- The only way to fight this problem is to open up the channels of information so that all the falsehoods are exposed," answers Torgny Tholerus in my Zoom interview.

- On what do you base this optimism?

- You need communication to make a society work. The more communication there is, the better it works. A prerequisite for people to be able to cooperate is that they talk to each other.

- But what can that lead to?

- I think it should lead to the eventual end of all wars. When communication has become sufficiently well people will realize that it is better to cooperate than to fight.

World peace is not here yet. Quite the contrary. But what about the nudity meetings? They did happen. For a few years, the student bathhouse lent its facilities for nude bathing at certain times. In one of our email conversations, Torgny Tholerus explains:

- For example, regarding the "nude dates", I have now realized that this is the wrong way to go. They were not wrong in themselves, but it was wrong to start with them. There are a lot of other things that need to be done first. It's no use taking off your clothes if you're still wearing them in your head. That is, you must first do something about the blockages in your brain, the lack of love, the involuntary loneliness, the psychological damage from frustrating childhood experiences. Only then can taking off the clothes bring people closer together.

Don't help the dark forces

The lack of reporting in the mainstream media on honor culture, clans, immigrant-related crime, and the economic motives for immigration is a journalistic and political failure. Based on the false notion that the journalist should "help the little guy", a kind of benign self-censorship has developed over many years around anything related to the lack of integration of "newcomers". This inability or unwillingness to see or describe problems was also present in the political environment. The reporting and discussion that was suppressed so as not to strengthen the "dark forces" led to its opposite, to suspicion of the media and increased xenophobia. Only in the 2020s did the floodgates open. Now the opposite is true and there is no end to the misery that immigration brings. A xenophobic party with roots in the Nazi era sits at the center of power in Sweden, and now it is rather difficult for those who talk about social issues, economic disparities, and lack of education to be heard when there are demands for tougher measures.

When news reporting is done with the intention of describing reality in a certain way for political reasons, it fails. Both today and historically. The present situation has deep roots.

When the little town Södertälje south of Stockholm received the large wave of Assyrian refugees in the late 1970s, the media avoided reporting on the economic reasons for the wave of refugees. Ekot, the national news in radio, and reporter Anders Thunberg learned the hard way in the new year 1980/81 that they should not talk about anything other than that the immigrants were being persecuted. Swedish Radio had sent Thunberg to the immigrants' home regions to find out why so many Assyrians were coming to Södertälje.

It was supposed to be a few features to be broadcast during the Christmas holidays, but it became a major news story. Anders Thunberg wanted to understand why so many people from the Christian enclaves in Syria were coming to Sweden. He asked about the motives of the migrants. Ekot investigated the oppression on the ground and the consequences of the large and rapid exodus in the communities the Assyrians left behind. Anders Thunberg reported on the emptying of villages, the disruption of old structures, and the disruption of the balance of power. Many Assyrians first moved to what was then West Germany, where they heard about another country further north that took better care of refugees. The Assyrians were Christians and found special support in the Christian communities in Sweden. The left had previously protected Vietnamese deserters and refugees from Chile. Now the Christian churches were given a profile with their own refugee group to protect.

The picture that Anders Thunberg painted was more complex and multifaceted than many might have thought or even wanted to know. Christians who remained in Syria regretted the exodus and rejected claims of widespread repression. Ekot was told that many of those who left were motivated primarily by economic reasons. The migrants had heard of a land of milk and honey and were attracted by new opportunities in the small town of Södertälje. There they were welcomed by Christian communities who wanted to defend their fellow believers.

Anders Thunberg did not take a stand. He did not pursue his own line on whether it was good or bad for Assyrians to come to Sweden. He reported what he had heard and seen, complicated the established picture and gave more explanations for the refugee flow than just the severe oppression of a Christian minority. He should not have done so. The fiercest attack on Anders Thunberg came from Harald Ofstad, professor of practical philosophy at Stockholm University. In Sweden's largest daily paper Dagens Nyheter on February 1, 1981, he wrote a major article on "racial prejudice" and made a violent personal attack on Ekot's reporter, condemning his reporting with words such as irresponsible and stupid:

> "The latest example of the reluctance and
> mistreatment of the Assyrians seeking asylum is a
> series of programs produced by Ekot at Swedish
> Radio. Here we learn that Assyrians lie and deceive
> the Swedish authorities. They claim to be persecuted
> when in fact they are living in very good conditions.
> They take advantage of the humanity and naivety

of Swedes, a naivety that goes so far that even
a three-year-old Assyrian can deceive us. This is
incitement against ethnic groups. We recognize the
tone. If you want to denigrate an ethnic group, the
best way to do it is with money and sex. This is how
blacks were slandered in the United States, and the
German Nazis did the same thing to the Jews: the
Jews used Germany's wealth to prey on Aryan girls.
We all have prejudices. But some of us are a little more
aware that we have them and do more to combat
them than this naive or malicious reporter."

The tone could be harsh and unforgiving long before social media. The renowned professor condemned Anders Thunberg as naive and malicious, and compared his reporting to the Nazi persecution of Jews. This was costly for a reporter who, without an agenda, met those who had an agenda.

Anders Thunberg was assisted on the ground in Syria by the Swedish diplomat Ingmar Karlsson. In his memoirs, he vividly describes the immigration of Syrian Orthodox Christians to Sweden and how whole families and clans broke up for good and moved to Sweden. He could not report any persecution of the Christians, but forged documents to support unfounded applications for asylum. Ingmar Karlsson writes:

"The Syrian Orthodox Church therefore viewed the emigration to Sweden with great concern and as a

manifestation of what one abbot called "a perverted
humanity that threatened an ancient culture and the
survival of the Church."

Ingmar Karlsson's diplomatic warnings back to Sweden went
unheeded, and the social climate of the time demanded reporting
that was not neutral regarding the consequences. This sad mood
was also present in parts of the journalistic profession and among
some of Anders Thunberg's colleagues at the radio. This became
even more clear later during the great battle over the persecuted
Kurdish refugees who were forced to hide in a church in the
interior of Northern Sweden in the early 1990s. The battle over the
Åsele refugees was one of the first major asylum fights in Sweden.

In 2010, two Kurdish brothers, Rashid and Ziya Sincari, came to
Sweden seeking asylum. They claimed to be politically persecuted
Kurds from Saddam Hussein's Iraq. They were quickly granted
a residence permit and later joined by the family, their two wives
and ten children. But then an investigation by the Immigration
Department (now the Migration Board) revealed that the wives
and children had Turkish passports. They were called Gümüscü
and came from Diyarbakir in Turkey. The families were not
who they said they were but came from a different country
than they claimed and could not prove that they were politically
persecuted. In 1993, the Immigration Department revoked the
families' residence permits. On the same day the decision was
made, the evening of October 19, 1993, the families fled to the
church in Åsele, where they "hid" while the appeal process dragged

on. The priest, Roland Haglund, opened the church and told
Dagens Nyheter:

> "As a priest and a Christian, I could not act
> otherwise. I followed the golden rule of Christian
> teaching: Whatever you want people to do for you,
> you should do for them."

The case eventually became a matter for the government and
Prime Minister Ingvar Carlsson. As popular support for the
so-called Sincari families grew, the government tried to deal with
a formal case called the Gümüscü families. No matter how the
government turned the issue around and discussed it in several
internal meetings, it could only conclude that the families had no
grounds for asylum. The government's reasoning was that there
must be something to international conventions. Without asylum
rights, the families could not be allowed to stay. The government
did not want to let temporary public opinion control such a
decision.

Leif Blomberg was the Minister of Immigration, and the case of
the refugees in Åsele Church was probably his most difficult case.
He stubbornly maintained that everyone must be treated equally
before the law. Prime Minister Ingvar Carlsson said in afterwards
that there was "no good decision to be made, only two bad ones,
one worse than the other". He wrote in Dagens Nyheter:

"If the families had been allowed to stay in Åsele,
it would have sent the wrong message. It would
have been a message that you can sabotage your
way around the laws we have in Sweden; a message
that parents of refugee children do not have to take
responsibility for their actions that also affect the
children."

The government's line was that there were no grounds for
asylum. The Immigration Appeals Board found that the families
did not have "sufficiently strong humanitarian reasons to obtain
a new residence permit" and found no reason to change previous
rejection decisions. According to the Board, there was no risk
of return to Turkey and no evidence that the fathers would be
harmed by illegal political activity.

The families were to be deported, and on January 11, 1996, the
apartments in Åsele where the families had moved were raided.
A large police force with dogs cordoned off an entire residential
area. The two fathers were not there, and the eldest son, Shiyar,
managed to escape into the forest. The people of Åsele protested,
and after an angry scene, the two mothers and nine children were
arrested and immediately flown to Diyarbakir in Turkey.

The tone of the debate was very high. Journalist Jan Guillou
called it all the government's "draft policy". The Migration
Agency's employees "are the ones left over when the rest of
the government rationalizes," wrote editor Rolf Alsing in social
democratic evening paper Aftonbladet.

"The Migration Agency is the modern equivalent
of the executioners of the past," said Nils Schwartz
in newspaper Expressen, while Carl Otto Werkelid
in conservative morning paper Svenska Dagbladet
wrote: "Our regulated state mercy risks being defined
by many as the work of Satan."

One of the main pieces of evidence that the Sincari families were politically persecuted was a Wanted advertisement published in the Turkish newspaper Mücadele on August 27, 1990. It named the fathers of the family as dangerous PKK sympathizers, and a copy of the newspaper advertisement was submitted by the families' lawyer. This "evidence" was presented several times but was rejected by the immigration authorities. It reappeared in a new submission by the lawyer in the spring of 1996. The "evidence" again became news in the media and was also published in SVT Swedish Televisions' regional news program Nordnytt.

The publication of the advertisement strengthened the families' case that they were politically persecuted and should be allowed to stay in Sweden. The journalistic assessment was that this was true and relevant news. Ola Nilsson, reporter for Nordnytt, still thought there was something strange about the wanted ad. It looked pasted on, and how could the two brothers be wanted under a name they didn't have? Ola Nilsson and a photographer from SVT in Umeå went to the archives of the Turkish National Library in Ankara. Like the Royal Library in Sweden, all printed material is stored in Turkey. Ola Nilsson managed to find the original issue of Mücadele from that day. The articles around the wanted ad corresponded to what the lawyer had submitted, but where the ad should have been, there was a soccer report instead. The so-called "wanted ad" was obviously a forgery. The main evidence cited simply did not exist, and the families' case was now weakened by these new revelations. Did they really have the right to apply for asylum as political refugees? On March 7, 1996, Ola Nilsson did a "stand-up report" in front of the National Archives in Ankara and explained his findings. The report was broadcast in both national and regional tv-news, but his local colleagues gave him a hard time. After all, he had "ruined" the case for persecuted refugees. But he was just doing his job. He later explained:

> "My job is not to make things easier or harder for the
> Sincari families. My job is to get the facts and present
> them to the viewers. If I deliberately withhold
> information to make people think the way I think,
> then I am not working as a professional journalist
> but something else entirely. There are many other
> things I could choose to do. I could do advertising,
> propaganda or information for a political party or
> a company. Then I would be free to work in that
> way and only bring out what speaks in the "right"
> direction. But as a journalist, I am an extension of
> the public and have the immense privilege of being

curious and seeking facts during my paid working hours."

Reporter Ola Nilsson was severely criticized by his colleagues. He had revealed that the two fathers had falsified crucial evidence of political persecution. As a result, critics said, he had made it impossible for them to stay in Sweden. The situation at Nordnytt became so infected that daily work was hardly possible for several weeks. Many local TV, radio and newspaper journalists were members of the support group *Friends of Sincari* and felt it was their duty to defend the persecuted refugees.

On a bright early summer evening, May 30, 1996, the Ethics Committee of the Swedish Journalists' Association organized a debate at a restaurant in Umeå with the question "How was the reporting handled?" I was there to talk about impartiality. The atmosphere was hostile, the divisions still strong. Many of the journalists felt it was their duty to defend the refugees: "We should be on the side of the little person, we should give a voice to the weak."

The news director of the local radio station said he was proud of how they had tried to investigate the powers and how it had acted to defend the family, but he was critical of the fact that Nordnytt had started to dig into the old wanted ad. A local radio reporter, however, thought that things had gone too far, that the editors had taken up the families' cause. The stories had been edited so as not to hurt the families. For example, one reporter had filed a story about how popular the families had become in the small community. One resident described how she had an entire freezer full of cloudberries they had picked. Others had received help painting houses and repairing cars. But the editor thought it sounded like moonlighting, so he edited out everything but the cloudberries.

Several reporters became friends with the families. The regional paper *Västerbottens Kuriren's* Åselereporter became good friends with the families from the moment they arrived, and the newspaper's managing editor explained that the refugees were "citizens of Åsele, a part of our society - and they are treated like that...". But other reporters at the paper felt that the local reporter in Åsele should be removed from the coverage because he had become so involved in the families' cause. The distrust between the different camps in the north of Sweden was universal. Some simply did not want to believe Ola Nilsson's report about the forged ad. They saw his report as a hit job for the government. Others thought that the newsrooms had been turned into campaign organs for the families.

The evening discussion in Umeå ended in total disagreement about the journalistic mission. Those who defended reporting in support of the Sincari families relied on the journalistic convention that the reporter should be on the side of the weak. Is there anyone weaker than a refugee fleeing persecution in a church in the hinterland of Norrland? Surely it is the reporter's job to help such a person in need?

But the reporter should neither help nor hinder. It is not the journalist's job to help President Kennedy or Prime Minister

Gandhi. The reporter should tell what he or she knows and believes the audience wants to know. Yet there is a notion that the newsroom should be on the side of good, whatever that good may be. This is a false notion. The journalist should not be on the side of anyone, that is the point of the mission and the professional role. This is what the reporter Ola Nilsson tried to tell his colleagues, almost in vain. But his colleagues found it difficult to be objective in their reporting. The Board of Review for Radio and Television received thirty complaints that the programs about the Åsele refugees were inappropriate and biased in favor of the Sincari families. Most of the reports were cleared but with criticism, and the Board noted that "throughout the broadcasts there was a certain imbalance between participants who opposed the government's decision and those who considered the decision to be correct. Some of the pro Sincari stories were censured:

> "A report in *Kvällsöppet* on January 1, 1 on SVT
> 2 did not give a background to the rejection
> decision, which should have been done. The report
> therefore violated the requirements of impartiality
> and objectivity. The presenter of the radio program
> "Karlavagnen" on 16 January took a stand against
> the rejection decision in a way that, according to the
> Board, violated the requirement of impartiality, and
> a number of segments in T V4's News on 15 January
> failed to meet the requirement of objectivity."

Should a news organization withhold information that it has determined to be true and relevant because it may cause harm? The answer should be crystal clear. Ola Nilsson and Nordnytt's careful investigation showed that the wanted ad was forged. The Immigration Appeals Board had also rejected it, so the evaluation of the advertisement was important for how the authorities and ultimately the government handled the case. Thus, the false advertisement was relevant to understanding the outcome of the case. The public should have a right to know, even if the Sincari family was unfortunate and even if someone had legitimate reasons to falsify an advertisement. Since the enormous attention in the mid-1990s, the reporting about the Sincari/Gümüscü families have been very quiet. The friendship association has closed, but several family members have managed to find a life and a future in Sweden despite their deportation. The son Shiyar was later granted a residence permit on humanitarian grounds, while the fathers Asid and Siyapos Gümüscü went into hiding and unsuccessfully applied for a new residence permit. They were arrested by the police in February 2000, and after being rejected by the Foreigners' Board, they voluntarily returned to the country in April 2000 to their families in Diyarbakir.

Author Astrid Lindgren paid for the two girls, Rojda and Jinda, to return to Sweden to study for just over a year. Rojda became a dentist and a surgeon. The girls' brothers, Ahmet and Diyar, followed her to Sweden to study. Ahmet finished his doctorate in social work at Umeå University in 2019, and I contacted him in

November 2020 to find out what had happened to him and his family. The answer came by return mail.

In the end we did well, but I must also say that we were all deeply affected by the dramatic expulsion that took place with police action and emergency landings. We were very grateful for all the help we received from Friends in Åsele and others involved all over Sweden. After being expelled in 1996, I lived in Diyarbakir until 2002. I came to Sweden in 2002 as an exchange student and studied social work. After the program I got a job and stayed in Sweden. I finished my Ph.D. last year and I work half time at Umeå Municipality and half time at the Department of Social Work at Umeå University. My older sister is a doctor and a surgeon at a hospital in southern Sweden, and my younger sister works as a skin therapist at a private clinic. My brother works as a coordinator for a government agency in southern Sweden. All the siblings returned to Sweden after the deportation to study and then stayed. Since we grew up here and considered Åsele our home, we could not adjust to Diyarbakir. So it was only natural for us to come back.
Greetings
Ahmet

The Åsele refugee controversy is a clear example of what happens when the media fails in its reporting duties. But the Gümüscü families are not the only example of how the media and politicians find it difficult to deal with information that could be harmful to refugees, immigrants, or people with a non-Swedish background.

The murder of the young girl Sara in Umeå became one of the first known honor killings. On Sunday, December 16, 1996, fifteen-year-old Sara was found dead in a snowdrift in Västra Ersboda, five kilometers north of Umeå. She had been strangled with a belt by her 16-year-old brother and 17-year-old cousin at around 2 a.m. and left to die hidden in the snowdrift. The two boys turned themselves in to the police the next morning and showed them where the body was.

In the first days of coverage, the motive seemed very unclear. There was talk of a "fight" or an "argument" between the teenagers, who were traveling on the same bus from a disco. Sara, her brother, and her cousin were from Iraq. But questions about what happened and the ethnic backgrounds of those involved were put off. Honor killings did not exist.

I remember an angry discussion in the newsroom at the TV-news at the time. The producer thought that we should not report in a way that could benefit the xenophobic forces. Instead, the murder in Umeå became part of the "incomprehensible street violence". The media silence was first broken by journalist Kerstin Vinterhed in Dagens Nyheter. Three days after the murder, she wrote an article about the "culture of shame".

"The teenagers in Umeå who killed the 15-year-old Iraqi immigrant have restored the family's honor. The fact that they turned themselves in is part of the story. Such an act should be known. Iraqi-born psychiatrist Riyadh Albaldawi told DN that the girl's close relatives, a brother and a cousin, were the ones who killed her. "Remember that this is a shameful crime," Albaldawi said. What one person does can tarnish the whole family. It is up to the male relatives to clear the family's name. "In the patriarchal family, power is concentrated in the hands of the man, with the grandparents coming next," he says. Then comes the mother, and then the sons of the family. The eldest son, in particular, is charged with being the father's deputy in defending the family's honor. At the bottom are the daughters, who are closely guarded. Albaldawi emphasizes that this is a matter of tradition, not religion - read Islam. What is at stake here are millennia-old customs, family traditions that are older than any religion. It is when this ancient family structure meets a very different society with very different gender roles and norms that such a disaster can occur, he points out."

Kerstin Vinterhed broke a taboo with her article. It must have struck a chord, and she needed the help of an Iraqi psychiatrist to push her thesis. Sara's murder in Umeå became the first known honor killing in Sweden. In January 1997, the two boys were charged with murder. In interviews with the police, the 16-year-old said he had direct orders from his uncle to check on Sara, how she was dressed and what she was doing. The father had asked his son to make sure Sara was living as an Iraqi girl, not a Swedish one. Both boys were eventually sentenced to several years in prison for the murder.

The conflict over honor culture has been alive and well in Swedish society for decades. Immigration, integration, gang crime in vulnerable areas, honor violence and honor culture have been explosive topics in politics and the media. Xenophobia and opposition to immigrants have been a breeding ground for populist right-wing parties. In this situation, refraining from presenting different perspectives or facts that may be uncomfortable for certain immigrant groups, so as not to feed xenophobia, is likely to have the opposite effect.

"The well-intentioned restraint that has characterized some of the sentiments in the major newsrooms or in the cultural sphere has actually increased suspicion and xenophobia, thus strengthening the forces that should be fought. This has created the image that the media cannot be trusted. That facts are withheld for propaganda purposes becomes a perception that spreads and can be exploited, which has now backfired with full force on mainstream media."

The bitch got what
she deserved

The small village of Grytnäs is situated in the beautiful countryside of Dalarna, opposite Leksand, by Österviken in the southern part of lake Siljan. It is a real Dalecarlian village with red timber farms, lily of the valley meadows down to the glittering lake with the blue mountains in the background. When I was growing up, timber was still floated on the lake and my father paddled a canoe across the bay to work in Leksands-Noret, the central part of the municipality, with a church and a provincial medical center. These were the summers of my childhood, in Prosgården, opposite the village cottage in the middle of Grytnäs. Prosgården, named after the old Pros family, was an old farmhouse with a surrounding yard, a large barn, a cottage and the main building. Dad supported the family by substituting for one of the few country doctors in Leksand during the summer, so we had long vacations with the whole family. The rest of the year we lived in Uppsala, where my father was a professor of medicine at the university. This was my father's childhood home. My grandmother was Präst-Märtha, daughter of the vicar in the neighboring parish of Siljansnäs. Many uncles, aunts and cousins lived and still live on Stenbacken in Siljansnäs, separated from Grytnäs only by the villages of Sunnanäng, Fornby and Tasbäck.

At Prosgården I lived in the farmhouse, next to an old grindstone overgrown with wild roses and with a wonderful view of Siljan. Here I and the boys of the same age from the village could sit in peace and talk and play cards. I could probably count myself as one of the villagers with at least three generations of ancestors in the cemetery and my father as "the doctor in Noret".

I still know large parts of the famous village play *Himlaspelet* by heart. I sang in the boys' choir in Rune Lindström's story about the poor painter Mats Ersson who went to God in heaven to ask for justice for his fiancée Marit, who had been burned as a witch. When I was a little boy, I used to cycle the seven kilometers from Grytnäs to Noret, where the performance took place, every evening for many years. I don't remember any boys from neighboring Mora in the cast. Himlaspelet was for real people, from the Leksand community.

There was a big difference between being a Leksand boy, a Rättvik boy or a Mora boy. Dad learned this early when he was in the church rowing team. There was a fierce battle between the village boys to be the fastest to row across Österviken in Siljan to Leksand in the big old long narrow church boats. Dad from Siljansnäs quickly learned to mock and despise the boys from the neighboring parish of Sollerön, and of course those who came from even farther away, Mora and Rättvik.

I got the mistrust of the boys from the neighboring parish with my mother's milk. We Grytnäs boys in my cabin really knew what shady characters the Mora boys were. When we got older and could drive around Siljan on weekends in the old cars or when it was time for the hockey games between Leksand and Mora, it was deadly serious.

The Mora boys steal and fight, stab and rape. They also have access to the deadly Mora knives. This is a truth that rarely appears in the politically correct media, which hides the truth about the Mora boys. I miss the clear headlines about what is happening:

Mora-Bengt slit his wife's throat.

Mora-Sten stole the golden crucifix in Sollerö church.

Morag gang cut off the ear of Rättvik boy.

Girl from Leksand raped by the Morag gang.

Mora-Mats strikes again.

Mora knives are the most common murder weapon in Sweden.

If I chose to focus only on the crimes and misdemeanors committed by Mora boys, I could fill a daily news site. I could go through the indictments and convictions in the Mora District Court and select only crimes committed by Mora men. In the unlikely event that I find something about the Leksand or Rättvik boys, it has no place on my news site. If I poured out stories like this about the Mora boys day after day, a picture would soon form, a picture that creates horror and rejection. Each individual story might be factual, but through a biased selection I could present a propaganda picture.

That's how they work, the right-wing nationalist online hate sites. I made up the headlines about Mora-boys to illustrate the mechanisms. To understand, I have long followed the right-wing news sites and discussion groups on Facebook and X, formerly Twitter. Much of what is written is presented in some sort of journalistic format. It looks and sounds like real news, but through selection and bias, it is to be understood as crude propaganda. The recurring narrative is that Muslims and young men from the Middle East and Afghanistan are more dangerous than ever. This is the message that washes over those in the far-right opinion bubble.

A small selection of "Sweden-friendly" websites:

McDonald's Mohammed to Sara: "I will fuck you and then I will stab you".

Immigrant mob cuts off teenager's hand - "White bastard, it's our land" Arabs crawl, swim, climb and dig their way into the EU

The balcony migrant case shows the failure of Swedish migration policy

Nurses forced to apologize for being white

Arab family angry they didn't get extra taxpayer support

Why should immigrants be exempt from the law?

Crime brings Sweden close to anarchy

Bloody chaos in shop when asylum seekers suddenly try to slit a customer's throat

Swish Afghan who wanted the municipality to pay the maximum subsidy Layla rented out her room - murdered with 30 stab wounds

Somali IQ even lower than previously thought

The shift in public discourse is that these propaganda sites have become part of everyday media life. Open racism against Arabs, Blacks, Muslims and Afghans. The hate is open and massive and flows online every day. The story is that young men from the Middle East pose a deadly threat to our way of life, our security and our well-being. The perpetrators come from the same part of the world. It is possible that behind each case there is a real event, but this is irrelevant, as it is the sample that provides the propagandistic picture. Statistics from the Swedish National Council for Crime Prevention (BRÅ) that 64% of all fatal violence against women was committed by men with whom the victim or perpetrator was or had been in a relationship have no place among these "news".

Gang violence, shootings and murders are real and obviously a large and growing problem. But the propaganda sites cherry-pick data about the role of immigrants to sow division and mistrust. Any society can be suspicious of foreigners, although this has not always been the case with Muslims and Arabs. Sometimes it is about the difference between boys from Mora and Leksand. The publication is not made to present something that the editor finds true and relevant according to the usual methods of news evaluation. It is done to influence the opinions and behavior of others.

Swedish press ethics rules state that the media should not emphasize ethnicity in their reporting, and the difference between established newsrooms and right-wing propaganda sites is therefore significant. The extremist online bubbles influence and spread their message in society. They engage in propaganda under the guise of journalism to achieve certain effects. There is a systematic attempt by extremist forces to destroy democratic institutions. Public service is at the forefront of the attacks, followed by established newspapers such as the largest morning news paper Dagens Nyheter.

The political party Swedish Democrats (SD) is the party that has invested heavily in building a "conservative news outlet" online, with many visible and invisible threads. Developments in Poland and Hungary have obviously been an inspiration. SD ideologist Linus Bylund said in Expressen that journalists who report "biased" stories are working against the nation, and tweeted that they are "enemies of the nation." He followed up on this argument in Fokus magazine:

> "I would like to see a more personalized retaliation option for the Public service Review Board. There are people responsible for the content of each program. There needs to be personal responsibility. There are some tools today. But these are financial things that affect the companies, not the individuals. Nobody loses their salary for two months or gets fired. The threat has to be there... If you overstep your authority as an employee of the people's media channel and deceive the people, because it is an anti-democratic act to spread fake news, to take a stand on what is perceived as news, then you are abusing a very heavy trust that you have received from the people for the people's money and not to turn opinion against the people."

It is a recurring rhetorical figure to accuse the mainstream media of spreading fake news, which is exactly what these alternative media do themselves. My concept of consequence neutrality has sometimes been used to hide what right-wing nationalist media do when they engage in activist journalism against immigration and refugees. When they agitate against blacks and Arabs, they claim to ignore the consequences, but that is to turn the whole idea of my argument into its opposite. When extremists engage in propaganda under the guise of journalism, it becomes more important than ever for real journalism to defend its independence and refuse to become a player, either for or against immigration or any other political issue.

The polarization of the news that has been so evident in the US is now being established in Sweden. This became very clear during the 2022 election in the many SD-affiliated media. For example, there was a vicious campaign against the then leader of the Centerparty, Annie Lööf, as some kind of "Sharia Annie". Conspicuously present in the SD media channels are stories about problems caused by immigration.

How dangerous this can be is shown by the US trend of increasingly polarized media. The right-wing radio talk show hosts do not engage in journalism, even though they are broadcast on platforms that used to be journalistic. During Donald Trump's presidency, Fox News became an increasingly partisan propaganda channel for him, with commentators and hosts who were a direct part of the then-president's support team. After the election and Trump's defeat, when Fox News cautiously tried to take a more independent stance in the newsroom, it was met with hatred from Trump's trolls, who turned to even more hateful, spiteful, and conspiratorial right-wing outlets. The extreme outlets Newsmax and Parler were among those that began to take over Fox News' audience.

Online hate and threats against journalists, politicians, influencers, comedians, and musicians are a major and growing problem. In the spring of 2021, the situation became almost unbearable for staff at the Swedish National Board of Health and researchers studying the coronavirus. The media institute Fojo at Linnaeus University published an anthology in February 2021 to depict the growing hatred and threats. Head of operations Kersti Forsberg writes:

> "If someone had told me ten years ago that in 2020 Sweden would have a special investigator to protect democratic society. I would have laughed and said it was a bit of an exaggeration. We can certainly talk to each other without having to investigate how. If someone had told me seven years ago that by the end of the decade Fojo would be teaching professional journalists how to recognize the influence of information, how to protect themselves and not just their sources. I would have wondered what country we were talking about. Russia?! [...]

If someone had told me five years ago that SVT's editorial security costs would be four times higher in 2020 than they are now. I would have said it was unreasonable. If someone had told me three years ago that Sweden would fall in the Reporters Without Borders press freedom index in the next two years because of the hatred and threats against Swedish journalists, I would not have believed it. But that's where we are today. How did we get here?"

One of the contributors to the anthology is Carl Heath, special investigator for the Committee for the Protection of Democratic Discourse:

"First, news and information are now disseminated without any journalistic accountability. False claims and hateful messages can spread and go unchallenged in ways that were not possible before. The recipient of information has a greater responsibility to assess its credibility. In addition, fewer people are paying for journalism, and the economics of media have become more strained. The number of journalists has decreased, and local journalism in particular is suffering. In addition, social media make journalists more accessible and more vulnerable to hate and threats."

Threats from extremist groups are now taken more seriously by police and law enforcement agencies, but few cases have been prosecuted and convicted. For those who are threatened, it has a chilling effect on what they want and can report, and the conditions for free debate are disrupted. The act of violence during the Political Week in Visby in 2022 shows how far right-wing extremist violence can go. The regions psychiatric coordinator was stabbed to death in the street, and the leader of the Center Party and the Director General of SVT were other intended victims. The heads of the major media houses must now have extensive personal protection. Hatred and threats against politicians distort the entire social climate.

Not even the highest representative of the Church is free. On Easter weekend 2021, then Archbishop Antje Jackelén was finally forced to leave her Twitter account, where she had been quite active.

"Taking a Twitter break," she wrote. "Disgusted that my tweets are being used to spread threats, hate and lies about faith, the Swedish Church and society. You who do this may feel like winners for the moment, but: the true winning side is always the side of truth and love. Switch to it!"

To explain herself, the archbishop posted a screenshot of some of the hateful tweets she received:

Sick just looking at her, the Islamist hugger

She's a threat to Christianity and humanity

The bitch is crazy

SEND THIS BASTARD TO THE KINGDOM OF ALLAH

I understand the archbishop. The possibility of anonymity makes many people go crazy.

I'm a small player in this context, but I know what it feels like to face the hatred, like when I received this message on Facebook:

"Hahahahahahahahha the bitch got what she deserved."

The message to me from "Tommy Lefevre" on Facebook was short and to the point. I don't usually post anything private on social media, but I made an exception this time. My mother Ulla died in July 2019 and one of her high school friends had written a beautiful in memorial in UNT. I linked to it and received many warm greetings from friends on Facebook. And the hateful comment from this "Tommy Lefevre". What had I done to deserve that? Well, I had written my weekly column in Fokus magazine, based on an idea I had while reading a new translation of Homer's Odyssey over the summer. It was a really good story, I thought, and I made it the subject of my first column after summer. The article reflected on our cultural heritage. Odysseus fled across the seas in a fragile boat, fighting giants, trolls, and sirens. But wherever he landed on unfamiliar shores, he was well received by the people who lived there, I noted in my column:

> "What Homer teaches us is that strangers should
> always be received well and with the greatest
> generosity. Otherwise, the wrath of the gods will
> be aroused. Nor is this something unique to the
> ancient Greeks. This basic moral imperative can be
> found in most religions and cultures. It is therefore

also part of what could be called "Swedishness",
part of our common cultural heritage [...] Perhaps
(conservative political leaders) like Jimmie Åkesson,
Ebba Busch Thor and Hanif Bali should also sit
down by the fishy sea and read the classics. Then they
might be reminded of what happens to those who
are most dismissive of poor beggars and refugees.
Like Melanthes, the goatherd of Ithaca, who was
the worst at insulting and mocking Ulysses when he
came home dressed as a beggar. When the time for
revenge finally comes, he follows Odysseus' orders:

Tie his hands and feet behind his back and throw him
into the chamber, tie him firmly to a board, tie a tight
rope around his body and hoist him high up on a
pillar to the ceiling, so that he may first be severely
tortured for a while before he dies. After he had hung
there for many hours, the goatherd, who had thus
violated the laws of Zeus, was taken out into the yard.
They cut off his nose and ears with a ruthless knife,
then pulled out his genitals and fed them to dogs, and
in their fury they cut off the victim's feet and hands."

My column ended with these powerful quotes from Homer. I
also made a short video version that was posted on social media.
I should not have done that, because now the trolls have been
awakened. It's hard to comprehend the scale, ferocity and hatred

of those who write about immigration policy. The raw hatred quickly flowed towards me. Now the trolls could rejoice that my mother was dead. There were quickly thousands of hateful posts, especially on Twitter at the time. Nevertheless, the hate directed at me is a pale reflection of what has been going on for a long time against other high-profile writers, media profiles, or radio and television personalities. But the hatred quickly becomes personal.

The xenophobic right-wing online newspapers followed suit. The "newspaper" *Fria Tider* wrote: "Fichtelius wants more immigration because the god Zeus demands it", while another site, *Samhällsnytt* wrote: "SVT profile threatens immigration critics with torture and execution". Both newspapers referred to criticism of my article on social media. There are communication vessels between the extreme online sites and the hateful tail. Not only did the hate storm escalate online, I received breathless phone calls and written death threats against me and my family in the mail. I filed a police report, and the new police hate crime unit took the matter seriously, but failed to track down the threateners in a small, anonymous, handwritten note in the mail:

We will kill you and your family.

Warm Regards

NMR (National Movement of Resistance)

Frighteningly, a small article can lead to a lot of hate. It was unpleasant enough to make me uncomfortable writing about it again. Extreme violence is real and needs to be taken very seriously. The social climate has become such that the consequences of a single article can influence the individual writer. Journalists, writers, and freelancers who do not have the backing of large and resourceful media companies with robust security departments will find it particularly difficult.

The so-called news sites run by the far right incite, the tail acts, and the sites refer to the tail in a vicious cycle. More established and "clean" bloggers and writers write and point, but perhaps rarely directly cross the line of what is legal or tolerable. But the tail understands and acts, and I got to feel that in my column on Odyssey:

Erik is a real asshole! Fucking asshole... and you call yourself a journalist!

Fucking psychopath. I guess the public service is full of people like you.

What mushrooms have you been eating?

You are beyond magically stupid.

You threaten people with torture, come and say it to my face, you old fat bastard, and you'll see.

The art of burning
a marijuana plant

Hate and threats from online trolls and right-wing nationalists are one thing. But when the threats come from the country's police, who are supposed to defend democracy and freedom of speech? It's easy to panic and become paranoid. So much so that one day I was afraid of what was in my flowerpot.

I went out on the balcony and tried to light a large marijuana plant. The smell of hashish spread all over my quarters. But the flames around the fresh green leaves wouldn't catch, and I panicked as the distinct and special scent spread across the western part of Stockholm. I put out the fire and went back to the kitchen. Just throwing the pot in the bucket under the kitchen counter was not an option. The police could go through the garbage. I was afraid of the police. The whole Stockholm police force was out to get me.

I tried flushing the plant down the toilet. That didn't work either. The leaves just floated to the top. How do you get rid of a potted plant? The big garbage can down in the yard did not work either. That could be searched by the police.

I was not a hardened drug addict or a marijuana grower. But I had a summer house north of Stockholm. At the entrance to the cottage was a bird feeder that had spilled some of its contents on the ground during the winter. During the summer we discovered a small herbaceous plant with lobed leaves under the bird table. Without really thinking about what it was, we took it home to the apartment in Stockholm, where the flower grew in the window. Eventually, some visiting friends asked us why we had started growing marijuana, and then we finally understood what happened to the hemp seeds spilled by the birds. But the plant was beautiful and stayed in the window among other flowers.

Until April, 1980, when the police came after me. There were big black headlines on the front page of *Kamraternas Föreningsnytt* - the magazine for the *comrades*, the association of Stockholm police officers. Gunno Gunnmo, the chairman of the union, wrote the words in big black capitals:

Erik Fichtelius

A danger to society - a threat to freedom of the press and the rule of law!

The president of the police union demanded that I be stopped. This would be read by every policeman in Stockholm. I was afraid, the spirit of the corps was strong. It's best to get rid of compromising material at home.

What had I done wrong? The police representative drew two high-profile stories.

I had broken a story that, in today's news climate, would certainly have had a different ending. Through a small-time gangster, I had made contact with various prostitutes in order to clarify some of the suspicions and rumors in the wake of the Geijer affair, i.e. the suspicion that the then Minister of Justice, Lennart Geijer, frequented a brothel. One thing led to another, and I got in touch with some young women who had gotten into trouble in various ways. They were 14 years old and had been placed in a juvenile home outside the city of Västerås in mid Sweden by the social services.

One of the girls had managed to escape and come to Stockholm. On Sergels Torg in the city, near the main train station, she was picked up by two men, patrolling police officers. She should be taken back to the juvenile home from which she ran away. But instead, the two officers took the broken girl to a room the subway personel used and to which the officers have access. There, the 14-year-old is raped by both officers before being dumped in the city.

The girl eventually contacts my sources and I hear her harrowing story. Ekot documents how a 14-year-old girl on the run from a juvenile detention center is raped by two police officers. The story in Ekot gets some attention in the evening press, but it does not cause the outrage it would in today's post #metoo world. Ekot's allegations were fairly easy to verify, but the newsroom refuses to give away any names or information beyond what was published on the radio.

The police's half-hearted investigation of the case went nowhere, and no charges were ever filed. According to Gunno Gunnmo, it was the police officers who suffered from the publicity. The case was particularly serious because I had previously exposed a serious case of alleged police abuse. This had attracted more attention and anger. Ekot's report in February 1980 about what happened in cell number two at a city police station shocked many people.

Late in the evening of December 4, 1979, 65-year-old Gösta was taken by ambulance from a detention cell at the police station to Sabbatsberg Hospital. His face was completely torn apart, his head swollen and round like a football. Gösta was between life and death. What had happened?

A few hours earlier he had been picked up by a police patrol under the Skanstull bridge, clean but drunk. He had been taken to the cell under the law on the care of intoxicated persons, to protect him from himself. Whatever happened in that small cell, it was unacceptable by all accounts that he was fatally injured a few hours later.

Ekot broadcast a special one-hour documentary on the case after several months of investigation. The police had completely failed to investigate what had happened. There was never any question of suspecting or investigating any police officers.

"The staff is free of any suspicion. They are nice guys who help them," explained the police inspector in charge.

The officer on duty had a vivid description of how the drunken Gösta had somehow managed to injure himself by falling repeatedly and then banging his head on the bars in the cell, causing injuries to his face and the back of his head. But the police officers and prison staff were not to be examined or questioned. One police officer dismissed the case without investigating the scene, without contacting the prosecutor, or ordering a forensic examination. He said it was impossible for the police to have attacked a peaceful man who had done nothing before. The public and politicians disagreed, calling for new regulations and a prosecutor-led investigation. Anonymous critics put sticky notes all over the city with the gruesome picture of the beaten uncle Gösta under the headline:

Help the city police - beat yourself up!

Uncle Gösta survived, but he never recovered and could not tell what really happened. The investigation, which started too late, was without result. But according to the police union, it was the police officers who suffered, and the dangerous reporter should be stopped. That's why I was so scared when I realized what was growing on my windowsill until I figured out what to do.

I cut the plant up and separated the leaves into several different small plastic bags. With a pounding heart and a constant glance over my shoulder, I stalked around the island of Långholmen in the city, distributing my dangerous cargo among the island's small garbage cans, where it mixed with dog poop and empty beer cans.

Celebrities, facts, relevance and news

When Swedish singer Anita Lindblom died on September 6, 2020, it was big news. One of Sweden's most famous and popular pop singers with songs like "Such is life" and "The ballad of the blue Barret" died at the age of 83. Many know her deep, sensual voice. She lived a stormy life and was married to the light weight champion Bosse Högberg for a few years. She died in her home on the French Riviera, in a village near the Italian border. Anita Lindblom moved or fled to France as early as 1969, because of large tax debts and trouble with the tax authorities. When I met her in Paris one early morning in 1974, she was wearing a large, fluffy white bathrobe.

I had just moved to Paris to learn French and try to make a living as a freelance journalist. Since I was living in France, I was able to make an agreement with the evening newspaper Aftonbladet that I would be available for freelance work, and in early February 1974 I got my first assignment for the newspaper:

- Anita Lindblom is returning to Sweden. Interview her! The evening editor of Aftonbladet sounded very excited. What a thing! Anita Lindblom had made a deal with the bailiffs and was moving back to Sweden. It was a big deal for me, too, but maybe not quite what I had in mind. I was supposed to be covering big, important news, not celebrities in trouble. Still, it was my first assignment, so I said I could handle it. Anita Lindblom was in the phone book. I hopped in a taxi to her apartment in central Paris. It was almost ten o'clock at night, and the concierge at her building explained that Madame Lindblom had moved a few months ago. I was given an address in the suburbs and thought I would have enough time to meet the deadline the next morning. Anita Lindblom's money had apparently not been enough to keep an apartment in the fancier neighborhoods. She now lived in a high-rise in the east of Paris, where the taxi dropped me off. I had a street and a number. But the concierge hadn't written down whether it was entrance A, B, C, or one of the twenty other stairwells with the same number. Now it was so late that the doors were locked. Too bad, but it was probably just a matter of giving up temporarily.

Maybe I would make it to the morning, because in the seventies the evening papers were still evening papers and the last deadline for the last editions was 10 o'clock in the morning. I returned early in the morning to the high-rise buildings in the suburbs and began to look for Mrs. Lindblom among the names in the doorways. Now I found her and could knock on the door. A sleep-deprived celebrity appeared in the apartment building, wearing a fluffy, wide bathrobe. I introduced myself and asked for an interview.

- Yes, she replied in her deep voice. It costs 5,000 crowns.

I asked her to wait. I had to check with the editors. It was a lot of money; 5,000 kronor is the equivalent of more than 3 000 US dollars in 2023. In the café on the street corner, I made a collect call to Stockholm. It was almost the first time I learned to use French really well, to spell my name in the new language:

Françoise - Isidor - Colette - Hector ...

Now the morning editors had taken over and I proudly explained that I had found Anita Lindblom and that she was willing to do an interview. The problem was that she wanted to be paid.

- What the fuck! shouted the editor. Five grands! To that old bitch! Why should we interview her? What's the big deal?

What had been big news the night before was now an irrelevant, or at least too expensive, request from an old woman. It was the same person, the same story, but the evaluation of the news was different between the evening and morning news. News is not an exact science. The question is whether it is science at all.

I went back to a snotty Anita Lindblom and explained apologetically that Aftonbladet was no longer interested. She was 37 years old in 1974 and would live another 45 years, until the fall of 2020. By then, she was still so well known that her death had become news everywhere, but the estate did not demand payment.

What is news? I have struggled with this question all my life. My thesis is that the value of news should not be determined by who benefits or is harmed by a piece of news, as long as it is true and relevant. The editor should choose news because it is news, not because it suits a particular ruler, party, or government. This is about what should *not* be the basis for evaluating news. But what should? What is it? News is what a news editor says is news. The problem is that different news editors can say different things.

In the evening papers, there was a huge difference between the evening and morning teams. At certain times in the seventies, it was not uncommon for the tough morning editors, who had the final say before the paper went to press, to throw out more than half of what the "pussies" in the evening newsroom produced. This may have been fine as long as the money flowed in, but later generations of editors-in-chief were forced to make the evening and morning news evaluations more similar. If only for economic reasons.

News is supposed to be true and relevant. The concept of truth deserves its own chapter, while relevance in this context refers to the concept of news, i.e., its importance to the intended audience. Is the story interesting to the readers, listeners and viewers of your newspaper, radio or television station? Then it is news to them. What is news in *Horse and Hound* magazine may not be news in New York Times. If the news is about a movie set in outer space, there aren't even horses in the movie, and it's definitely not of interest to Horse and Hound magazine. This is said with a wink to anyone who, like me, loves the movie Notting Hill. But again, what is news?

It is more a matter of feeling than of precisely definable values. An experienced news journalist feels what is good news but has difficulty explaining it in intellectual or academic terms. As a visiting professor at the JMK School of Journalism at Stockholm University in 1996 -97, I was to write a textbook on news journalism, and I started by going to the department's library. I asked to borrow all the books that said what news was, but the librarian just laughed at me.

- That's not possible, she said.

I thought the books were on loan and asked to be put on the waiting list. Then I was told I was naive.

- There are no such books!

There is no common academic definition of the concept of news. Yet news is an entire field of study. Håkan Hvitfelt, a professor at JMK, has both researched and written about news. He follows a research tradition from Norway, where a young scholar Johan Galtung studied several morning newspapers in the 1960s. The sociologist Johan Galtung, who later became known as a peace and conflict researcher, began his academic career by cutting and pasting newspapers at home. He was able to derive the concept of news and systematize what topics could be expected to make the front page. Galtung speaks of thresholds of intensity and proximity that must be crossed for the news to be published. The probability of publication increases when the news is close in time and space. Once the initial resistance to a particular news story has been overcome, it becomes easier in the future for that particular type of news.

In a follow-up study twenty years later, Håkan Hvitfelt found that it is more likely that a story will be produced, published and placed on the front page if it is about:

- A traditional topic
- with a short distance
- to actual events

- that are both sensational and surprising
- involve specific individuals
- and are simple
- important or relevant
- occur over a short period of time, but as part of a theme
- are negative
- and derived from traditional sources.

Comfort to a tiger's heart. To find out what's going on, academics look at what editors tend to value most. The practical expertise I have acquired over the years carries some weight. What comes out on top depends on an elusive sense of news. For me, this was very evident when I joined Ekot in the early seventies. As a new substitute, I often had to take the harsh early morning shift. We would sit there with a few reporters and evaluate what news should be broadcast. If Ekot classified something as news, it was easier for others to make the same assessment. It felt both heavy and responsible. But how did we know? We went with our gut. Even though there was an older editor in the group with more experience, it was very clear that judging news was a fluid concept.

Over the years, I have tried to approach the concept of news in a number of ways. I wrote a textbook on news that has been translated into about ten languages and used around the world. In that book, *News Journalism - Ten Golden Rules*, I formulated a set of criteria for what is news. It should be important, fresh, unknown, close in time and space, unusual, personal, exciting and original. A persistent misconception can also be news. I have also written a more light-hearted book in which I try to define the concept in one hundred and one questions and answers. The closest I come is the last question and answer in the book:

What is news, really?

Short answer: A change, sudden or slow, that is interesting enough to make the newscast or the front page.

Long answer: This book has thus become a long search for an elusive concept. However, it is possible to roughly define what this mystery is. The basic element is that it is a change that can be captured and told. It is not enough that it has happened, we must be able to understand it. And there has to be someone who can observe and tell the story in an interesting way. We have to bite the bullet and realize that a lot of it is about cultural conventions about what we have learned to consider news. But also understand that the need to know what is going on around us is a basic human survival instinct.

What makes this so difficult is that it involves tacit, practical knowledge. What you might say is "in the walls". But these walls are permeated not only by smoke, but also by the zeitgeist and a cultural heritage. During some years Ekot had several reporters who covered the situation of inmates in prisons and several labor market reporters, a specialization that has almost disappeared today. But then there were no climate reporters or European Union specialists. Saucepan-journalism was the pejorative term for consumer issues when Konsumentekot started in the mid-eighties and brought the topic into the real news. Editorial priorities change over time, and news evaluation vary from country to country. In several Latin American countries, for example, news about UFO:s is on the agenda. Icelandic media, of course, have news about fairies and goblins, which are very much a part of everyday life in Iceland, but not in Sweden. Ghosts appear more often in Indian media. Since the U.S. defense establishment and mainstream media have begun to pay more serious attention to unidentified flying objects, the reporting has changed and is no longer routinely dismissed as nonsense.

There is also a geographical limitation to news coverage. For a Swedish news consumer, one injured person in the municipality of Skövde is more important than five hundred dead people in Mumbai, India. For those who live in Skövde, it is more interesting to know what is happening at home than what is happening far away with people with whom they have no relationship. The opposite is true for people living in Mumbai. The news value decreases with the square of the distance. This is about local news value, not human value.

News is emotion, convention and expectation. News is not only what journalists choose to publish as news, but also what audiences have come to recognize as news. Research shows that if a newscast or newspaper does not contain 80% of what the audience expects, it will not be perceived as news. Thus, the delivery of news is governed by convention and sometimes by prejudice.

Change is at the heart of the concept of news. There are sudden changes, like a plane crashing, someone being murdered, a party winning an election. Change that happens immediately. But there must also be room for slow change. Sooner or later, land rise should become news. Climate change is big news, even if it doesn't happen overnight.

There is a real difference between views and news. In a newspaper, editing and headlines can clearly show the distinction. At the same time, commentary journalism can create a gray area. Views can be disguised as news, and a biased selection can be hidden in a journalistically neutral form. When journalists and anchors move effortlessly between being opinionated commentators and news reporters in the same program or newspaper, the lines become blurred. But they are boundaries that can be maintained by whoever decides to maintain them. News consumers can also make demands, and through their viewing habits or media purchases, reward those who strive for impartial and objective reporting.

Sham Marriage and Smuggling

One night in the late summer of 1971, my car rolls off the ferry from Ystad to Świnoujście in Poland. The headlights are dazzling, guards in long brown coats with automatic weapons slung over their shoulders are shouting orders in an unknown language. "Passport" and "control" are understandable, even if they are in Polish. I am traveling with a friend from Uppsala, but I am scared. I'm on a reporting tour for Swedish Radio, but I've also accepted another secret mission. There are two bags in my trunk. One with clothes and toiletries, the other with forbidden literature. Half of the luggage consists of exile literature, including books by the Russian writer Aleksandr Solzhenitsyn. Such dirty literature was banned in Poland during the Soviet occupation.

One of the guards waves his submachine gun at the trunk lid in the dark. I have time to think that this is it. The soldier points to my travel companion and taps one of the bags. I protest incomprehensibly, no, that bag is mine. But the inspector is unrelenting and forces me to open it. What have I gotten myself into? It is a large, paved area in the port area, an inhospitable customs station. The weather is rough and cold. The roaring guard has chosen one of the bags and is rummaging through shirts, underwear, toothbrushes, and soap. He shakes his head, slams the bag shut, and raises his hand to the trunk. Close it!

It was enough to examine one of the bags. The one I didn't "want" to examine. The dangerous bag was never checked. We could close the trunk and continue into the darkness. Into communist Poland. Only in retrospect do I realize how careless I was. On a reporting trip for Swedish Radio, I was smuggling banned opposition literature to one of the regime's most hated resistance groups, those who would eventually help overthrow the dictatorship.

I was part of the circle of hope, as my friend Gienek Smolar called it. He gave me the content of the bag, but he himself could not go to Poland. He was a political refugee in Sweden. Gienek and I were fellow students at the Department of Sociology in Uppsala in the early seventies. His full name is Eugeniusz Smolar. He and his wife Nina are Jews, and they decided to leave Poland in 1970 because of severe political and anti-Semitic oppression. Gienek and Nina were part of a small group of left-liberal intellectuals who formed the vanguard of what would become the Solidarity trade union. The group gathered around historian and journalist Adam Michnik and organizer Jacek Kuroń. The group eventually called itself KOR - *Komitet Obrony Robotników* (Workers' Defense Committee). Also supported by the Smolar brothers, KOR would play a major role in modern Polish history. KOR leaders and hundreds of their sympathizers were persecuted and harassed by the authorities and often ended up in prison.

Gienek and his brother Aleksander were among the organizers of the great student protests in Warsaw in March 1968. The students revolted against repression and censorship, and soon the demonstrations had spread to all the universities and technical and medical colleges in Poland. Many young workers joined in. The regime responded with mass arrests, anti-intellectual and anti-Semitic propaganda. Aleksander Smolar was arrested and imprisoned; Gienek initially escaped. But when Gienek led new student protests in August 1968, after the Warsaw Pact invaded Czechoslovakia, he was arrested and imprisoned along with many others. Many lost their jobs and study permits, while hundreds were sentenced to prison. Gienek was sentenced to 18 months in prison and suspended from the university.

This also became an anti-Semitic campaign by the Polish government. Within a few years, more than 15,000 Jews were forced to emigrate from Poland. When Gienek was released from prison in 1970, he, his brother Aleksander, and Nina were among those who chose to leave the country. Aleksander moved to Paris, while Gienek and Nina ended up in Uppsala, where we became fellow students. Gienek studied sociology and Nina continued her doctoral studies in cancer research in biochemistry.

With Aleksander in Paris, Gienek and Nina in Uppsala, and Michnik and Kuroń still in Poland, they decided to do what many other Polish exiles had done before them - publish books and newspapers. They started the quarterly *Aneks - Annex to the Censored Press in Poland*. The magazine featured articles and essays by the great thinkers and writers of Poland and

Europe: Samuel Huntington, Alain Besançon, Hannah Arendt, Arthur Koestler, Alexandr Solzhenitsyn, Andrei Sakharov, Roy Medvedev, Zbigniew Brzezinski, Leszek Kołakowski, and Zygmunt Bauman, to name just a few of the top names. Many also wrote in the Paris-based exile magazine *Kultura*.

Newspapers and books were produced and distributed in the seventies through a combination of samizdat, tamizdat, and radio, in what Gienek Smolar has called the "circle of hope". Samizdat is illegal literature printed in the country, while tamizdat is literature printed abroad and smuggled into the country. *Aneks* was a tamizdat publication, printed in 2,000 copies, 1,500 of which were smuggled into Poland by various means. There it could be distributed further in samizdat form or through articles read on BBC broadcasts throughout Poland. It became a circle of information, news and literature.

Gienek and Nina opened the doors to another world for me. Both the one in front of me and the one far away. My friends thrived in Sweden and we spent lots of times together. But they carried with them the legacy of Soviet oppression that still plagued Sweden's neighbor, Poland. I was probably not surprised when they asked me for a favor in the winter of 1971.

- Could you go to Warsaw and marry Ewa? It's her best chance to get out.

Ewa was one of their friends. The border was closed, and Ewa found herself on the fringes of the circle of oppositional young Poles. Her boyfriend Stanislaw had managed to escape to Sweden and was granted political asylum. Ewa would not have been able to leave Poland so easily. She and Stanislaw had a little girl, Magda, who was not even a year old when Stanislaw managed to get out of Poland.

It was a hell of a thing. A single man in Stockholm, a single young woman with a small child in Warsaw, trapped under oppression. Thus. on a spring day in 1971, six months before my smuggling trip, I find myself in the town hall of the Wola district of Warsaw, the capital of Poland.

- I don't understand what he's saying, but you should just repeat what I've said, says the young Swedish student who was acting as interpreter.

The mayor of the gray concrete block administers the marriage oath in Polish. The Swedish student tries to instruct me so that I can repeat the oath in Swedish. It works, but no one but me and the interpreter understands how crazy it is. We stumble through the ceremony.

Bengt, the interpreter, described the scene many years later as a Monty Python sketch, long before Monty Python. The street where the City Hall stands has since been renamed Solidarity Alley.

In 1971 I went to Warsaw to marry Ewa so that she could leave communism and be reunited with Magda's father. It was a classic sham marriage. Not primarily so that Ewa could come to Sweden, but so that she could leave Poland in an orderly fashion. I married Ewa the day after I met her. Before that, we had been exchanging hot love letters for several months to give the letter censor something to bite into. When we had both taken the oath, the officiant pressed a little button under his table and Mendelsohn's Wedding March crackled through the poor speakers. There is something strange about Eastern European boredom. Everything in the gray smells of turnips. Ewa's friends are throwing rice at us outside the dreary building. Ewa has her daughter Magda in a tight grip.

Then we celebrate for several days in Ewa's small apartment in the center of Warsaw. Brown, smoky and with a deadly gas flame heating the shower water. Ewa is a photographer and art historian, and many of her friends are journalists. Several of them work for state television, and at night they drink vodka in large glasses and smoke stinky unfiltered cigarettes. It is at night that I learn the truth. Ewa and her friends say they live a life of lies and occupation. Some of them think that Russians should be hung from lampposts, and that the only truths they are allowed to report on the news are about US abuses in Vietnam. When it comes to the Vietnam War, there are no major restrictions on what can be said. Otherwise, there is strict censorship, which is best drowned in vodka on dark evenings in the tired and gray Polish capital. They were deeply pessimistic, and there seemed to be no hope for the future.

Gienek Smolar didn't just ask me to go to Poland and help. More than six months later, I went to Poland on a reporting trip for the radio, and Gienek helped me with contacts and information. This time he asked me to bring the bag with the dangerous literature.

The big suitcase with the forbidden literature was hot. It was to be delivered to Gienek's friends in Warsaw. To shake off any potential pursuers, I had to switch between bus and taxi and make my way to an address several blocks from the apartment where the group's leader, Adam Michnik, and his friends were waiting. There were no security police pursuers in sight. I dragged my luggage up the narrow stairs of a run-down apartment building. It's like Christmas in the warm and dark apartment when I arrive. Soft, battered furniture and a small kitchen with a gas stove. With eager hands, the small group throws themselves at the books. I realize that each book I have smuggled will be passed from person to person in many stages as part of the circle of hope. Adam Michnik is pale, having just been released after six months in prison. But now his eyes shine.

I feel stupid and ignorant because I have hardly read any of the books that my Polish friends are so happy about. The kitchen is crowded and everyone's talking. They ask me to smuggle something else back to Sweden. They explain that they have managed to hide a unique historical document. It is an eight-hour recording of a strike meeting at the Szczecin shipyard on the night of January 23-24, 1971, a dramatic moment in Polish history. A month before the shipyard meeting, in December 1970, there had been a shocking increase in food prices, leading to violent protests throughout the country, especially in the major shipyards around Gdansk, Gdynia and Szczecin. Large numbers of military and police forces were deployed to the coastal shipping industry, and on December 17, clashes left more than seventy people dead and about a thousand injured. The situation was very tense, the regime was shaken and party secretary Władysław Gomułka was dismissed. He was replaced by Edward Gierek.

At the end of January 1971, the shipyard workers were still
on strike and occupied their workplaces. The new party secretary
Gierek went there as soon as he took power. Late in the evening
of the 23rd he simply knocked on the doors of the occupied
shipyard in Szczecin. Edward Gierek entered with a handful of top
party officials. He has with him the Prime Minister, the Minister
of Defense, the Minister of the Interior, and several other party
leaders. It's a serious situation, but this is long before Lech Wałęsa,
who was one of the strikers in Gdansk, appears on the national
stage.

Edward Gierek is placed on a podium next to the leaders of the
striking workers. For everyone in the shipyard to hear what is said
during the meeting, microphones and loudspeakers are used in an
internal PA system. It also allows someone to secretly record the
incredible meeting. To loud applause, the striking workers' leaders
read out a twelve-point list of demands, including a reduction
in food prices, free union elections, no reprisals against striking
workers, an end to harassment by the security police, and demands
for more and accurate and free information in the media about
what is happening. Interestingly, most of the strongest demands
are for democracy and freedom of expression, rather than food
and wages. The tape is clear and dramatic. The leader of the party,
Edward Gierek, is occasionally interrupted by shouts and screams,
which are carefully noted in the later transcript. When he finished
speaking, a meeting began that lasted all night. The shipyard
workers testified about their lives and complained directly to the
new leader. The chairman of the meeting gives the floor freely, and

everything that is said and heard is written down verbatim from the secret recording:

- Who wants to speak? Who is ready? The delegate from K-1? Yes?

The delegate from K-1:

"... But does Comrade Gierek know that we can no longer count the corpses here, because it is difficult to calculate how many were picked up on the street. (Shouting and screaming in the hall.) Oh, it may not be the number, but people fell, the bullets whistled. And those bullets - how were they bought? With money from our sweat. That is what is so hard to bear. How is it possible that the working class can be turned against the working class?

I ask, what is the purpose of this militia? To beat up honest people and protect parasites? The methods of the militia need to be changed. And the leaders must also be changed, the aristocracy that steals everything. (Loud applause.) If we really want to elect our representatives, we must get rid of all those who have elbowed their way into their comfortable chairs, where they have been sitting so long that their pants have begun to mold. They are useless. We are fighting to change the representatives. Especially at the base. It's like a fish, the head rots first, but it has

to be cleaned from the tail fin upwards. All this is
not directed against comrade Gierek. I am finished.
Thank you!"

The party secretary is forced to listen, apologize, and promise reforms. The night rally is a unique event in the history of Poland and Europe. The recording is now in a small apartment in Warsaw. The opposition group I met has several tapes with copies of the recording, but no one has managed to get it out of the country.

- Could you possibly...? asks Adam Michnik.

Together with Ekot's Polish-speaking correspondent, Göran Skånsberg, I made a radio documentary in January 1972 with the unique material and the voices of the shipyard workers. Neither we nor the Swedish audience really understood the importance of what we were broadcasting late on a weekday evening on P1. The program was not even considered important enough to be saved in the Swedish Radio archives, and it no longer exists.

My friends Gienek and Nina in Uppsala worked hard to have the recordings of the dramatic night meeting transcribed word for word. They published the whole material with one of the exile publishers in Paris. Newspapers and magazines all over Europe reproduced long excerpts and summaries, but no one was told how the secret tapes had gotten out of Poland.48 Books containing the printed transcripts were smuggled back into Poland and distributed within and by the opposition, in the very circle of hope that Gienek called it. The material formed the basis of a filmed drama-documentary of the events. In 1976, the British television company Granada produced the film *Three Days in Szczecin*, which reenacted the dramatic meeting at the shipyard. Almost twenty years before the fall of the Berlin Wall, the shipyard workers in Poland showed the direction of development. That was the documentation I was able to get out of Poland.

My sham marriage to Eva was of a more private nature, but the other thing I did in Poland was totally against my role as a reporter. I preach objectivity. Here I had become an activist smuggling documents back and forth to an opposition group where the leader of Solidarity, Lech Wałęsa, would eventually emerge as the leader. In the early seventies, I was not a neutral reporter, but active in the struggle against the Polish regime. This was hardly compatible with the role of a radio reporter. But my bosses knew nothing about it, no one was informed about my secret work, and it could hardly have been approved. I had crossed the line rather unknowingly.

My former colleague and managing editor, Stig Fredrikson, did something similar when he was a correspondent in Moscow for the TT news agency. He became a courier for author Aleksandr Solzhenitsyn, smuggling the future Nobel Prize winner's manuscript to the West for publication. But Stig had at least informed his superiors and received their approval. Personally, I acted entirely on my own. Willful and stubborn, a little too young to understand the context. What I did was part of a larger democracy work that, if it had become known, would probably not have been condemned in Sweden, but would have resulted in heavy prison sentences in Poland. I became a small cog in a well-organized resistance that was much larger than I understood at the time.

My friends Gienek and Nina Smolar were right, there was repression against our neighbors, and Swedish youth were demonstrating mostly against the US war in Vietnam. This was a blind spot for many in Swedish politics. But that did not give me the right to leave the role of journalist to become an activist. It is important to realize what this role is and what it requires, which is perhaps easier to understand for those who have violated principles, as I did with both smuggling and a sham marriage. At the same time, I have learned about lies and hypocrisy. I don't want to be a part of that.

Six months after the wedding, Ewa came to Sweden with her and Stanislaw's daughter. A few days later she called me in despair and said in broken English:

- Erik, I have to talk to you ...

Also living in Stanislaw's small apartment in the center of Stockholm, was Maria from Portugal. She was eight months pregnant. Stanislaw had met someone else. What would Ewa do in Sweden now? My family, Gienek and Nina and some Poles in Uppsala had to try to help her. Ewa moved to Uppsala, where she found an apartment and began studying Swedish. It was a real sham marriage in the sense that we never even kissed. When we got divorced and had to go to compulsory mediation, Ewa began by saying in broken Swedish that it was a long and lasting separation. The mediator, a local politician, just laughed:

- Aha, it's a sham marriage.

Ewa and Magda moved back to Poland and after a few years
we lost contact. I never heard from her or about her. Our mutual
friends Gienek and Nina Smolar finished their studies in Uppsala
and moved to London after a few years. Nina continued her cancer
research, while Gienek got a job at the Polish branch of the BBC.
After a few years, he became head of the Polish broadcasts and
a member of the editorial board of the BBC World Service. Part
of the content of the programs was material from Aneks, which
was read aloud during the broadcasts. Samizdat - Tamizdat - Radio
- smuggled books, newspapers and documents - The Circle of
Hope.

In November 1988, during the last year of the Cold War, when
British Prime Minister Margaret Thatcher was scheduled to visit
Poland, both Warsaw and the Gdansk shipyards, Gienek Smolar
was registered as part of the BBC delegation. The Poles initially
refused to accept this renegade. Gienek Smolar is still proud
of Thatcher's stubborn reaction: "No Gienek, no visit..." was
Thatcher's immediate reply to the Polish ambassador in London.

Gienek received a three-day visa and was able to visit Poland
for the first time in 18 years. It is not for a government to
decide which reporters can cover a story. But Gienek had a
dual role, both as a BBC correspondent and as an unofficial
adviser to Thatcher. He helped her prepare for the meeting
with General Jaruzelski and other Polish leaders. Gienek attended
Thatcher's meeting in Gdansk with the Polish government
and some 20 Solidarity leaders, including Lech Wałęsa and

Tadeusz Mazowiecki, who would later become Poland's first non-Communist prime minister.

- This was a problem, says Gienek, not only in this case, but in all my activities, smuggling materials, courting politicians and trade unions, and so on. It was stressful at times, but I built a strong Chinese wall between the two missions. Not only in the way I did my own reporting, but also in the way I managed the whole Polish bureau.

Gienek Smolar's bosses were fully informed and supported him. Exile writers, books, and the work of the opposition group KOR paved the way for the Solidarity trade union movement and its leader, Lech Wałęsa. It contributed to the fall of the Polish communist regime and later to the fall of the Berlin Wall.

The Smolars were finally able to return home. Wałęsa became president and was awarded the Nobel Peace Prize, Jacek Kuroń became minister of social affairs, and Adam Michnik became editor-in-chief of Poland's largest daily newspaper, Gazeta Wyborcza. Aleksander Smolar became an advisor to Prime Minister Tadeusz Mazowiecki. Gienek joined the management of Polish Radio as program director.

Talking to Gienek on the phone now, he sighs deeply: "I never thought I would have to become a democracy activist now again.

In the late 1960s, Gienek was fighting communist oppression. In the 2020s, it is the onslaught of right-wing nationalist forces. The Polish authoritarian regime has attacked public service, replaced managers and journalists and turning radio and television into the same kind of propaganda channels they were under communism. Once the right-wing government took control of the public service, it went after newspapers, courts and universities. Through state-controlled companies, the regime even gained control of major regional newspapers and took over all newspaper distribution in the country.

Since 2016, Gienek Smolar has had to resume his work to fight for Polish democracy. The circle of hope he spoke of has not closed. Adam Michnik, Gienek Smolar and their friends have fought a long battle. Perhaps it was not in vain. In the Polish elections in the fall of 2023, the right-wing authoritarian regime lost its majority, and hope for liberal forces was rekindled.

But what happened to Ewa, whom I married? Ewa's boyfriend Stanislaw stayed in Sweden, but he became ill and died a few years later. I lost contact with Ewa. In the new year 2020/21 I finally get Ewa's address with the help of the Swedish student who reluctantly interpreted the wedding ceremony fifty years ago. The interpreter's language is no longer so fragile. His name is Bengt Samuelson, and he has become a prominent translator and interpreter of Russian and Polish literature into Swedish. His latest work is a new edition of fourteen volumes of Dostoyevsky.

When we get in touch, Ewa tells me that she lives in her old parental home in a small village outside Warsaw. She has forgotten Swedish and speaks little English, so her youngest daughter translates for her. The oldest daughter, Magda, lives nearby and has children of her own; Ewa met a new husband when she moved back and had another daughter who learned English well enough to translate her mother's letter to me. When the communist regime fell, Ewa helped run a local citizens' committee to get people to vote in the first democratic elections in June 1989. She became editor of the small community's opposition newspaper. Then, when more individual initiatives became possible, Ewa got involved in a school for students with special language needs and with space for children with Down's syndrome.

Today, she dreams of making a film about the growth of the Polish silk industry. "I started to write a script," she says. "But then the corona came. I'm a little harmed and tired. But I know my eldest daughter, Magda, wants me to be richer and smarter."

Censorship
– The Antithesis of Consequence Neutraliy

It was the day of the ceremonial awarding of the "Farmer of the Year" prize to Poland's most industrious farmers. On an autumn day in the late seventies, the party secretary himself, Edward Gierek, was to present the prestigious award to a farmer in a small village in the middle of the countryside. This required preparation. On the farm of the selected farmer, the local party committee set up a borrowed tractor and drove cows and pigs to make the farm look more prosperous. All the houses along the road to the farm had to be painted before the visit. The rough gravel road across the fields was not considered comfortable enough for the waiting cortege, so it was decided to pave it. My old colleague from Aktuellt, the 9 o'clock News, Jacek Stanczyk, was then working as a sound engineer for Polish state television. He accompanied Comrade Gierek on the trip and, together with a photographer, documented everything for the evening news.

Jacek Stanczyk and his wife and TV colleague Elisabeth told me about the visit.

The new paint had only been applied to the facades, so the gables and sides of the houses were still worn and peeling. Unfortunately, the local party administration had only managed to get one color. All the facades facing the street were pink. It had also been difficult to obtain a steamroller, so the actual paving of the roads leading to the farm had only begun the night before the visit. It was a cold and damp morning when the First Secretary of the Central Committee arrived in the village in his caravan of black Tatra cars. Jacek had left early to record the high-level visit.

The motorcade rolls slowly across the fields toward a long row of pink houses. The idyll is disrupted by an old lady who comes cycling up a path toward the road, just where the motorcade is about to pass. A security guard jumps on the terrified woman and knocks her into a ditch. Just as the party secretary passes by, she lies screaming in despair, bouncing on the side of the road with a security guard on top of her. Edward Gierek must hear the noise, but he stares straight ahead.

The newly laid asphalt is still hot as Edward Gierek's large black motorcade makes its way to the farm. Steam from the hot asphalt forms a cloud nearly a meter high over the fields. Polish television gets great footage of a long line of black cars floating in a sea of fog with pink houses in the background.

Unfortunately, Polish TV viewers never got to see this surreal film. The Polish censors had very detailed and specific rules about how the First Party Secretary could be portrayed, and they were particularly careful about how he looked on television. Every picture of First Party Secretary Comrade Gierek that was to be published had to be approved in advance:

"Before publication, all pictures of the First Secretary of the Central Committee and other pictures of the party leadership must be approved by the Press, Radio and Television Department of the Central Committee PZPR," the censorship regulations stated.

The public was also never told what happened after the celebrated and well-orchestrated visit. The farmer who suddenly received a tractor and new cows and pigs on his farm and refused to let them go when the Communist leader went home.

"They are mine," said the farmer stubbornly now that he had Edward Gierek as a witness. No one dared to take the valuable props from him.

Censorship is strong and oppressive in many countries. More than thirty years after the fall of the Berlin Wall, it is difficult to understand or remember how total the control was and how the censorship worked. How the possible consequences of even the smallest piece of news had to determine whether it could be published or not. At the same time, it is the threads of the old Soviet structure that we see today when the Russian regime lies about its war of aggression against Ukraine.

Censorship has a long history and is very well documented in Poland under communism. This is thanks to censor no. C-36, Tomasz Strzyżewski. One day in February 1977, he boarded the ferry from Szczecin to Sweden. Wrapped in plastic, mixed with newspaper clippings, and taped to his legs and back, the fugitive censor had with him about seven hundred pages of documents that he had stolen or copied from the Krakow Main

Office for the Control of the Press, Printed Matter and Public
Performances. These were documents that Tomasz Strzyżewski
had been carefully collecting since the summer of 1975. The straw
that broke the camel's back for him was the regime's attempt to
hide the truth about the Katyn massacre, in which thousands of
Polish officers and other leaders were murdered by the Russians
at the beginning of World War II. Soviet historians blamed the
killings on the Nazis, and censorship rules prevented the names
of the victims from being published. One of them was Tomasz
Strzyżewski's own grandfather.

Thanks to the defection of Censor No. C-36, the world got
a unique insight into how censorship worked under the Polish
communist regime. This is a relief for today's censorship and
propaganda under authoritarian regimes. Tomasz Strzyżewski was
given detailed instructions and decisions on censorship. They
showed how far control extended into the smallest corner and
how obviously the party leadership feared that the truth about
conditions in Poland would reach its own people. The instructions
were collected in a loose-leaf system with black covers, commonly
referred to as the Black Book. The documents were published in
Polish in 1977 by the exile publisher Aneks in London and then
smuggled back to Poland, where they were secretly distributed
according to the well-established method of the Circle of Hope.
Again, my old friends from Uppsala, Gienek and Nina Smolar,
were the driving forces.

When the exiled censor Strzyżewski landed in Sweden, he first
approached Radio Free Europe to hand over his documents, but

they refused. They could not believe that such absurd censorship rules were authentic. Thomas Strzyżewski then contacted Aneks. Gienek and Nina examined the smuggled material and found it to be authentic. The Black Book was published in Polish and translated into English under the title *The Black Book of Polish Censorship.*

The Polish Censorship Office was a very large and powerful organization, with headquarters in an alleyway next to the party headquarters and large regional offices throughout the country. But being a censor was not a high-status job, although the power over the media was great. Many censors were politicians who could not get jobs elsewhere, hired through contacts or relatives higher in the party hierarchy. The lack of expertise meant that instructions to staff had to be extremely detailed. It is also the level of detail in the documents that is so frightening. The instructions were strictly secret, even the very existence of a censor was secret, except to the journalists who had to deal with the rules. But the people understood and knew that the news was controlled and false. The leading editors, of course, knew about the censorship, and they could negotiate with the censors or try to have the decisions reviewed higher up in the Party. The editors themselves were high-ranking Party members, except for the tightly controlled Catholic press, which was not controlled by the Party. All this led to a high degree of arbitrariness and opened the door for rival forces to make different decisions in their own interests.

The whole point of the operation was to present conditions in Poland as a happy paradise and to prevent any criticism of the Soviet Union. Citizens and the outside world were to be convinced that in Poland there was no crime, no accidents, no alcoholism, no serious or contagious diseases. Cities and countryside were clean and well-maintained, and there was no environmental degradation. Workers and farmers worked happily for good wages with ideal working conditions. Women workers had no problem balancing work and family. Food and consumer goods were always plentiful at fixed prices with no inflation. No one, neither celebrities nor political leaders, lived better than anyone else. Athletes were role models and young people were well educated. Families were well provided for, and the elderly well cared for. Not even the flu could darken the bright Polish sky. Of course, no one wanted or even tried to leave this paradise.

It sounds fantastic and crazy at the same time, but this was the image the regime wanted to portray of Poland. This was how the picture was to be painted, and anything that did not conform to this would be censored. Everything required total control of the media and instructions down to the last detail. My two good friends and colleagues Elisabeth and Jacek Stanczyk and I worked together at Aktuellt in the 1990s. Elisabeth was a film editor, Jacek a photographer. Both had previously worked for Polish television. But in the spring of 1981, Jacek and Elisabeth began to sense where things were headed. They managed to get to Sweden before the military coup in December that year. What was broadcast on Polish state television, especially the evening news, was a top priority for the party leadership. Senior party officials were present in the clipping rooms, in addition to the usual censors. There were some film sequences in particular, that Elisabeth always had to cut out before the reports were given the go-ahead to be broadcast. Pigs were never to be shown in the news. Polish housewives were not to be reminded of the existence of such animals in Poland, as there was no pig meat in the shops. The pork was exported to the Soviet Union and what little remained in Poland was reserved for the nomenklatura, the party bosses and their families. Ordinary people found it very difficult to obtain pork and it was best not to remind them unnecessarily. This was also reflected in the instructions in the Black Book:

> No information regarding Poland's meat exports to
> the USSR is allowed.

> *Section IV, paragraph* 12.

Any foreign trade statistics was sensitive information. The population associated empty shop shelves with the export of valuable goods and it was strictly forbidden to suggest that Western goods were better than Polish ones. There was no mention of coffee consumption, to "make it impossible to calculate how much coffee is exported".

> Information about the licenses purchased by Poland
> from capitalist countries should be eliminated from
> the mass media. This ban applies to both new and
> old license agreements. A lot of such information

could lead the average reader to the conclusion that
the usual way to modernize our economy is to buy
licenses from advanced capitalist countries.

Information note No. 3, 1975.

The secret bans were explained in detail so that the censors
could understand the reasons for the regulations. Since the lack
of food under communism was one of the causes of growing
popular discontent, there were extremely numerous and detailed
censorship regulations concerning food and food production.
Nothing could be said about the shortcomings in the ability of
department stores to buy beef and pork from farmers, nothing
could be published about the harvest or comparisons between this
year's and last year's harvests. It was allowed to write about sugar
shortages in other countries, but nothing about the sugar shortage
in Poland.

By reading what was not allowed to be published, it is possible
to understand what was missing. The population would be
prevented from understanding the extent of the abuses. As one of
the directors of the Press Department of the Central Committee
explained to a group of journalists:

- Until we say it is bad, it is good.

Did censorship serve its purpose? Jane Leftwich Curry, who
edited and translated *The Black Book of Polish Censorship* into
English, argues in her conclusions that censorship had quite
the opposite effect than intended. It made it impossible for

communist party to govern Poland. Instead of increasing the popularity of the regime, the people learned that the press lied and that the communist leaders who controlled it also lied. Instead of increasing control for the leaders, the gap between reality and the regime's images widened. By denying any wrongdoing, the leadership lost its authority and opened the door to the opposition and the independent trade union movement. One of the most important tasks of the KOR opposition group from its inception, in addition to providing intellectual support to the protesting workers, was to help build an independent and underground news service like that operated by Gienek Smolar in London and his comrades in Poland. Thus, despite the vast apparatus of control, despite the repression and the detailed instructions to the censors, the regime failed to achieve its goal.

As Gienek Smolar puts it, censorship had another fundamental function under communism. It was to create the impression that there were no alternatives. The Soviet Union was powerful, the West was in crisis and would not help. The current situation was the only option for Poland and the Poles. The Soviet Union would be the leader for centuries, so keep your mouth shut, don't revolt, don't get involved in politics, or else...

Censorship is a very strong word, but it is often misused. Censorship is an act of the state, associated with repression and lack of freedom of speech and of the press. It is not censorship when a publisher rejects a manuscript, a newspaper rejects a letter to the editor, or a private social media platform removes hate speech or incitement to violence. Most importantly, censorship is much more than a bureaucrat cutting, deleting, or stopping entire articles or books. It is also a proactive system of giving instructions on how to angle and emphasize things, what to choose, and what image to convey. The purpose of censorship is to exercise power to achieve certain intended effects with what is published. Therefore, censorship is the antithesis of consequence neutrality.

This is very clear in the Polish censor's instructions on how the party secretary should be photographed, or in the additional instructions when the Polish cardinal Karol Wojtyła was elected pope in 1978. Wojtyła was the Cardinal of Krakow and thus one of the leaders of the Polish Catholic Church, along with Cardinal Stefan Wyszyński, the head of the Church. The Church was tolerated by the regime, which could not cope with the strong Catholicism in Poland. The Catholic Church was an independent force, and when one of its leaders became Pope, this potential opposition movement was naturally strengthened. How would the censored media react to the news of Wojtyła's elevation to Pope John Paul II?

Elisabeth Stanczyk told me how panic broke out in the TV newsroom in Warsaw. "Everyone was running like scalded rats," she said. Could this news be broadcast? If so, how would it be presented? This was so unique that there were no guidelines. No one dared to do anything but remain silent. The fact that for the first time in history a Polack had been elected as God's representative on earth was not reported on the television news. Nothing on the first day, when the news was new, nothing on the second day, when the news was still trickling over the borders, nothing about the jubilant people gathered in the square in Krakow. The news was proclaimed from the pulpits, heard in Polish on foreign radio broadcasts, and spread by word of mouth. On the third day, the situation became precarious; it was no longer possible to remain silent. Finally, instructions came from the highest level:

- Publish but keep a low profile!

The telegram about the new Pope came last and very briefly in the television news on the third day, just before the weather. Then came the instructions from the censors that future coverage of the Pope's activities would be extremely restrained and cautious. The Pope was not to be photographed in front of large crowds, but only from below in solitary majesty. He should preferably be called by his old name, Karol Wojtyła, and not as Pope John Paul II. This man was not to be glorified in any way.

This caution was rational and understandable from the point of view of the regime. The Polish Pope became a real threat to the Communists, and his very existence contributed to the weakening of the regime and the strengthening of the opposition. The election of a Polish Pope was one of the events that led to the fall of the Wall.

Censorship thus regulated not only what was to be removed, but also how what was to be included was to be framed and presented. The proactive element in the mechanisms of censorship becomes even more apparent when it comes to literature. This was insightfully described by one of the giants of the library world, Robert Darnton. He was the longtime director of the Harvard

Library in Boston, the initiator of the Digital Public Library of America and an honorary doctor at Uppsala University. Darnton became an important inspiration and mentor for me when I was commissioned to write a national library strategy 2015-2019.

Robert Darnton has studied literary censorship in three historical periods. During the French Revolution in the eighteenth century, during British colonial rule in India in the nineteenth century, and during communism in East Germany, the GDR, in the nineteenth century. In his book on the history of censorship, he shows how literary censorship is more complex and intricate than the news scene.

One of the common features throughout history is that book censors work closely with authors, publishers, and printers. Censors become part of the literary process in a very specific culture of negotiation. Sometimes authors, publishers, and censors even swap jobs. This has manifested itself in various ways over the centuries, but it is particularly evident in the administrative and hierarchical nature of East Germany. A few months after the fall of the Wall in November 1989, Robert Darnton happens to know some GDR censors who have suddenly become idle. They try to justify themselves to Darnton, but also share previously secret instructions and rules.

All literary production in East Germany was planned in advance by the regime. It was, of course, part of the five-year plans that were developed and decided upon in a very hierarchical organizational scheme, with the party secretary at the top, down to the officials in the book production department of the Ministry of Culture.

Censorship was formally prohibited in the GDR, where the constitution provided for full freedom of speech and of the press, with the small addition that production and printing permits were required before a book could be written and published. Each book was outlined down to the smallest detail, and some words were not allowed, despite the supposed freedom. For example, "ecology" was forbidden because it could be associated with the large-scale environmental destruction caused by state industry. No references to Stalinism were allowed, and words such as "Stalin's opponents" were changed to "opponents of his time," and references to the 1930s were changed to "the first half of the 1900s. The word "criticism" was also deleted as it could be misleading.

Robert Darnton was given a copy of the plan for 1989, the last literary year of the five-year plan before the Wall came down. It was a plan that had taken several years to develop in the cumbersome bureaucracy, covering all literature scheduled for publication in 1990. A total of 625 titles, with a planned total print run of 11,508 950 copies. 1989 was the year in which the first forty "glorious years" of the GDR were to be celebrated. According to Party Secretary Comrade Erich Honecker, the literary year 1989 could be defined both by the present and the past:

"Our Party and our people are rooted in a revolutionary and humanist tradition of centuries of struggle for social development, freedom and the rights and value of humanity."

Socialism was advancing everywhere, and all curves were pointing upward. This would be reflected in literature with an "energetic anti-fascism that is consistent with the principles of social realism and the promotion of the historical struggle of the working class for social progress."

Then the people tore down the Wall, but censorship lives on elsewhere. The threads of the past are a relief for what is happening today. Russia, China and Hungary are recent examples. For example, what happened to a close associate of Hungarian Prime Minister Viktor Orbán in Brussels in the fall of 2020 was not allowed to be published in the state-controlled media in increasingly authoritarian Hungary. This is shown by the events surrounding a sex party in Brussels with loud music, shouting and noise. Despite all the Corona restrictions, a huge party took place in an apartment on Rue des Pierres in the center of Brussels on the evening of November 2020. Neighbors alerted the police around 9 p.m., and officers soon stormed into a drug and sex orgy for gay men. Law enforcement encountered about twenty guests, mostly men, some of them completely naked. One of the guests tried to escape by climbing out a window and down a drainpipe. But down the street, the fleeing man was caught with ecstasy tablets in his backpack and identified as József Szájer, a Hungarian member of the European Parliament.

József Szájer is one of the founders of Hungary's ruling Fidesz party and has been one of Prime Minister Viktor Orbán's closest allies. He has been a leading advocate of fighting LGBTQ rights and co-authored the law banning same-sex marriage. It is big news when such a man is arrested at a gay group sex party. József Szájer was forced to resign the very next day. Even if everyone's sexual orientation is a private matter, this is hypocrisy of the highest order, and it attracted a lot of attention all over Europe. Of course it was big news. Except in Hungary.

There was silence in the state-controlled media. Hungarian Prime Minister Viktor Orbán controls almost all the press, radio and television. This kind of news is not appropriate. On the day of the MEP's arrest, the main Hungarian TV channel headlined its news with "Never before have Hungarians been so happy with their prime minister".

Russian censorship and propaganda are palpable and terrible. So is the Chinese surveillance society and state monopoly on information. Authoritarian regimes, even in EU countries, use the same methods. Not only Hungary and Poland, but also Austria, for example, has a modern history of the government influencing news coverage through bribes and ad buys to strengthen the prime minister. What's interesting is that all these influence operations have such a long history, and that the threads from to the former Eastern Europe are so strong.

The wall was never really torn down, but rather rebuilt. Lies, propaganda and censorship have reached new heights. This is when a society needs journalism.

State TV?

State TV in Belarus, Poland, Hungary, and Azerbaijan is not true public service. Yet they call themselves public services as part of the new political language. But state-controlled and censured media do not serve the public. What we see today in many authoritarian countries is a far cry from the public service we have in the Nordic countries and Northern Europe. On the other hand, to call Swedish Radio (SR), Swedish Television (SVT) and Educational Broadcasting (UR) state television is simply malicious and wrong. It is an abuse of the word and a mockery of those who work and have worked there. It is also an insult to the people who are forced to live with real state television under a communist, authoritarian or fascist dictatorship. Reserve this term for what is truly state-controlled broadcasting.

When Polish TV is silent about the Polish Pope and cuts out all pictures of pigs, when Hungarian TV does not mention anything about the LGBTQ rights opponent in the European Parliament who was arrested with his underwear down, or when Russian state TV constantly praises President Putin, *that* is state TV. When Russian state news channels lie every day about the war in Ukraine and turn truth into lies, that's state TV.

Swedish public broadcasting is not state television. Independence from government, as well as freedom from advertising, is the very hallmark of public broadcasting. Over the years, increasingly strong barriers against undue pressure have been built into the model. Several mechanisms are in place to ensure independence. Pluralism is stronger because Swedish public service is organized into three independent broadcasters. Television, Radio and Education. There are several layers between the government and the companies, and an administrative board appoints the boards of the broadcasters, whose members may not be active politicians. The special public service fee is set for several years and is kept separate from the annual state budget, although it is a tax. Ministers or other politicians are not able to control news or programming. This does not prevent the independence of the public service from being further strengthened for a new license period, contrary to the efforts of right-wing nationalist forces.

There are political forces in Sweden that, like the regimes in Poland and Hungary, want to gain political control over an overly independent public service or cut it back. But the current Swedish system works, I dare say, after more than fifty years in public service, often in positions that were sensitive in terms of integrity.

I have been a crime reporter, a consumer reporter, managing editor of news on the radio, a political reporter and commentator on television, the initiator and editor of the political programs on SVT 24, the CEO of Educational Broadcasting (UR) and member of the Review Board. But not once have I been subjected to what could be called institutional political pressure, i.e. an attempt by a political authority to control the provision of news. A reporter may hear whining and complaints from all sorts of sources, but I have never experienced a member of the government or parliament trying to tell me what to do. Independence has worked in practice, not just on paper. But it has not always been easy to explain or make credible. This became clear during a study visit Ekot received in the early 1990s. The Baltic states were in the process of establishing their independence with democratic institutions about a year after the fall of the Berlin Wall in 1988. A Baltic government delegation of ministers, deputy ministers and agency heads from Estonia, Latvia and Lithuania came to Swedish Radio. As head of News, I told them about my responsibility for finances, personnel, technology - but above all about my responsibility for content, i.e. what news should be broadcast and what should not. The head of Ekot is the responsible publisher, and I made it clear that this meant that I alone had the final decision on what news would be broadcast on national radio. The Baltic visitors looked at me wide-eyed and skeptically, a forty-year-old boyish reporter.

- Yes, they said, smiling and laughing. But who is in charge?

- It's me, I tried again.

- Yes, yes, but who decides?

- Actually, it's me.

- Well, well, but above you?

- There is the Director General of Swedish Radio, but he doesn't control the news, that's my responsibility.

One of the visitors, a deputy foreign minister, got angry.

- I have heard enough lies, he shouted. We know this from the Soviet era. Don't talk shit. Who is in charge of the news? You can't be that!

When I insisted, he got so angry that he left the room and slammed the door. In state radio, the news cannot be controlled by a young journalist down in the newsroom. Enough propaganda! Another, equally skeptical visitor that day made a more pointed criticism after I talked about the concept of consequence neutrality.

- I have an idea, he said. If all media are as consequence neutral as you say, maybe one media outlet would be enough. I have a suggestion as to what it might be called. How about Pravda?

His point, of course, was that it is so difficult in practice to meet the requirements of impartiality and objectivity. So, a prerequisite for a functioning news service is pluralism, that different newsrooms and publishers compete, complement and balance each other. If one fails in its task, it can be pointed out by others.

The independent role I tried to describe to the Baltic visitors has not always been the case for the public service. It is an independence that broadcasters and journalists have gradually fought their way into over the years. Public service broadcasters in Europe have had to fight for their independence for a long time and gradually build up their positions. This is also true of the flagship, the British BBC, which has been under intense pressure throughout its existence. One of the biggest crises came during the Suez War in 1956, when the BBC reported critically on international reactions to British actions. The BBC stood by its independence, and even during the Falklands War in 1982, the BBC did not fall prey to the hyper-nationalist propaganda that characterized much of the British tabloid press coverage. The BBC chose to refer to the warring parties in neutral terms, such as "British soldiers and Argentine soldiers". Margaret Thatcher wanted the wording changed, but the BBC refused to budge, despite the Prime Minister's threats of major budget cuts and radical changes to the BBC's regulations and license. The attack was stopped by her own Tory colleagues, including the then Chairman of the BBC, who, in an angry argument with her, shouted that:

"Maggie, the BBC does not belong to you or to any party, it belongs to the British people!".

It was not until after the Second World War that Swedish Radio, founded in 1925, got its own news service. In its early decades, radio news coverage was controlled by the newspapers, which wanted to avoid competition. For a time in the early days of radio, the head of the news agency TT was also the head of the radio and was therefore known as the "double-excellence". TT had a monopoly on radio news broadcasts, and Swedish Radio was not allowed to report what was happening in its own live broadcasts. Radio reporter Gunnar Helén violated this news ban when he reported live from the peace celebrations on Kungsgatan in Stockholm on May 7, 1945. Gunnar Helén later became a leader of the Liberal Party and eventually chairman of the board of Sveriges Radio.

During the war, radio, like the press, was subject to strict control. Throughout the war years, the State Information Service (SIS) distributed small grey notes daily to the managing editors telling them what to publish and what not to publish, with good advice on emphasis and angles. SIS was part of the Ministry of Foreign Affairs, which had a special "Advice and Exemption Department" to issue instructions to the press and radio. The Foreign Office could rely on an order prohibiting publication of "certain specified military and other conditions".

One of those who wrote these little gray notes was a young diplomat who later became Director General of Swedish Radio, Olof Rydbeck. He had been a Foreign Ministry official during the war and radio director between 1955 and 1970, when he was appointed ambassador to the U.N. in the fall. When I joined the radio in 1969, Rydbeck was still head of Sveriges Radio, which was then a single company for both radio and television. The period up to the seventies can probably be better described as a kind of state radio. Olof Rydbeck's memoirs clearly show how closely radio and television were linked to the state and the government. Rydbeck made no secret of his ambition to control and centralize power over news coverage, but he did not quite succeed.

It was not often that the Director General gave direct orders about news evaluation, but Olof Rydbeck wanted to keep a daily check on the situation. In order to ensure a "balance" in the coverage, he set up daily meetings in the fall of 1961, where all current affairs and news directors would report on the content of the day's broadcasts. Every day at a quarter to twelve, the program directors for radio and television and representatives of TV, radio, the International Program, the Central News desk, and Cultural Programs met in a conference room at the top floor in the Radio House. Ekot and Aktuellt did their best to hide their news from each other, waiting to present their own unique features. At noon, Rydbeck disappeared for lunch.

Coverage of the Vietnam War in the late 1960s was a sensitive issue. On one occasion, Olof Rydbeck tried to stop a piece by the US-critical writer Sara Lidman on *OBS! Kulturkvarten*, but after protests and much discussion the program was broadcast anyway.

The Russell Tribunal in Stockholm in 1967 was of particular concern to Olof Rydbeck. It was a privately organized war crimes trial investigating the U.S. war in Vietnam, with testimony of abuse, torture, and napalm. Led by British philosopher Bertrand Russell and French writer and Nobel laureate Jean-Paul Sartre, it attracted international attention. But the director of Swedish Radio dismissed the tribunal's sessions as "pure propaganda".

At his quarter-hourly meetings, Rydbeck gave instructions that the tribunal could be observed, but not be given special attention. When a reporter wanted to interview Sartre, Rydbeck ruled that the interview could only be about the author's literary work, not about the Tribunal. Many journalists protested loudly against this kind of internal censorship.

Anders Wilhelmsson, the former head of national radio news, was present at the meetings, and he told me how Rydbeck once snapped back at the critics that this was nothing compared to the gray notes he had written during the war.

Radio and television reporters had gradually increased the autonomy and independence of political reporting in the 1960s. The radio journalist Herbert Söderström with his sharp voice and pointed questions, and the television reporters Lars Orup, Gustaf Olivecrona and Åke Ortmark, the three O's, with a more aggressive tone in their questioning. In the run-up to the 1966 municipal elections, Prime Minister Tage Erlander was asked what advice he would give to a young homeless couple in Stockholm. Erlander's answer that they could get in line for housing did not impress, and the question influenced the election. Olof Rydbeck wanted to put even more emphasis on political coverage and hired three political "powerhouses" as reporters, one blue, one green and one red. Known as the Surf Brothers (after the laundry detergent SURF with different colored "grains"), they had different political backgrounds but would now use their skills and contacts in the service of journalism. They were Sam Nilsson from the Conservative Party, Ivar Peterson from the Centre Party and Allan Larsson from the Social Democrats. Sam Nilsson eventually became the head of television, and Allan Larsson was later involved in finally crushing the attempts to politically control news coverage. It was during "Kris á la Malta", during New Year 1970/71.

In the fall of 1970, Olof Rydbeck was replaced as radio director by then chairman of TCO, the trade union for civil servants, Otto Nordenskiöld. The state budget was presented in early January, traditionally by Minister of Finance Minister Gunnar Sträng, who solemnly presented the "merciful bundle". Prior to that, reporter

Allan Larsson and his colleague Christer Pettersson had filed a story for the 9 o´clock news Aktuellt about what was to be expected in the budget. Gunnar Sträng was falsely accused in a newspaper of having leaked the news. The finance minister was furious, called the radio director and ordered him to stop all news about the budget before it was officially presented by the government. Nordenskiöld was about to go on vacation to the island of Malta, but he had time to do as Gunnar Sträng said.

When the reporters at the different news departments of radio and television heard about the Director Generals news ban, they went wild and everyone started hunting for forbidden budget news. Otto Nordenskiöld announced from Malta that the ban on budget news remained in force.

Allan Larsson managed to get a new news story about the financing of a health and safety fund and edited a ready-made report on the subject. He put the roll of film and tape on his desk next to a letter of resignation. He told the management they had to choose between the story and resignation, he later told me, and he also documented his story in a letter to his old workplace. "Kris á la Malta", named after a popular Christmas dish, was raging at Swedish Radio and Television.

Otto Nordenskiöld lost his authority. Allan Larsson's story was broadcast, and all the newsrooms now did their utmost to uncover more budget news. Otto Nordenskiöld's position was permanently weakened, and it was clearly impossible for ministers to give instructions on news. Even for Allan Larsson, who many years later became minister of finance minister himself.

Internal control and attempts at political control during the first decades of radio, yes. Self-censorship in various forms, perhaps. But censorship as under the dictatorship with state television, no.

On the other hand, Swedish public broadcasters of today can be criticized for maintaining alliances with the increasingly controlled public broadcasters of the former Eastern Europe or with broadcasters in the rogue states of the former Soviet Union. The European Broadcasting Union (EBU) has not only the BBC and Norwegian NRK as members, but also state-controlled broadcasters in Hungary, Poland, Belarus, and Azerbaijan. These are companies that do not meet reasonable standards of independence and autonomy from their governments and whose programming policies are anything but neutral. Through their membership in the EBU, the regimes in these countries borrow prestige from the EBU and glory from EBU events such as the Eurovision Song Contest. This was particularly evident when Azerbaijan won the contest and was given the honor of hosting the 2012 final in its capital, Baku.

The EBU likes to talk about media independence and the importance of a democratic infrastructure. The more influence its anti-democratic members have, the more hypocritical it becomes. During my time as Director General of Educational Broadcasting, UR, I also participated in the work of the EBU. Eva Hamilton, then Director General of SVT, took the initiative to create a Northern European faction to try to defend the democratic core values of the EBU. In a special "Tafelspitz group", the Nordic public broadcasters held preliminary meetings with their colleagues from Germany, Switzerland, Austria and eventually the British BBC before the EBU General Assembly meetings. The idea was that public broadcasters, free from their governments, would be able to respond collectively and proactively to the representatives of authoritarian states.

It was embarrassing that Azerbaijan managed to nominate itself to host the 2011 EBU General Assembly and to hold the meeting in Baku. The situation was not helped by the fact that Azerbaijan would host the Eurovision Song Contest the following year. The question was what to do if Belarus won next time, or if their dictator Alexander Lukashenko wanted the next EBU meeting in Minsk.

I was one of the more critical Director Generals and together with some Nordic colleagues we thought we had to act. As a result, UR was asked by the EBU to organize a seminar on democracy and freedom of expression in Baku the day before the opening of the 2011 General Assembly.

This was a diplomatic challenge, not least for my interpreter Veronika Menjoun who organized the seminar. We invited speakers, researchers, and experts from several countries as well as the European security organization OSCE. Representatives of the fragments of the opposition press in Azerbaijan were given a place on the podium to meet one of President Ilham Aliyev's closest associates and advisors. The most sensitive topic was the situation of some imprisoned bloggers who had posted a satirical video on YouTube depicting the president as a donkey. The bloggers had been beaten by the police and sentenced to several years in prison.

The opposition press seized the opportunity during the seminar and there was a long and fierce debate. The president's man was forced to answer for the murdered, abused and imprisoned journalists. The opposition newspapers ran full pages the next day on how the regime had been grilled by critics. The government media was silent.

But the EBU had shown democratic muscle and proposed a resolution to be presented to the General Assembly. The European Broadcasting Union planned to state the importance of free and democratic news coverage. The abused critics would be named and the EBU would protest the imprisonment of the young satirical bloggers and demand their release. The Azerbaijani TV director panicked. When he saw the draft resolution, he realized that this would be the end of his career. He presented the EBU management with an ultimate challenge:

- If you list the names of imprisoned bloggers who should be released, I will turn off the power in the meeting room!

The EBU management did not dare to call his cards and deleted the mention of names. The final resolution was watered down to a more general document on democracy and freedom of expression. Instead, the EBU leadership requested a personal meeting with the President to present their concrete demands for the release of named prisoners. The meeting took place without publicity in Azerbaijan and the imprisoned journalists remained in jail.

During my presentation at the EBU General Assembly to report on the democracy seminar and play the hated video clip of the President as a donkey, the internet connection in the room suddenly went down. Audio and video could not be displayed and the report from yesterday's debate was not as concrete as it could have been.

Eventually, the EBU adjusted its statutes to specify democracy requirements and tried to regulate the possibility of excluding member countries that do not meet these requirements. Nevertheless, problems persist and are exacerbated when the EBU has member companies that are not independent, that have fired 'disloyal' journalists and where managers take orders directly from the government.

Swedish Radio Director General Cilla Benkö has been a member of the EBU board for many years, de facto representing the Nordic countries. She has waged a rather lonely and unsuccessful battle to criticize and respond to the state broadcasters of the authoritarian countries. Although the Northern European public service broadcasters cannot be accused of being state television, they organize themselves together with broadcasters in authoritarian countries. In the run-up to the Eurovision Song Contest 2021, it was once again possible to see that the EBU has not really managed to understand that music and politics are linked. For too long, Belarus and other dictatorships or authoritarian regimes have been allowed to remain members of the EBU and thus compete in the Eurovision Song Contest. It was only when the Belarusian entry in 2021 came from a group that mocked those protesting against dictator Lukashenko that the EBU reacted, demanding changes of the content of the song or a new entry. Belarus was threatened with expulsion from the contest for violating the contest's "non-political stance". It was not until the end of May 2021 that Belarusian state television was expelled from the EBU. By then, BTRC had broadcast the obviously coerced interview with the captured journalist Raman Pratasevich, who had been arrested on the Ryanair plane that Belarus had hijacked in the air on its way to Vilnius and forced to Minsk. The EBU was acting against its affiliate, not directly against the regime.

All this tardiness and caution casts a shadow over the concept of public service.

Republican or Royalist?

"Your Majesty, dear Felipe... I have been king of Spain for forty years, and during all these years I have wanted the best for Spain and for the Royal House. With great affection, your father."

Juan Carlos I to his son on August 3, 2020

With these last lines, the old king announced to his son, king Felipe, that he was leaving the country. Juan Carlos' flight from the royal Zarzuela Palace in Madrid was the culmination of months of revelations and scandals. But for a long time, the king was protected from criticism by the media, which simply kept quiet about his mistresses, lavish lifestyle and corruption. After all, king Juan Carlos saved Spanish democracy. Without him, the country would probably never have made a peaceful transition from general Francisco Franco's dictatorship to a parliamentary democracy. Appointed to replace Franco in 1975, the newly crowned king surprisingly turned out to be a democrat and introduced general elections. When the old Franco supporters attempted a military coup in 1981, including the occupation of parliament, Juan Carlos I donned his commander-in-chief's uniform and stopped the coup plotters. It was a symbol of power that the fascist officers had to bow to. Without the king, Spain would not be a democracy, and Juan Carlos was loved by the people.

But the public long remained unaware of the king's luxurious life, secret mistresses and bribes. These included contacts with Sheik Mohammed bin Rashid Al Maktoum, the ruler of Dubai, who gave the king two Ferrari cars. From the Saudi royal family, Juan Carlos received 65 million euros in suspicious payments to a Panama account for the king's involvement in the sale of the Spanish AV E super train to Saudi Arabia. Some of the money went to the king's German mistress, Corinna zu Sayn-Wittgenstein.

This was first revealed in the summer of 2020 by the newspaper *El Confidencial*. Until then, the king's business and private life had been protected by informal censorship of both the press and politicians. While Spanish journalists would gossip to foreign colleagues, they would not write anything in their own newspapers. Once the lid was lifted, Spaniards were inundated with an avalanche of revelations about the ex-king's life. Eventually, the old king was forced to pack his bags and flee to Abu Dhabi.

The new young king, Felipe VI, renounced his inheritance to distance himself from his disgraced father, who, despite pleas, was not allowed to come home for Christmas. Support for the monarchy began to swing wildly, and the media made new revelations about gifts of riding horses from a Mexican tycoon and mysterious payments into the ex-king's accounts.

It is not easy to report on a popular monarch. I learned this early on from Swedish king Carl XVI Gustaf's First Court Marshal. It was the late summer of 1975, and the then 29-year-old king was about to take one of his first Royal tour in the country. The tradition is that a new king pays a visit to every county in the land. This was before Carl Gustaf had become engaged to Silvia, and he was far from enjoying the self-confidence, popularity and respect he later gained over the years. But crowds of people came to see the shy young monarch as he toured the country. Every county had to be visited. I had managed to convince my bosses at Ekot that this was newsworthy. Maybe we could even get an interview with the king? He rarely gave interviews. The king's next trip would be to Älvsborg County in southwest Sweden.

I requested an audience with one of the highest officials at the court, First Court Marshal Bjorn von der Esch. He was genuinely surprised by Ekot's interest when he received me in his great golden room at the palace, wondering what I was after. News departments of radio and television didn't usually care much about what the king was doing, he reasoned. We were probably all Red Guards. He reacted spontaneously to my plan audiences to cover the king's tour with this line:

- It won't be easy for you, son. Either you'll have all the old hags from the fancy apartments on the good quarters of Östermalm against you, or your colleagues!

I was stunned. In the large, magnificent room at Stockholm Palace, the First Court Marshal explained the dilemma I faced. To the best of my ability, I tried to explain that it was interesting that the king was attracting such large crowds, and that Ekot wanted to report on it. In addition, we were interested in interviewing the king about how he saw his role and mission. The First Court Marshal looked at me with amusement and skepticism. I had long hair, typical of the time but I had dressed neatly for the visit to the palace. Björn von der Esch was a landowner from the south of Sweden and a classic gentleman in a well-tailored suit. After his years in the king's service, he became a conservative member of Parliament with an independent agenda. We kept in good contact over the years. He was a nationalist and argued that Sweden should stay out of the EU. Euroscepticism was a common conservative stance in Europe, but in the Conservative Party the whip swung so hard that the party eventually kicked him off the parliamentary list. But von der Esch stood for honesty and integrity.

In 1975 he was still the king's confidant, with the key to the coveted interview and access under the royal tour. Somehow, I gained the Marshal's trust, and he explained my dilemma to me in no uncertain terms. If I was too kind and submissive to the king, my fellow journalists would despise and slander me. If I was mean to the king, his supporters might get angry. But to call the king's friends "old hags in Östermalm"?

I assured the First Court Marshal that I understood the request and that my intention was neither to ridicule nor to praise the king.

I wanted to report something newsworthy. Preferably topped off with an interview with the king?

- We'll see, the marshal said.

I went on the tour and reported on the meticulous preparations and interviewed a Social Democratic mayor in Borås who had no intention of bowing to the king or going to dinner at the residence in the local capitol Vänersborg. I stood behind the barriers when the king passed by and tried to get the Marshal's attention. What about the interview?

When the king visited Steneby Vocational School and the aqueduct in Håverud, we recorded a lot of sound. The sound engineer and I stayed up all night in a hotel room mixing a long sound collage, almost without any spoken text - just royal sounds. It was really cute when an elderly lady in broad dialect at a ditch encouraged her granddaughter to wave the flag.

- Wave, there's the king! Not there, it's the police...

... But now!

You could hear the delighted silence of the crowd as the king's big black car slowly drove by.

- What fun! the grandmother sighed happily to her granddaughter.

Ekot aired the long audio collage all morning. My colleagues liked the piece. The royal hysteria seemed comical and ridiculous to those who initially thought so. At noon, the tour arrived in the city of Borås. I managed to whisper a question to von der Esch as he passed by on a red carpet. What about the interview?

- We'll see, he replied quickly. Come to Grand Hotel at two o'clock. And bring me a story you've done, so I can hear it first!

Now I would be put to the test. Have I managed to strike a balance between the royalists in Östermalm and my republican colleagues? The sound engineer and I meet the First Court Marshal in a small antechamber of the king's suite at the hotel. We have the long audio collage broadcast on Ekot that morning with us and play it on our tape recorder. Björn von der Esch listens and is delighted. When we reach the ditch with the encouraging grandmother, he almost applauds. How wonderful! The old hags in Östermalm will love it. The listeners get to be part of the journey.

I get the interview with the king. The large double door to the Royal Suite opens, and the Monarch emerges. He talks surprisingly long and coherently about what it is like to sit and wave to the people. The interview is broadcast, if possible, more often than the morning's audio collage, and it is so unusual that the biggest evening paper Expressen prints the entire interview on a large centerfold under the headline "The people want to see me".

It is quite reasonable that a series of radio reports from the king's tour could be appreciated by both royalists and republicans. By being more neutral, by simply holding up a microphone and letting what happens happen, I can allow the audience to read their own opinions into what is being reflected. Anyone who thinks it is a silly flaming of an outdated institution can think so, and anyone who is happy to hear fanfares, tributes and royal speeches can have

theirs. My own opinion of the monarchy has nothing to do with
it.

The Swedish king is relieved of most formal duties, except for
opening the annual session of Parliament and chairing meetings of
the Foreign Affairs Committee at the Palace. Nevertheless, the king
retains considerable symbolic power and is expected to rally the
nation in times of crisis and hardship. For many years, the Swedish
monarchy hung by a thread. Before Carl Gustaf started a family,
only he and his uncle Bertil had the right to ascend to the throne.
Prince Bertil had retained his right to the throne only because he
had not married. Instead, he lived in "sin" with the woman he
loved. Her name was Lilian Craig, she was not a noblewoman, and
she had been married before. If they had married, like his brothers
Sigvard and Carl Johan, who married commoners, Bertil would
have lost his title as a prince.

Prince Bertil and Lilian's relationship was not particularly secret
among the insiders. But the press remained silent out of respect for
the monarchy. Prince Bertil had succeeded in appealing to the most
important managing editors to exercise discretion in this matter.
Princess Lilian herself wrote in her memoirs about the agreement
with the press:

> "I was not there at the time, but I have heard that
> he spoke early with his friends in the journalistic
> community: [...]. You can ruin our lives if you want
> to,' he said. Of course, we will be grateful if you do
> not. In that case, I promise to let you know as soon

as our situation hopefully changes for the better. [...]
His plea worked. We were able to move as we pleased,
avoiding newspaper mention and speculation, and
were grateful for it. Could something similar happen
today? I doubt it."

It was not until 1972 that the public secret was revealed.
That summer, the reporter Jan Mosander was covering the
Olympic Games in Munich. The young Olympic hostess, Silvia
Sommerlath, registered him as an accredited journalist. Mosander
was then the correspondent in Germany for *Expressen* and was
initially given an assignment that had little to do with the games.
He was contacted by the newspaper's managing editor, Edgar
Antonsson:

"Prince Bertil and Lilian Craig are on their way to Munich. We
will be the first to announce that they are a couple. That will be
the end of it. You write when they arrive. We must have a picture
of them together!"

Expressen took a picture of Prince Bertil and Lilian getting
off the plane, but Mosander didn't know much about royalty.
He secretly got help from Kid Severin, Expressen's legendary gala
reporter, who was traveling on the same plane as the prince and his
mistress. Kid Severin knew everything, of course, but she didn't
want to ruin her relationship with the royal family by writing
about Bertil and Lilian. Instead, she gave Jan Mosander all the
details he needed for his article. The Expressen ran the news on its
front page:

PRINCE BERTIL SHOCKED:
CAME WITH LIILIAN!

Inside the newspaper:

Prince Bertil causes scandal in Munich. Europe's
royalty and nobility are appalled. He is living with a
woman without being married!

The ice was broken. The monarchy was still hanging by a thread,
but the Munich Olympics saved the day. It was there that the king
met Silvia for the first time. The rest is history.

When and how should the king appear before the people? The
only rule laid down in the Constitution is that the king must
declare the session open when Parliament begins its work for the
season. Initially, when the king was young, he opened with a few
short words lasting less than a minute. Over the years, he has
evolved to speak at length about things he considers important,
such as the environment, nature and defense. But what should the
king do on other occasions?

On September 28, 1994, the whole of Scandinavia was hit by
a huge disaster. 852 people from the countries around the Baltic
Sea lost their lives in the cold, stormy waters when the passenger
ferry Estonia sank. 137 passengers were rescued. Sweden needed
some words of comfort from its regent, but there was no tradition
of royal addresses to the nation. It was by no means a foregone

conclusion that the king would speak. I was a reporter at Aktuellt, and during the morning in the newsroom I raised the issue that we should try to get a speech or at least a few words from the head of state.

The royal court seemed almost surprised when I called to suggest that the king make a speech to the nation.

The court pushed back. "We don't usually do that ... how can we do it?" they said. The king can't receive many different media at the palace, his staff objected.

- We'll take care of it, I said. This is a national disaster, so we should not compete with each other. If Aktuellt is allowed to go there with a photographer and a sound technician, we will make sure that all other media have immediate access to sound and images. We will record and share.

Of course, I have my own personal opinion on whether or not Sweden shall be a monarchy. Allowing the king to address the nation can be interpreted as strengthening the monarchy. But my private views on the constitution have nothing to do with the news evaluation. In the case of a major national disaster like Estonia, it is appropriate and relevant that the head of state be allowed to speak.

The court was aware of the situation after the sinking of Estonia. After the staff managed to reassure the king that there would be no media frenzy, only a small team from Aktuellt coming to the palace, I was told that I was welcome.

The king is calm and serious, but clearly uncomfortable with the situation. Reading speeches from a written script is not Carl XVI Gustaf's forte. We set up the camera in a golden salon, arranged the lighting and set up a microphone. A reporter from Ekot has come along and connects to the microphone so that the radio has its own recording. The king has a typewritten memo with a one-minute speech in front of him and is reading it:

> Sweden and Estonia are deeply saddened by the serious ferry disaster that occurred last night in the Baltic Sea. Deeply shocked by the reports of the large number of lives lost, I have today sent a telegram to the President of Estonia expressing my condolences and those of the Swedish people. In a message to the shipping company, I expressed my deepest sympathy to the relatives in their tremendous grief. We are all thinking of their difficult situation. The extensive rescue operations were carried out in an admirable manner. I would like to express my sincere gratitude to all those who made great efforts to save lives under extremely difficult circumstances. Thank you very much!

The king looks earnestly into the camera. But he gets stuck and must start over. Not once, but more than ten times. I try to calm him down and give him some instructions. "Please, a little slower, Your Majesty, look into the camera..."

In the end, the king's short speech is as it should be, and we hurry back to the studios. We barely have time to load the tape before the king's speech is broadcast. Aktuellt sends a copy to

Rapport and TV4. Elisabeth Tarras-Wahlberg, the king's press officer at the time, explained to me long afterwards that this was a decisive turning point in the way the king was treated by the media, and that he began to be seen as a head of state who appeared at important moments.

We have the system of government we have, and you just have to deal with it as a reporter. If I want to change it, I have to vote for a party that really wants to establish a republic; if I want to keep the kingdom, there are parties that stand for that. The point here is that it is important for the audience to hear entire speeches by leaders and officials, heads of state, ministers, or party leaders.

But televised speeches are by no means self-evident. In fact, there has been a fierce battle over journalistic focus and priorities. For me, during much of my professional life, it has been a struggle for integrity and authenticity in news reporting. I believe that public radio and television should offer its audience live political events, such as major parliamentary debates, important court cases, party rallies, political speeches or lectures at universities and public educational institutions. Give space to the players in politics, science and education to express themselves, not just filtered through a reporter's account. Many of my colleagues dismissed this as a kind of "Vremya journalism". Vremya was the name of the Soviet television news program that featured excruciatingly long speeches by the party secretary and other communist figures. It was simply a despicable "microphone journalism" to broadcast long speeches. The issue was highly controversial and ultimately about power over the agenda.

As head of radio news, I introduced live radio broadcasts of the main party-leader and thematic debates in parliament. This met strong resistance from feature producers and others, who sometimes had to move their programs, but the audience multiplied. The audience was even larger when Ekot broadcast live from the trial of Christer Pettersson, accused of murdering former Prime Minister Olof Palme, in June 1989. The authenticity and immediacy of a live broadcast is hard to beat.

But live is perhaps the wrong word to describe the Palme trial. Ekot broadcast with a ¾ second delay so that the name of the defendant could be whistled over when it was mentioned. Christer Pettersson had not been convicted and would remain anonymous on the radio until the verdict was reached. Producer Lisa Söderberg and I at Ekot took turns as managers to handle the button.

The idea that journalists, not politicians, should talk on TV is also deeply rooted in visual storytelling. A clip that often appears in various TV entertainment programs is from the September 1994 election night. I am at the Social Democrats' vigil, and the funny clip is of me trying to report from there in Aktuellt, but being trampled on the floor by all the rushing journalists. At least that's how it looks and is presented in the comedy programs. In reality it's a fight about what the TV news should report. It is shortly after 21:00. Aktuellt is on in the middle of the election night, just as the forecasts show that the Social Democrats have won and Ingvar Carlsson shall be proclaimed the new prime minister. Everyone is waiting for him to come out to his cheering supporters and thank them for the victory. The viewers of my program will be the first to hear what the election winner has to say. When Ingvar Carlsson comes out, I shout "Put it out!" in the internal communication to the producers and I come on the air just as Ingvar Carlsson starts to speak. The photographer insists that the reporter should be seen and heard, so he points the camera and microphone at me. I don't want to talk and point in vain to the podium where Ingvar Carlsson is standing. I can still see that the camera is pointed at me, and to indicate that it is Carlsson who should be in the picture, I crouch down on the floor. The photographer does what he thinks is right and tilts the camera towards me, but now the winner of the election disappears completely from the picture. "focus on Carlsson!" I whisper into the microphone, and only then does the camera turn. But then the winner of the election has almost finished speaking.

When SVT started its digital broadcasts in the late 1990s, I tried unsuccessfully to make it a Swedish version of C-SPAN, the American television network that broadcasts live from politics, Congress and political speeches, rallies and conventions in the United States. Instead, SVT launched a rather small digital news service that did not attract a large audience. So in 2002 I was asked to design a new start based on my ideas for a Swedish C-SPAN. The big question I was working on was whether there would be enough material to broadcast. The parliament and the political conventions were obvious and the political summer week in Almedalen was the flagship. I could also show that there were enough seminars and lectures to fill an entire channel. In January

2003 the TV management gave the go-ahead, and at the end of February SVT 24 Direct was launched.

For a long time this was controversial in journalistic circles. Critics argued that reporters should be interpreting events, not just holding a camera or microphone. One does not exclude the other, I argued, and when the people have elected representatives, we should be able to listen to what they have to say. Today, SVT Forum on SVT 2 and UR Samtiden on are an indispensable part of public service. The programs are part of the idea of providing a democratic infrastructure to complement the investigative and commentary news activities. Broadcasts in which not the broadcaster, but the speakers who are heard, may have an intention regarding the effect. A Swedish television should of course cover the parliament, political conventions, press conferences, political weeks, as well as education and research. But there were spaces that had previously only been covered by radio. The ceremonial meeting of the Swedish Academy on December 20 each year should of course be broadcast on television, not just on radio as it has been up to now, I thought as a television producer. It could be glossy television, with high-class intellectual content, crystal chandeliers, silver candlesticks, and inspirational speeches. But it would take time to woo and convince the aging members of the Royal Academy of something as modern as television.

It took almost a decade. It was not until I became Director General of Educational Broadcasting (UR) and in charge of the Knowledge Channel that I was able to get the Academy to agree to television broadcasts, perhaps in combination with the natural replacement of the Academy's older members.

The second radio monopoly to be challenged was a Christmas address, a "Greeting to compatriots abroad". It has been a tradition since the 1930s for the king to give a Christmas address on the radio to Swedes abroad. A greeting from home. It began with Gustaf VI Adolf when he was still crown prince and developed into a more general address to all Swedes. It was broadcast on television a few times in the late fifties, but then became a radio broadcast only. Given the current king's reluctance to memorize speeches in front of a microphone, it was understandable that he wanted to give the speech only on the radio. But most other European monarchs or heads of state give Christmas or New Year's speeches that are also televised. Why can't the king of Sweden do the same?

As managing editor of SVT 24 Direkt, I began courting the court. The speech after the Estonia catastrophe had gone well. The king's speech in the Stockholm City Hall after the tsunami at Christmas 2004 was a great success, far exceeding anything the elected head of government had to say:

> "Imagine if, like the king in the fairy tales, I could
> set everything right and end the story with a then
> they lived happily ever after. But like you, I am just
> a grieving, searching fellow human being..."

This may be the best speech Carl XVI Gustaf has ever given. Again, couldn't the king speak directly to the camera for ten

minutes? He doesn't have to sit and look at a piece of paper
all the time. I reminded the court that people on television use
teleprompters. The text scrolls in large letters on a screen directly
under the camera lens, and it looks as if the speaker knows
everything by heart, and the speaker can make eye contact with the
viewers.

But the king could not come to the newsroom to practice. It was
unthinkable that he would be subjected to such a thing. But we can
come to you, I suggested. We'll install a prompter in the castle!

One late evening in the fall of 2007, we discreetly carried the
equipment into the castle and set it up for His Majesty to test.
A friendly reporter, Mattias Forsgren, and a solid photographer,
Kenneth Boijertz, from the 24 Direkt newsroom installed the
camera and a well-functioning prompter and ran a cable through
a window to a recording truck in the castle courtyard. The king
could practice as much as he wanted.

After two tries, it went quite well. It became easier for the king
to read when he could try different text formats and colors on the
prompter. Finally, the editors made a sharp recording in Prince
Bertil's apartment at the Palace and took a DVD to Drottningholm
castle when the editing was complete. Crown Princess Victoria
and the First Court Marshal thought it was a success, and from
2007 the king's Christmas address was also made for television.
Nowadays, the king's Christmas address is considered a fine old
TV tradition, and everyone has forgotten that for a long time it
was only heard on the radio. Party leaders have followed suit and

now also give formal Christmas speeches that are broadcast on television.

Carl XVI Gustaf's speech on SVT 1 on prime time on Christmas Day has high ratings and the king's status and esteem has increased. It goes without saying that the king of Sweden, like the king of England or the king of Denmark, can address the nation both at Christmas and in times of crisis and disaster.

When the coronavirus crisis was at its worst, the king went into self-imposed isolation at Stenhammar Palace south of Stockholm. But from there, the king sent greetings and thanks to his people in a short, televised address. The king has practiced and knows what is required. He now prefers to speak without a prompter.

I might have contributed to strengthening the position of the monarchy. My only defense is that I acted consistently. It is not my job as a reporter to choose or reject content on television based on who or what is favored or disfavored. It is clearly news when the king speaks to the people.

Shoot the journalist!

- Shoot him immediately! Take him to the barracks and shoot him!

The answer came fast and crystal clear. It sounded especially strong in the local dialect in Dalarna.

It was at the business association in Leksand, in a classic assembly hall with a red exterior in the center of Leksand. One of hundreds of lectures I have given on consequence neutrality in Sweden and around the world. It's a lecture concept that works everywhere. For generals at the Swedish National Defense College, at the School of Journalism or, as here, for proud entrepreneurs in the summer town of my childhood.

I constructed the lecture as a war game. "I want you to think and act as if you were the president of the United States," I ask the audience, who are now participants in a game. "We are going to take a really great president from American history," I say.

Lincoln usually comes up as a suggestion, as does Roosevelt - but with a little nudging, everyone is soon on board with Kennedy. We choose John F. Kennedy for our game, and the participants should try to put themselves in his shoes and suggest what the president should do when the New York Times intends to reveal CIA- plans to invade Cuba in the spring of 1961. If it makes the newspaper,

Castro can read this while sitting with his cigar, his morning coffee and a large glass of cold yogurt.

- Oh, that's it, the CIA is going to invade the Bay of Pigs?! Maybe it's time to send in some soldiers and repel the invasion...

The US President must somehow stop the news from getting out! What can he do?

The answers to this question say something about the mindset of the audience and the mood of society. Most people I have met over the years suggest using deadly force against the journalist to stop the news. This was expressed most quickly in Leksand.

- Shoot him immediately!

Officials in the prime minister's office, businessmen from Kiruna to Lisbon, politicians, pensioners and even journalists are quick to resort to murder to solve the president's problems. The only ones who tend to hesitate are the senior officers in the military's leadership courses. The colonels and generals know that shooting is dangerous. People can die. They have also thought through their own constitutional role – often in the form of a war game. We have a military first and foremost to defend our democratic system of government. The territory is a bonus. You don't just shoot journalists at random.

For almost a decade, I taught at Defense's legendary leadership summer course in Solbacka. Every year in August, the nation's leading decision-makers gather at the old boarding school to practice in the stunning greenery of Sörmland what might happen if war comes. The army band plays on arrival, and the highest judges, members of parliament, business leaders, deputy ministers, party leaders and party secretaries, media managers, royalty, academics, governors, director generals, colonels and generals spend a week testing the capabilities of the national defense in advanced war games. That's where my Bay of Pigs scenario came in handy. It was particularly fascinating to see how the civilian participants, government officials and business leaders, were the most belligerent - not colonels and generals. Repressive measures against troublesome journalists seems not inconceivable in a crisis situation.

Sometimes, in Solbacka and other places, I felt that the solution "shoot the journalist" was in the air, but no one dared to say it as clearly as in Leksand. If you scratch the surface, the idea is there, get the reporter out of the way! But in my game scenario, this solution faces some obstacles. When the assassination proposal comes up, it is interesting to ask the players how many journalists need to be shot. After all, we are talking about several reporters, and probably the editor-in-chief, managing editor, and front-page editors of The New York Times. A few hours before publication, there are quite a few members of the editorial staff and their families who must be liquidated if publication is to be stopped.

Then things get complicated. Apart from the more legal and moral aspects of this killing, there are some logistical problems. How do you kill a few dozen leading Armenian journalists and their families in a matter of hours? What happens then? What will other journalists do? Will anyone start to wonder? And does the president have the right to kill people just like that? In the US?

The "kill the journalist" line, however deceptively simple it may sound in Dalarna, must be abandoned pretty quickly. It is then usually suggested that the journalist be arrested and imprisoned. Again, the problem is that there are a lot of suspects to be rounded up and the question is what will be in the indictment. America's leading newspaper is about to expose its own government's illegal and unlawful invasion of a neighboring country. Under what laws could the journalists behind such a story be imprisoned?

The best answer came dramatically from a journalist when I spoke in Odessa, Ukraine:

- Under Soviet law, of course!

It was a drafty lecture hall on the Black Sea. Tired journalists with fresh memories of the Soviet era when colleagues were killed or imprisoned for being wrong. But now it's after the fall of the wall, and before the Russian invasion, so fortunately Soviet law no longer applies in Ukraine. But such laws are needed to arrest journalists on their way to expose the Bay of Pigs invasion. What would the law have to be?

American journalists are prohibited from exposing illegal actions by the U.S. government and president.

Legitimate defense secrets exist in all countries to protect the military operationally. But now there is more to it, the Bay of Pigs invasion would be a violation of international law and the preparations are against US law. Therefore, President Kennedy would need Soviet laws. It cannot be a legitimate protection of national security to prohibit news about an invasion that violates the UN Charter, the treaty between the American states, international law, and American law.

This far into the war game, many participants are scratching their heads. Other repressive measures? One drastic proposal was once called the "Serbian solution." Bomb the entire newspaper building to smithereens! A milder version of this measure was to cut off water, toilets and electricity so that the newspaper could not get out. Upon closer inspection, the measure was not very efficient or effective.

- No, better to bribe the journalist!

Great idea - but how much can it cost? How much does it cost to silence a journalist? Here, the price tag varied greatly between countries and contexts, but a common conclusion was that bribery is an unsafe way to go. When millions of dollars are involved, it can be difficult to get the money quickly, and there are a lot of people on the payroll. Also, an attempted bribe could be exposed and used to corroborate the newspaper's story.

- But the reporter could get a top job in the White House?

Sure, but what fun is that compared to breaking a world scoop and winning a bunch of prizes? Surely, in journalistic circles, it's nicer - and probably more profitable - to win the prestigious Pulitzer Prize than to carry binders for the president.

One creative suggestion is to simply move up the date of the invasion. The Bay of Pigs is invaded before the New York Times is printed! Give the order to begin immediately! The problem is that this involves transporting troops by sea. The invasion force will travel by boat from Nicaragua to eastern Cuba. It takes far too

long; the newspaper is published before the invasion force arrives.
Even though the operation could miraculously begin immediately.
Whoever makes such a suggestion has obviously not served in the
Navy.

The question is, how can a president stop what he considers to
be a damaging publication? After all, the president is elected by the
people. He must be able to act with authority and legitimacy. The
people did not elect the journalist. What mandate does a reporter
have compared to a president? We are talking about a democracy,
right? Should the journalist really be able to place himself above
the elected president? What kind of self-appointed authority is the
reporter? Does he have some kind of divine mandate?

No, neither divine nor self-appointed, but part of an idea. The
power of the journalist comes from an idea of how democracy
works. It is the idea of separation of powers, checks and balances,
between the different branches of government. The executive
branch is not above the legislative or judicial branches - and
none of those three branches is above the fourth - the free press.
The whole point of the American Constitution is that these
four powers are equal and balanced. That's why the president
can't arbitrarily lock up a critical journalist, let alone shoot
him. A similar concept of separation of powers is found in the
Swedish constitution, although not as strong as in the American
one. In Sweden, the free press is considered the third branch
of government, not the courts, which do not have the same
constitutional status in Sweden as in the United States.

The power of the journalist is not divine, but neither is it executive, legislative, or judicial. The power of the journalist is to investigate and report, freely and independently. This should not be stopped by an ever so kind-hearted and popular elected president but should be protected by law. The president is not above the journalist and the journalist is not above the president. They are equal parts of a power-sharing system designed to make democracy work. The president with all his power is powerless against the journalist!

Do not kill. Do not imprison. Do not bomb. Not to bribe. Not to invade. Will the most powerful man in the world watch his plans to rid the world of a communist dictator be sabotaged by a bloody journalist? What remains in the game, after most proposals have been rejected, is a test of the President's symbolic power. The young, charismatic president knows the editor-in-chief, of course. As we now understand the game, the President cannot force or order, but he can appeal in the national interest. Can the President possibly convince the editor-in-chief to voluntarily cancel or at least delay publication?

The first person in the game to suggest such a solution will become the sole president in my scenario. The other participants will be Orvil Dryfoos, publisher of the New York Times. The newly appointed president of the game must now do his best to convince his friends and colleagues in the audience not to publish.

But why should they? Their job is to publish what they know and what is important to their readers. All the news that's fit to print, as it says on the front page of the New York Times.

Participants who started out advocating the shooting of journalists are now fighting tooth and nail for the freedom to publish. Now they are publishers! Presidents who have never been so eloquent will find it hard to argue against this commitment.

Scenarios and dilemmas in a war game are a fascinating teaching tool. It begs the question of why we have journalists. One of the most charged war games on the Bay of Pigs I ran was at the Ho Chi Minh Academy in Hanoi. It was an adventure just to get there through Hanoi's traffic chaos. The interpreter, Thuy, drove me on a motorbike from the Army Hotel through the crowded streets, and I was terrified all the way there. The academy is housed in a white palace with wide staircases and open arcades facing the courtyard, with faculties for both propaganda and journalism.

The Vietnamese students are curious and friendly. They ask me if I can sing something and encourage me to take the lead in the large open stairwell. More than a hundred students listened in amazement as I sang the FNL's fight song in Swedish. "Free the South". A beautiful student thanks me by singing a cappella the theme song from the movie Titanic. But then the students ask if I don't know any real Swedish songs?

I sing all the verses of the folklore song "Who can sail without a wind". Now I am approved as a visiting professor at the Ho Chi Minh Academy and can present my war game scenario to the students.

The future Vietnamese journalists are asked to pretend to be the President of the United States. Just a little putty. Ordering the newspaper not to publish was quite simple and fully in line with Vietnamese press law in the service of the party. But in the game, after the twist, the task is instead for the President to appeal to the newspaper to voluntarily refrain from publishing. The participants now act against the president as if they were the publisher of the New York Times. The ceiling fans in the palace of the Ho Chi Minh Academy hum in the tropical heat. The participants are arguing against their nemesis, the U.S. president, who wants to stop the publication of an important story. The young Vietnamese journalists now all want the news of the Bay of Pigs invasion to reach the people, and they argue strongly and passionately. The job of the press is to report important, real news. The president should not be able to stop it. The news is free. Genuine news is what you feel in your stomach. I have tried to explain this to the students many times.

The war game short-circuits the whole party-controlled system. Vietnam's press law is very clear and detailed. Journalists must:

- Defend the Party's line, views, and policies, promote positive conditions, and fight against wrong ideas.

- Follow the directives of the Press Administration, its purpose and content.

- Contribute to political stability, build and defend socialist democracy and the socialist motherland of Vietnam, and report good examples.

Journalists should simply follow the orders of the government. But when it's an order from a U.S. president? Confronted with this contradiction in news evaluation, one participant explains:

- I feel in my Swedish stomach ...

My lectures in Vietnam were part of a Swedish democracy support organized by FOJO, a journalist education center, in cooperation with the Swedish Parliament. Perhaps one or two seeds have been sown. Talking practically about consequence neutrality has been a way to convey knowledge about a democratic infrastructure, and this has been important, not least in countries with different systems. There was a lot of interest, not least in the former Soviet Union or the former Soviet republics.

When an updated version of my book *News Journalism* was published in Russian in 2006, I was invited to speak at the journalism faculty of Minsk University in Belarus. The students were already familiar with the first edition, and when I arrived at the university, I was greeted like a rock star by several hundred students in the foyer. They wanted pictures, autographs and dedications. The auditorium was filled to capacity, and together with the interpreter Veronika Menjoun, I gave a six-hour lecture.

The administration of the faculty was of the old Soviet type, and they probably did not really understand what they had invited. It was a good lecture in democracy when one of the teachers of the faculty had to act against the students in the game and try to persuade them not to publish an important news item in the role of President Kennedy. The lecture I gave then would probably not be possible to repeat today.

Sometimes, as a lecturer, I make up one or two details when I have forgotten or missed something. It happened in Dnepropetrovsk, a then hidden old military town in eastern Ukraine, long closed to foreigners, where the Soviet military launched rockets and satellites. The hotel where we stayed looked like a dream for the reporters of the nostalgic Swedish TV program K-märkt. Purple galleon sofas, green carpets and orange steel lamps. The breakfast dishes in pressed metal under bright neon lights. Out in a city field, a shabby C branch of the Moscow Circus with a drugged cow as its main attraction. On the other hand, the entrance fee was only a few kopecks. The city has since been renamed to its Ukrainian name of Dnipro, a name that does not sound as unfamiliar as it once did before the Russian invasion.

Also in Dnipro, I spoke about the imminent invasion of the Bay of Pigs and accidentally added that the training camp was in Nicaragua. Again, a worn-out lecture hall with peeling paint and poor lighting. In the back of the room sat an older, thin man with sharp features and dark hair. Suddenly he stood up and protested:

- No, Professor Fichtelius. We were not in Nicaragua. We were in Guatemala.

- We?

Who was this man? The Bay of Pigs documents show that the Soviet Union and Fidel Castro knew a lot about the impending invasion, but Castro did not know the exact place or time. What Castro knew had nothing to do with what was or was not in the New York Times. Castro had agents and informants in Miami and throughout Latin America. The Soviet Union had no shortage of agents on the continent, and they reported back home. Castro was as prepared as he could be.

Had I met someone who was really there? He said "we"?! Perhaps a former intelligence officer, now retired in a run-down Soviet military town? Not entirely impossible. KGB or GRU? To this day I am sad that the man left the lecture before I could ask any questions.

A Perfect Double Failure

The small boats glided as quietly as possible in the moonlight toward the shores of the Bay of Pigs just before three o'clock in the morning on Monday, April 17, 1961. U.S. Navy aircraft carriers and destroyers lay at a safe distance in international waters. A small army of 1,500 Cuban exiles, Brigade 2506, equipped and trained by the CIA, would liberate Cuba from communism and overthrow the dictator, Fidel Castro. Once they had established a beachhead at the Bay of Pigs, they intended to set up a government-in-exile that could ask the United States for open support.

Things went wrong from the start. Several of the landing craft ran aground on large coral reefs that the CIA had mistakenly dismissed as sea grass on aerial photographs. As the first invasion soldiers approached the beach, led by CIA agents Gray Lynch and Rip Robertson, they were spotted by a Cuban patrol in a small jeep. But the patrol in the jeep thought they saw the lights of a fishing boat and flashed their headlights to warn the "fishermen" of the coral reefs. The first shots were fired by the invaders, who shot up the jeep and stormed the shore. Farther up the beach was a small bar in a shed at the edge of the forest. The Cubans' preparedness and communication skills were greater than the CIA had anticipated. There was a newly installed telephone in the bar, and the alarm was quickly sent to Havana. Cuba is being invaded! Fidel Castro was awakened and jumped into a jeep headed for the Bay of Pigs. This was the Cuban leader's own fishing paradise. Castro's first order went to the pilots of the few planes Cuba had.

- First, sink the invasion force's ships. Leave the soldiers on the beach - shoot down the ships!

It would be a bloodbath.

Cuban pilot Captain Enrique Carreras was the first to reach the Bay of Pigs after sunrise. At 06:30 he hit the side of the large cargo ship Houston. On board were a field hospital, 130 soldiers, tanks, armored vehicles and much of the invasion force's weapons and ammunition. The ship did not explode but drifted burning and sinking toward a coral reef at Playa Larga. Scores of soldiers jumped into the sea and drowned. 45 minutes later, the second of the invasion force's five ships, the Rio Escondido, was hit off Blue Beach. With 200 barrels of gasoline on deck, the fire was intense, but most of the soldiers had made it to shore after the first air strike.

Two Alabama Air Force B-26s with four American pilots flew in from Nicaragua to attack Castro's troops on the beach. The first plane was shot down in the sea by Castro's pilots, and the second was shot down over land. One parachute pilot survived but was killed on the ground when he tried to throw a hand grenade. Both planes would have received discreet air cover from the carrier Essex, but the planners had overlooked the one-hour time difference between Cuba and Nicaragua.

Air domination was crucial. The invasion force soldiers made it to the beach but were fired upon from the air. They desperately called for air cover on their communications radios. Bleeding to death, they were at the mercy of the enemy. But President John F. Kennedy had made a clear decision that stood firm. No direct American involvement, no American warplanes! The invasion force was lost without air support and with supplies shot down. Soon they faced the Cuban army on the ground and were defeated in a few days of fierce and bloody fighting. The brigade was forced to surrender.

It was a failure for the U.S. in every way.

The Bay of Pigs has come to be known as the perfect failure. A CIA-led covert invasion force was about to invade Cuba, but it all turned into a major disaster for the US and its newly elected young president.

The Bay of Pigs casts its shadow far into the present. The story has it all. The Cold War, Nixon, Kennedy, presidential elections, revolution and counter-revolution, Castro, the Soviets, international law, secrets, spies, war, threads to Watergate - and last but not least - the question why we have journalists.

A little more than two years before the attempted invasion, in January 1959, the American Society of Newspaper Editors (ASNE) had a problem. The organization was planning its annual meeting in April, but it had no compelling names for speakers. They needed something new, something surprising, something that everyone would be curious to hear. Someone threw out a bold idea. What if ...?

The eyes of the editors fell on a young, charismatic, and handsome guerrilla leader who had marched down from the Sierra Madra mountains in Cuba a few weeks earlier. With a few hundred comrades, he had overthrown the U.S.-backed mafia dictator Fulgencio Batista. A few weeks after New Year's Day 1959, Fidel Castro marched triumphantly into Havana and was cheered by the crowds. Who was this Castro? Bird or fish? Was he a nationalist and liberation hero who could be a natural partner for the United States? Or was he a dangerous communist who would socialize American property and fall into the arms of the Soviet Union?

In the spring and winter of 1959, the jury was still out. Many American liberals saw hope in Cuba's liberation from the corrupt dictator Batista and his bloody regime. Several senators and other leaders hailed Castro as an American friend. The bold idea of the newspaper editors was simply to invite the new Cuban leader to be the keynote speaker at their convention. Fidel Castro accepted, and in April 1959 he came to New York and Washington for an eleven-day visit.

It was a resounding success. The 33-year-old Fidel Castro, in full camouflage uniform, cigar and beard, received a hero's welcome in New York. Cheering crowds shouted. "Viva Castro" and "Hi Fidel." He said what everyone wanted to hear. He told the newspaper publishers that he was for a free press and declared himself the enemy of every dictator. The assembled editors gave him a long round of applause.

Before the Senate Foreign Relations Committee, Fidel Castro gave assurances that U.S. assets would not be expropriated.

On NBC's Meet the Press, he declared himself against communism and on the side of the Western democracies. He laid wreaths at the Lincoln and Jefferson monuments in Washington, declaring that President Thomas Jefferson understood what a revolution would accomplish. Admirers were told by Castro that he stood for Cubanism, not socialism.

Fidel Castro moved from his luxury hotel in downtown Manhattan to a simpler black hotel in the simpler parts of Harlem. The public's applause was unending. But there were also critics and skeptics. President Dwight Eisenhower was cautious and did not want to receive the Cuban visitor. As a precaution, the president went off to play golf, leaving the unwelcome guest behind to his vice president, Richard Nixon.

An inveterate communist hunter, Nixon was skeptical from the start. He also did not want to give the Cuban leader any official status through a formal public reception but was forced to sacrifice a beautiful spring Sunday for a meeting with Castro in his office next to the White House. It was April 1, 1959, Castro arrived in his guerrilla garb, and the two met for three and a half hours, far from the flashbulbs and official protocol.

This was the seed of what was to come.

Nixon asked Castro why there were no free elections in Cuba. Castro replied that the Cuban people did not want them because they would make for bad governments. Nixon asked why the Cuban government did not have fair trials for its opponents, and Castro defiantly replied that the people did not want trials for their enemies. They wanted to shoot them as quickly as possible. Nixon wondered if Castro was not afraid that the Communists in his government would try to take over.

- I am not afraid of the communists, Castro said. I can handle them. Castro spoke at length about the country's illiteracy, poverty, unemployment, and the need for agrarian reform. Nixon was not impressed. He wrote down his impressions and a summary of the meeting in a memo to President Eisenhower. Nixon described Castro as a teenager, a bit artificial, not a heavy man, but still with elusive leadership qualities.

- Castro is either incredibly naive about communism, or he is under severe communist discipline," Nixon summarized.

That's putting it mildly. From that day on, Nixon was convinced that Castro had to go. Nixon later wrote that he had become the "strongest and most persistent advocate for setting up and supporting a secret effort to remove the man who had forced him to work that afternoon."

The choice was made. But President Eisenhower was a cautious general. He knew from experience that a commitment might require the U.S. to be willing to go all the way. And all the way was a full-scale, open American intervention. But Cuba was an independent state, recognized by the rest of the world and with its own seat in the U.N. An invasion of Cuba would be a violation of the U.N. Charter and the agreement with the American states. An open war between the U.S. and Cuba could provoke the Soviet Union to support Castro. An American intervention could ultimately lead to a third world war. At the very least, a Soviet response could be an offensive in Southeast Asia or an annexation of West Berlin, the Allied part of Berlin. The Berlin Wall had not yet been built.

But there might be a way out. A few years earlier, a covert CIA operation had succeeded in installing a pro-US military regime in Guatemala. In 1954, with only a few hundred men and almost no gunfire, the CIA was able to overthrow a government critical of the U.S. and install its own puppet as president of the country. President Eisenhower had personally paid tribute to the successful CIA agents at a reception at home. The president proudly declared that they had succeeded in preventing a Communist beachhead in the Western Hemisphere. This was a wake-up call. If overt intervention was impossible, perhaps a new covert CIA operation could solve the problem? After all, Castro himself had managed to overthrow a president with only a few hundred men. Surely the CIA could succeed in a counterrevolution with a larger force? But it would have to look like an internal Cuban affair. It would be Cubans landing in Cuba, led by Cubans, supported by opposition figures on the island. Even if they were recruited, equipped, and trained by the U.S., this involvement would be kept secret and denied. Once a Cuban exile army landed in Cuba, a beachhead would be established, the people would join, a new government could be proclaimed, and U.S. support requested. Then the United States could go in with full force and liberate Cuba from communism.

Many Guatemalan veterans stayed with the CIA. Chief among them was Richard Bissell, the CIA's director of planning, effectively the head of all covert operations. With a Ph.D. in economics from Yale, he was considered a genius, and it was he who had successfully managed the U2 project of secret signals intelligence planes over the Soviet Union. Now he was the closest man to CIA Director Allen Dulles. The CIA leadership began drafting a top-secret four-point plan. The U.S. would create a responsible and unified Cuban government-in-exile. It would launch a vigorous propaganda offensive, develop a clandestine espionage and resistance movement inside Cuba, but above all, recruit, train and equip a paramilitary force of Cuban exiles outside Cuba.

Richard Nixon was hanging on. He asked more and more often how the "boys at the institute" were doing. Nixon was also worried for personal reasons. He was going to run for president and wanted to take credit for overthrowing a communist dictator. Preparations were made in great secrecy during the fall of 1959 and were accelerated by the fact that in October the Soviets had clearly begun to approach Cuba and offer economic cooperation. The U.S. did not want a Soviet satellite in its backyard. The final decisions to continue 'Operation Pluto' were made in March 1960. On March 10th in the National Security Council, on March 14th in a special security group, and on March 17, President Eisenhower gave the green light to the CIA's secret plan. There was some resistance from the military leadership, which was concerned about the complexity of the operation and doubted the CIA's claim that an invasion would spark a popular uprising in Cuba. But the high level of secrecy meant that many did not know, understand, or could argue. The die was cast, and the recruitment of Cuban exiles in Florida began.83

The events leading up to the Bay of Pigs illustrate and can help understand the boundaries between the executive branch and the fourth estate. They show how the American press and media effectively bowed to the political power's definition of national security. What if, instead of remaining silent, the media had fulfilled their duty to publish? The first revelation of the invasion plans could have come as early as August 1, 1960.

Miami was home to thousands of Cuban migrants who had fled Fidel Castro's Cuba. They were a wonderful mix of old Batista men, liberals, and defectors from Castro's own forces. They were united by a dislike of Castro, communism, and a desire to bring a new, pro-U.S. government to the island. It was in this environment that the secret CIA army was recruited. The first troops began training at a farm south of Miami, Homestead Farm. Everything was supposed to be top secret. But recruitment was open, and it was hard to keep a secret in the middle of Florida. The farm's neighbors were awakened by roaring commands in Spanish over loudspeakers and could hear the troops training inside the farm.

Some local teenage boys were excited by the secret military exercises at the farm and went on a rampage one evening in August of 1960. They threw firecrackers over the fence but were not immediately met with laughter. The Cuban soldiers panicked, thinking it was Castro's agents attacking. They rushed out with their rifles and fired at the playing teenagers. One of the boys was seriously wounded, and local police began an investigation. Several suspected Cubans were arrested, but then it stopped. Someone in Washington managed to use "a secret request from federal authorities" to stop the local sheriff's investigation on the grounds of "national security".

Then the local newspaper, the Miami Herald, came to life. What kind of national security was being threatened on a farm outside Miami? The Miami Herald assigned its Washington correspondent, David Kraslow, to the case. He took a thorough approach. After weeks of digging and talking to sources at the FBI, the State Department and the White House, Kraslow finished a revealing and very comprehensive long article. He was able to describe how the CIA organized not only the Homestead camp, but a much larger operation. Kraslow found that both the Justice and State Departments were critical of this violation of the Neutrality Act, a U.S. law prohibiting the training of foreign troops on U.S. soil for intervention in other countries. The critical departments tried to pressure President Eisenhower to move all such training outside the United States. Kraslow was able to reveal that the exile soldiers were being trained at the Florida camps to be sent to Cuba to wage a guerrilla war against Castro.

The article was ready for publication, but the editors of the Miami Herald were concerned that they might compromise national security if it were published. They tried to get official guidance, including from President Eisenhower's press secretary. As a result, David Kraslow and the paper's Washington bureau chief were invited to meet with CIA Director Allen Dulles. The editors presented their findings. Dulles sternly declared that publication of the story would be "extremely damaging to the national interest".

The Miami Herald management bowed to this and decided not to publish anything. David Kraslow was disappointed but accepted it as a difficult decision. The secret was kept for now.

The next possible revelation of the secret plans was made by presidential candidate John F. Kennedy - inadvertently and without his knowing the full story. The presidential election was to be held in early November 1960. It was between challenger John F. Kennedy and incumbent Vice President Richard Nixon.

Late in the evening of October 19, some of Kennedy's staff were preparing for the last major televised debate against Nixon. The debate was to be on foreign policy, and the staff was worried that Kennedy would be seen as the soft-spoken rich boy who couldn't stand up to the Soviets and Communists. Many sympathizers had sent Kennedy questions and comments in advance of the debate. The voters' concerns were often about Castro and Cuba. The small group of advisers speculated that a strong statement on Cuba would be good and wrote:

- We must strengthen the non-Batista, democratic, anti-Castro forces in exile and in Cuba. They give us hope of overthrowing Castro. So far, these freedom fighters have received virtually no support from our government.

Freedom fighters sounded good. The speechwriters had no idea about the secret CIA plans, the exile army, or the camps in Latin America. To them, it was just a fancy phrase. This would make Kennedy tougher than Nixon, who was tough on Castro but limited himself to talking about some kind of "quarantine" of Cuba. Kennedy was already asleep, so the staff sent out a press release on their own. Nixon became furious.

He was convinced that Kennedy had received advance information about the invasion plans, and that Kennedy was now trying to steal Nixon's talking points. But Vice President Nixon was tied up. He wanted to save the operation at all costs, and the way to do that was to attack violently from the other direction. In the televised debate, Nixon hotly argued that Kennedy's line was irresponsible. He said Kennedy's proposal was the most shocking and reckless ever made by a presidential candidate. But now, suddenly, it wasn't Kennedy who was soft on the Communists.

Kennedy was considered to have won the debate. Not just because Nixon was sweating profusely in his heavy beard stubble. The Cuban issue played a major role, and the paradox was that Nixon had to argue harshly against his own secret plans in front of a clueless Kennedy.

After the presidential election in the fall of 1960, the CIA's secret preparations continued. Kennedy defeated Nixon, and although he was informed of the CIA's plans, it was still President Eisenhower's responsibility. Guatemala, with its CIA-installed president, was a suitable country for training. The brother of Guatemala's UN ambassador owned a large farm outside the town of Retalhuleu, where there was an abandoned military base, and the CIA renovated the old barns and barracks and built an airfield with runways for jets. The Cubans were trained by American officers and CIA experts in guerrilla warfare, explosives, sabotage, artillery, marksmanship and aviation.

Soon the Retalhuleu camp was an official secret throughout Guatemala. Then came the next opportunity for an international exposure.

On October 30, 1960, Guatemala's largest daily newspaper, La Hora, published a major front-page article about the camp. Its editor-in-chief, Clemente Marroquín Rojas, one of Guatemala's most prominent journalists, revealed that the CIA had spent a million dollars to build a heavily guarded military base near Retalhuleu. There, Cuban counterrevolutionaries were trained to land in Cuba. It was sensational and well-documented, but the article was not reported in the U.S. press and attracted no attention in the United States.

With one exception. Coincidentally, one of America's foremost experts on Latin America was in Guatemala on the very days La Hora made its revelation. Ronald Hilton was the director of the Institute of Hispanic American Studies at Stanford University, and he now realized that the CIA had a secret base in the country and what it was for. When he returned home, he wrote about it in the Institute's journal, the Hispanic American Report:

> It is widely known in Guatemala that the CIA
> is secretly training Cubans at a secret base in
> preparation for an invasion of Cuba.

Still no reaction anywhere. After all, it was just a small academic journal for Latin American scholars. But one of its readers tipped off the editor of the weekly magazine The Nation about Hilton's article, and the magazine in turn contacted Ronald Hilton to see what he knew. The Nation used Hilton's report as the basis for an editorial published on November 11, 1960. Under the headline "Are We Training a Cuban Guerrilla?" the paper referred to Hilton's statements and his allegations of a secret American training camp in the mountains around the town of Retalhuleu.

> We ourselves, of course, do not claim to have
> first-hand knowledge of the facts ... If Washington is
> unaware of the existence of the base, or if it knows
> of its existence but is innocent of any involvement
> in it, the appropriate authorities will surely want to
> quash all damaging rumors... On the other hand,
> if the reports as heard by Dr. Hilton are true,
> then public pressure should be brought to bear on
> the administration to abandon this dangerous and
> harebrained project.

The paper urged other media with resources and correspondents to verify the statements. The editors of The Nation, a weekly with a small circulation, were eager to spread their article. After the magazin went to press on November 11, the paper sent a press release and copies of the editorial to the leading newsrooms and news agencies in the United States. The main editors received a special print edition and the press release by courier. One of the paper's editors, Jesse Gordon, made his own calls to several newsrooms. He called the AP three times, and each time they asked him to send copies of the story, but somewhere higher up the hierarchy, the story ran into someone who didn't want to run the story. It was not quoted by UPI and was only mentioned in one newspaper, the York Gazette and Daily in Pennsylvania.

What about the New York Times, the leading newspaper? Jesse Gordon of The Nation sent his editorial to four different editors at the major New York newspaper. Finally, Peter Kihss, who covered Cuba, replied that he was interested and asked where he could find Ronald Hilton. But Dr. Hilton had no further information, and the New York Times Washington desk could find nothing. Nevertheless, the paper asked its reporter Paul Kennedy, who was traveling in Nicaragua, to go to Guatemala to verify the story. But he settled for an interview with President Ydígoras Fuentes. It took nine days for the effort to be noticed in the New York Times, in an unsigned article deep in the paper. The Guatemalan president was confronted with reports of a base set up with U.S. support as a training camp for military action against Cuba. New York Times wrote:

> The president branded the reports "a pack of lies".
> He said the base was one of several used by the
> Guatemalan army to train in guerrilla warfare. The
> goal of the training was to counter invasions such

as those recently seen in Honduras, Nicaragua, and Panama.

The New York Times made no assessment of its own, contenting itself with the expected denial from the Guatemalan president. The only paper that seemed to be "on" was the York Gazette and Daily, which wrote on November 25, 1960 about how the AP news agency had handled the story. There was a little buzz here and there, but the news of the secret CIA camp and its goal did not really spread.

On November 28, 1960, things may have begun to move again. One of the CIA's top executives, Inspector General Lyman Kirkpatrick, spoke at the Commonwealth Club in San Francisco. The meeting had a large audience and media coverage, and Kirkpatrick took questions after his speech. Someone in the audience spoke:

- Professor Hilton of Stanford says there is a CIA-funded base in Guatemala with plans to attack Cuba. Professor Hilton says it will be a black day for Latin America and the U.S. if this happens. Is this true?

After a long pause, Kirkpatrick replied:

- It will be a black day if we are found out.

Even this surprising admission went unnoticed. The CIA's third-in-command had effectively confirmed what was happening in a large public meeting. But the American public was left in the dark. Only a few small newspapers, the St. Louis Post-Dispatch and the Los Angeles Mirror, insisted on briefly reporting about the secret air base. Interestingly, the major news agencies, AP and UPI, were silent.

By January 1, 1961, however, there were widespread press reports indicating conclusively that there was an airfield and an American military base in Guatemala training guerrilla soldiers. By now, Fidel Castro had obvious reasons to believe that the U.S. was up to something. He publicly accused the US of planning an invasion and complained to the UN.

On January 8, the New York Daily News began publishing a series of articles that raised public awareness. They quoted former Cuban Prime Minister Manuel Varona, who claimed that an invasion force would land in Cuba.

On January 10, New York Times correspondent Paul Kennedy returned with a report directly from Retalhuleu. Following articles in the Los Angeles Mirror and the St. Louis Post-Dispatch, the paper had sent its reporter back to Guatemala, this time with orders to go outside the capital to find out what was really happening. The article broke some of the silence, but it was written very carefully. Nothing about the CIA and the American trainers. The big picture remained unclear, even though the news had now begun to penetrate the major New York newspapers. Still, President Kennedy was angry and thought they were writing too much.

The New York Times article prompted the Miami Herald to publish what it had known for months. On January 11, they began a series of articles about what was going on. In an editorial comment, the paper explained that it had waited to publish until others had written about the matter. On January 27, Time magazine reported that Castro may not have been making things up. The magazine wrote that the Cuban resistance movement, the Frente, was receiving half a million U.S. dollars a month from the U.S. and that the whole operation was run by a CIA agent named "Mr. B."

It was still as if the U.S. did not understand or know. The CIA planning continued. But there were also strong objections of a political, moral and legal nature. One of the main critics was Kennedy's special advisor, Arthur Schlesinger, a Harvard history professor. He wrote a memo saying that the last thing the Cubans should do was try to bring back the politicians who had gone into exile with gangster leader Meyer Lansky and other mafia bosses. The strongest internal critic was the chairman of the Senate Foreign Relations Committee, Senator J. William Fulbright. He, too, denounced the plans in a scathing memorandum to the president. The operation was ill-conceived, had weak or poor leadership, was already an open secret, and it would be impossible to conceal U.S. involvement, the senator argued. An invasion would be a violation of several international treaties, as well as U.S. law, which prohibits "enlistment or recruitment of foreign military forces in the United States, preparation of foreign military expeditions, equipping foreign naval vessels for attacks against friendly powers." The senator also had political objections:

- Covert support for this activity is the kind of hypocrisy and cynicism of which the U.S. constantly accuses the Soviet Union at the UN and elsewhere. This point will be clear to the rest of the world and to our own consciences.

Fulbright advocated tolerance combined with isolation of Castro. His summary judgment has become a classic: "The Castro government is a stab in the flesh but not a knife in the heart."

In the spring, scattered revelations appeared in the press. El Diario, a Spanish-language newspaper in New York, and the New York Mirror published the addresses of the recruitment offices. The various leaders of the exile groups could not remain silent.

On March 31, Richard Bissell of the CIA received a memo from Schlesinger at the White House informing him of a visit by Howard Handleman, a reporter for US News & World Report. Handleman had made a ten-day reporting trip to Miami and was getting details of the operation.

Cuban exiles told him that an invasion was about to begin. Recruitment to the training camps had increased sharply. The reporter knew how, where, and by whom the brigade was being trained. He understood that the CIA was counting on a popular uprising, but that they would eventually have to send in the Navy for the invasion to succeed.

Schlesinger panicked, but the reporter was convinced that the situation was delicate and refrained from publishing details. Schlesinger pointed out to the president that if a good newspaper reporter in Miami could get all this in a few days, Havana must be well aware of what was going on.

Just a few days later, a new revelation was under way. Gilbert Harrison, editor of the New Republic, sent Arthur Schlesinger a copy of a forthcoming exposé on the invasion entitled 'Our Men in Miami'.

The editor asked the presidential aide if there was any reason not to publish it. Schlesinger thought the article was careful and factual, but damning. Wondering if it was right for the government to ask an editor to withhold the truth, he gave the article to the president. Kennedy read it immediately and said he hoped the article could be stopped. The editor, Gilbert Harrison, accepted without question. Schlesinger thought it was a patriotic act, but later wrote that it gave him a strangely uncomfortable feeling.

Ten days before the invasion, the entire operation could have been called off because New York Times reporter Tad Szulc was on vacation. Tad Szulc was the kind of true grunt who has an uncanny ability to show up in the right place at the right time. A multilingual globetrotter with roots in Poland and studies in Switzerland. He was the New York Times correspondent in Rio de Janeiro. He spoke fluent Spanish and had an extensive network of contacts throughout Latin America. On Easter 1961, he was on his way home to new assignments for the newspaper, but he took a few days off and stopped in Miami on his way home to see old friends.

He checked into the simple McAllister Hotel in Miami's crowded downtown. On his first night in town, he sits in the hotel bar waiting for a friend. Then he suddenly sees an acquaintance from Cuba whom he met in the country the year before, a man who was then a supporter of Castro but has since defected.

- What are you doing in Miami? the man asks. You must have heard about the training.

Tad Szulc had heard a little, but he was skeptical. Refugees always talked about various plans to invade their old country. But this defector was serious, something was happening.

- Is it serious? Can I meet more people who know? Szulc asks.

He was allowed to. The next day, he met more Cuban exiles involved in the invasion plans. The reporter learned that traffic to Guatemala had increased. Cuban leaders had been asked to be prepared to travel on short notice. Szulc was given the names of several CIA agents. At a party, a friend pulled him aside and introduced him:

- This is one of our top Americans: Eduardo.

Behind the alias was one of the CIA's directors of Operation Pluto, Howard Hunt. He would later become better known as one of the organizers of the Watergate break-in.

An excited Tad Szulc called his boss Turner Catledge in New York. Szulc told him he'd stumbled upon a story he didn't want to talk about on the phone and was rushing home. That same afternoon, he sat in Turner's office on the sixth floor of the New York Times newsroom in downtown Manhattan. Sensing that something big was about to happen, Turner had asked the paper's publisher, Orvil Dryfoos, to join the meeting.

Szulc explained what he had learned and was immediately told he could consider himself stationed in Miami. He flew out that evening but stopped in Washington on the way to brief the New York Times correspondent and bureau chief there, James Reston.

"Scotty" Reston was perhaps the most influential political reporter in America. He was well-connected and trusted by President Kennedy.

In fact, Reston already knew a lot about the invasion. It would be the first major move of the Kennedy administration, he had heard. It seemed to Reston that Kennedy was trying to reduce direct American involvement. The president had told Reston that "all the guns would be in the hands of the Cubans. The invasion, the president said, would not depend on the United States.

After listening to Tad Szulc, James Reston went directly to the home of CIA Director Allen Dulles on P Street in Georgetown, Washington. They met in the library, with two agents guarding the entrance. Dulles was relaxed when Reston asked about the CIA's involvement in the Cuban invasion and denied everything. Reston felt the CIA director was lying through his teeth, but now he would have to wait for Tad Szulc to find out more.

Back in Miami, Tad Szulc pumped the Cuban exiles for more details. The Cubans kept saying that the landing would cause a general uprising. Szulc thought they were deluding themselves. How could a small brigade overthrow Castro? According to Szulc, they couldn't.

He finished writing his eye-opening article. Turner Catledge received it on April 6 and decided to publish the entire long and detailed story. The editor was proud of The New York Times' leadership and responsibility for the content, but accounts differ on the nature of the contacts between the White House and the newspaper. According to author and journalist David

Halberstam, President Kennedy realized that the New York Times was about to publish and called the paper's Washington bureau chief, James Reston. Kennedy spoke earnestly about the paper's responsibility and wanted the article stopped. The New York Times editors would have "the blood of the invasion force on their hands and could be responsible for stopping the whole plan. Reston informed Orvil Dryfoos of the call.

Author Richard Reeves gives an even more dramatic description of the events of April 6. Someone from the New York Times called President Kennedy and told him about the article that would be published the next day saying that an invasion was imminent. Kennedy is said to have exploded, slamming down the phone and talking about treason. When he calmed down he called Orvil Dryfoos and asked him to stop the publication. However, New York Times reporter Harrison E. Salisbury, in his book Without Fear or Favor, rejects all claims of direct telephone conversations between the President and Orvil Dryfoos. Author Peter Wyden, who wrote one of the most well-documented and credible books on the Bay of Pigs, *Bay of Pigs*, argues that it is established that the President was in contact with Dryfoos, but that it is far from clear who took the initiative. The president was angered by the newspaper's plans, and Kennedy is reported to have told Dryfoos that he had not even given the go-ahead for the operation.

In any case, Orvil Dryfoos was very concerned. Could the New York Times jeopardize national security by publishing this? Would the paper be held responsible if hundreds or even thousands of

Cubans died on the beaches? Or would the operation be called off and the paper be accused of sabotaging national security?

There were parts of Tad Szulc's article about which Catledge had doubts. He did not want to mention the CIA. There were other intelligence services. He preferred the obfuscating euphemism "US experts". The draft article said the invasion was "imminent. Szulc was reasonably sure it would happen on April 18, but had not written the exact date because he was not quite sure. Turner Catledge did not want to make any predictions about timing. Such things could easily go wrong.

Turner Catledge consulted James Reston by phone. Reston was against publication. He had no objection to the newspaper printing the facts. But he was against that New York Times would alert the rest of the world to the U.S. government's plans. James Reston argued that an invasion could not be called "imminent" with ten days to go. Dryfoo's concerns after hearing the President's protests, as well as the objections of James Reston and Turner Catledge, led management to make some changes. The managing editor ordered the removal of all specific references to the CIA, as well as any mention of a specific day or time of the invasion. The next order was the most drastic. The front-page editors had already drawn a four-column headline on the first page, with large war headlines in the left-hand corners. Instead, Catledge ordered a small, single-column headline in the center of the front page, with a continuation inside the paper. Assistant managing editor Theodore Bernstein and news editor Lewis Jordan were appalled by the order. The multi-column left cross was a signal of great importance to their own news. A one-column inferior space was meant to diminish the importance of the news. This was normally their decision and responsibility, they thought. The angry editors rushed to Catledge to protest that the paper was about to make a "terrible mistake". Lewis Jordan's face was white. His voice quavered with anger.

He and Bernstein claimed that never before had a front-page story been changed for political reasons. They wanted to speak directly to their publisher to justify his decision.

Catledge was furious. The managing editor's decision had never been questioned. But he swung around in his big swivel chair, called Dryfoos and asked him to come down to the newsroom. Dryfoos spent ten minutes explaining why he wanted to tone down the story for national security reasons. He was especially concerned about the men who would be fighting. The decision was his.

The story became a watered-down, one-column story with a less sensational headline: "Anti-Castro Units Trained to Fight at Florida Bases."

Tad Szulc was "disgusted" by the way the editors had handled his words. The reference to "American experts", not the CIA, came only at the bottom of the article, inside the paper. But Tad Szulc had been working informally with CBS television news, which ran the story the night before the New York Times. Ironically, below Szulc's article was a note referring to the CBS statement that an invasion was imminent and that plans were in the final stages.

Still, the article was enough to turn President Kennedy's face ashen as he read the New York paper on the morning of April 7.

- I can't believe what I'm reading," he exploded to press Secretary Pierre Salinger in the Oval Office. Castro doesn't need any agents here! All he has to do is read our newspapers.

But what did Castro really know?

The Cuban leader's analysis was that Kennedy would not change the Eisenhower-Nixon policy toward Cuba. Kennedy had tied himself too tightly during the campaign. The gap between East and West was widening, and Castro felt that Kennedy was stuck in the Cold War. The Cubans knew an invasion was coming. Castro had informants throughout Latin America and many agents in exile in Miami. In early November 1960, Cuban intelligence sent a report to Moscow that the CIA was training anti-Castro exile forces in Guatemala. In early April 1961, the CIA intercepted a telegram from the Soviet embassy in Mexico City, which correctly stated that the invasion was expected on April 17.

Nevertheless, Castro was unsure of the exact date and, more importantly, the place or places where the invasion would take place. He had long believed that the attack would come before Kennedy was inaugurated, and Cuba had been on high alert for months. This put a strain on the economy, and with the important sugar harvest in 1961, the state of readiness could not be maintained. Nor could Castro protect the entire coast of the country. It was too long and inaccessible. Therefore, various possible landing sites were manned by small military forces. Military aid from the Soviet Union was on its way, but it was not there, and in Castro's view, it was moving far too slowly. Regardless of what the Americans thought of the hundreds of pilots undergoing MIG training in Czechoslovakia, it would be months before the 50 inexperienced Cuban pilots actually trained would be ready. Castro could not imagine that the CIA really believed in an internal rebellion in Cuba. They should understand that he now had strong popular support. He realized that the invasion force would try to establish a beachhead and that the great danger was that the invading force would declare a new government that could openly ask for American support.

Fidel Castro was fortunate in one respect. In the fall of 1960, he had inspected the coastal area of Giron, where the Bay of Pigs is located, and decided that a resort could be built there. This became Castro's favorite fishing spot, and by the spring of 1961 there was a rapid development of roads, communications, and small bungalows. Castro had his own bungalow built and spent time there learning the geography of the area. All of this was apparently overlooked by CIA intelligence.

Despite all the objections and leaks, the American invasion plans continued. American pilots and aircraft were recruited from the Alabama National Guard, the part of the Air Force that still flew B-26s, and these could be repainted in Cuban colors and flags. Final decisions were made in early April. But John F. Kennedy wanted to reduce the "noise level" even further and prohibited the direct involvement of American warplanes. It was Cuban exile pilots in the repainted planes that would take out Castro's small air force. Step one was a Cuban pilot allegedly fleeing Cuba in his plane and landing in Florida. This would set the stage for future claims that the air strikes were carried out by defecting Cuban pilots and planes. With great fanfare, the defector and his plane were shown to the press. But this time, reporters were skeptical. Why was the pilot's name not released if he was now on display for all to see? The plane was admittedly painted in Cuban colors, with the Cuban star and the designation 333 FAR - Fuerza Aérea Revolucionaria, and the CIA had fired a few shots through the metal to make it look like it was in combat. But why did the B-26 have a steel nose cone when all Cuban planes had plastic ones? And wasn't there something odd about the supposed bullet holes? The CIA's elaborate bluff collapsed like a house of cards. The American government made an even bigger fool of itself when UN ambassador Adlai Stevenson was tricked into showing the picture of the alleged Cuban plane to the UN General Assembly. The Cuban foreign minister and the Russian ambassador were able to disclose the U.S. lies. Adlai Stevenson, who had been given no information about the CIA operation, was furious to see his credibility destroyed in public before the UN General Assembly.

The success of the operation depended on air superiority of the brigade. An initial attack was made with repainted B-26s with Cuban pilots flying from airfields in Nicaragua. While the invasion force was on its way over the sea, Castro's small air force was to be destroyed. The brigade plane attacked Campo Libertad airport outside Havana on the morning of April 16. Castro himself was awakened by the explosions. He thought the attack was insane. Now he knew the invasion had begun. But where would they land?

The air strikes succeeded in taking out five of Castro's planes, but not the entire air force. An unknown number of planes were intact, at least two T-33s and several Sea Furies. The invasion force requested authorization for further attacks, but Kennedy refused. Many of the Cuban planes that were hit and burned were dummies, old, inoperable planes used as decoys for an attack. The remaining planes were put on high alert. At all times, one pilot was in the cockpit, ready to take off, and a backup was sleeping under the wing. The pilots had to take turns every 30 minutes to complete the mission, but they were ready to respond at the first warning of new attacks.

The invasion of the Bay of Pigs beaches rolled toward disaster. As the invaders bled to death on the beaches, the CIA sent out victorious communiqués through a Manhattan PR agency, all in the name of the Cuban Resolution Council. The first was issued at midnight on April 17 and carried uncritically by much of the U.S. media.

Bulletin No 1

Before dawn, Cuban patriots in the cities and mountains began the struggle to liberate our homeland from the despotic regime of Fidel Castro.

The U.S.-led "Revolutionary Council" had been secretly flown to Opa-locka, Florida, where they were locked in a barn. To their surprise, they could hear their "own" communiqués on the radio.

And it was they who were supposed to lead the fight! They were not allowed to leave the barracks or make phone calls, while they were guarded by heavily armed American soldiers. The exiles became angry and resentful as their soldiers and sons bled to death on the beaches.

It was a grim outcome for the US:

114 invaders died in the assault.

1 189 soldiers were captured and taken to Havana for interrogation and long imprisonment.

150 soldiers never landed and made it back to the ships with the two CIA agents.

Cuban casualties were much higher. More than 1,800 Cuban civilians and military personnel were killed in the fighting.104 The captured soldiers remained in Cuba for nearly two years. Castro demanded $62 million in ransom, food, and medicine. The prisoners were released on Christmas 1962, when Castro agreed to $53 million in compensation.

Cuba was victorious. On Thursday, April 20, 1961, when the last of the invasion force had surrendered, Castro made a nearly four-hour televised speech with a pointer, confiscated documents, and maps. He triumphantly described his own actions and movements in the area. He gushed that the fighter planes destroyed by the "mercenaries" at Campo Libertad were dummies. He mocked "intellectual planners" from Yale, comparing them to his own heroes from the Sierra Maestra mountains. Castro mocked American spy reports:

- We don't have MIG plans, but I wish we did.

Cubans stood by their televisions and watched. After all, they were better and more accurately informed than the American public. At UN headquarters, things boiled over immediately after the faked and revealed defection of a Cuban pilot and the first air strike on Havana. Protesters outside the UN building chanted: "Cuba Si, Yankee No."

The General Assembly opened a debate at 10:30 a.m. on April 17. The U.S. was met with condemnation from around the world. Defeat everywhere. For Kennedy, it was an unmitigated disaster. He sighed to his advisor, Theodore Sorensen:

- How could I be so stupid as to let them go on?

Kennedy suffered from his defeat, but he did not shirk his responsibility.

- Victory has a hundred fathers, but defeat is an orphan, Kennedy said as he accepted the blame for what had happened. But he was still angry about the revelations in the press, even though so many editors had voluntarily refrained from publishing everything they knew. On April 27, 1961, President Kennedy delivered a fiery speech at the Waldorf Astoria Hotel in New York to the American Newspaper Publishers Association:

> I do ask every publisher, every editor, and every
> newsman in the nation to reexamine his own
> standards, and to recognize the nature of our
> country's peril. In time of war, the government and
> the press have customarily joined in an effort based
> largely on self-discipline, to prevent unauthorized

disclosures to the enemy. In time of "clear and present danger," the courts have held that even the privileged rights of the First Amendment must yield to the public's need for national security.

Today no war has been declared - and however fierce the struggle may be, it may never be declared in the traditional fashion. Our way of life is under attack. Those who make themselves our enemy are advancing around the globe. The survival of our friends is in danger. And yet no war has been declared, no borders have been crossed by marching troops, no missiles have been fired.

If the press is awaiting a declaration of war before it imposes the self-discipline of combat conditions, then I can only say that no war ever posed a greater threat to our security. If you are awaiting a finding of "clear and present danger," then I can only say that the danger has never been more clear and its presence has never been more imminent.

Nevertheless, every democracy recognizes the necessary restraints of national security – and the question remains whether those restraints need to be more strictly observed if we are to oppose this kind of attack as well as outright invasion.

For the facts of the matter are that this nation's foes have openly boasted of acquiring through our newspapers information they would otherwise hire agents to acquire through theft, bribery or espionage; that details of this nation's covert preparations to counter the enemy's covert operations have been available to every newspaper reader, friend and foe alike; that the size, the strength, the location and the nature of our forces and weapons, and our plans and strategy for their use, have all been pinpointed in the press and other news media to a degree sufficient to satisfy any foreign power; and that, in at least in one case, the publication of details concerning a secret mechanism whereby satellites were followed required its alteration at the expense of considerable time and money.

The newspapers which printed these stories were loyal, patriotic, responsible, and well-meaning. Had we been engaged in open warfare, they undoubtedly would not have published such items. But in the absence of open warfare, they recognized only the tests of journalism and not the tests of national security. And my question tonight is whether additional tests should not now be adopted.

The question is for you alone to answer. No public official should answer it for you. No governmental plan should impose its restraints against your will. But I would be failing in my duty to the nation, in considering all of the responsibilities that we now bear and all of the means at hand to meet those responsibilities, if I did not commend this problem to your attention and urge its thoughtful consideration.

I have no intention of establishing a new Office of War Information to govern the flow of news. I am not suggesting any new forms of censorship or any new types of security classifications. I have no easy answer to the dilemma that I have posed and would not seek to impose it if I had one. But I am asking the members of the newspaper profession and the industry in this country to reexamine their own responsibilities, to consider the degree and the nature of the present danger, and to heed the duty of self-restraint which that danger imposes upon us all.

Every newspaper now asks itself, with respect to every story: "Is it news?" All I suggest is that you add the question: "Is it in the interest of the national security?" And I hope that every group in America - unions and businessmen and public officials at every

level, will ask the same question of their endeavors
and subject their actions to the same exacting tests.

This speech alarmed the American press. They felt that the president was interfering with their responsibility to evaluate the news and were concerned about new demands for restrictions and information management. Despite the fact that in practice, with few exceptions, the American news media had already voluntarily submitted to the government's assessment of national security, the President made this anointed speech. The leaders of the American press therefore requested a meeting with President Kennedy. It was held at the White House at 11 o'clock in the morning on May 1, 1961.

America's leading news executives sat down in the Oval Office for a conversation with President John F. Kennedy. Eight smiling editors in suits, ties and crisply pressed white shirts, the heads of the AP and UPI news agencies, the American Society of Newspaper Editors (ASNE) and the American Newspaper Editors Association. Kennedy sat on the short end of the legendary rocking chair he had for his bad back, leaning slightly forward and smiling with interest at his guests. The event is documented in photographs in the Kennedy Museum.

The president opened the meeting by complaining that the newspapers had published too much about the plans to invade Cuba. He went through a whole list of what he considered premature disclosures of security-sensitive information. He was particularly upset about some articles in the New York Times, especially on January 10, 1961. Turner Catledge of the New York Times was chairman of the ASNE and he objected that several other newspapers, both in the United States and in Latin America, had published information about the invasion plans long before the New York Times. He mentioned both La Hora in Guatemala and The Nation newspaper.

- But it did not become news until it appeared in The Times, the president replied.

The editors' objections were clear. In fact, the New York Times had refrained from publishing everything it knew about the secret CIA invasion a month earlier, at the president's express request. Not only the New York Times, but newspaper after newspaper, major news agencies, and television and radio editors had withheld what they knew for more than a year out of a self-imposed concern for an alleged national interest. Kennedy was well aware of this, and in a fit of candor, the president leaned over to Turner Catledge:

- If you had printed more about the operation, you would have saved us from a colossal mistake.

This was not only a complete failure of American foreign policy, but it was also a failure of the entire "free" press, not just the New York Times. A double failure.

A news organization cannot leave it to a president, i.e., the executive branch, to decide what is in the best interest of national security. Each newsroom must make that assessment independently, based on the public's legitimate interest in knowing. In a war or crisis, the newsroom cannot become part of the nation's war effort in the sense that it chooses to withhold inconvenient news for the good of the government. If its own troops have violated international law, it must be exposed. If the president is planning an illegal invasion of a neighboring country, the media cannot remain silent because the president believes disclosure is against the national interest.

Of course, the president was fully entitled to try to influence the media, with good reason, based on his motives, by discreet persuasion and reference to national interests and security. But he had no power to stop publication by repression. His only power was to appeal. Kennedy, like his predecessor President Eisenhower, wanted to stop a communist dictatorship in America's backyard in the spirit of the Cold War.

The American media was also a child of its time, with the Cold War in full swing. Many American journalists and newspaper executives shared the government's view of the communist threat. This certainly contributed to their willingness to listen to the president's various proposals to keep quiet in the national interest. In the light of history, much of the American media thus failed in its mission to present true and relevant news.

Paradoxically, the person who most clearly expressed doubts about the wisdom of the cover-up of the planned Bay of Pigs invasion was President Kennedy himself. First, in his comments to New York Times editorial page editor Turner Catledge in the Oval Office, and then even more clearly a year later in a frank conversation with New York Times publisher Orvil Dryfoos at the White House on November 13, 1962:

- I wish you had run everything about Cuba ... I'm sorry you didn't tell it all then.

The local newspaper should have nice news and help the community

For a long time, the paper *Norra Skåne* has been suspicious of almost everything that happens in the name of the municipality. Politicians, employees and parts of the business community are singled out with headlines that are both insinuating and lying. The newspaper is a very destructive force in our community, and you should seriously consider whether you have any responsibility at all to convey a positive image of Hässleholm municipality. I hope for more serious reporting from *Norra Skåne* in the future.

This is what Pär Palmgren (Conservative) wrote to the editor-in-chief of *Norra Skåne* and the chairman of the newspaper's board on March 27, 2014. Palmgren was the chairman of the municipal council in the city of Hässleholm in sothern Sweden. The letter was also published as an editorial in *Norra Skåne*, and Pär Palmgren had to explain himself on the local radio station P4 Kristianstad the same afternoon:

- It's just misery. It gives a false picture of Hässleholm, says Pär Palmgren.

- Isn't it a bit strong to call the magazine destructive?

- Yes, but that is exactly what I think.

On the radio, Pär Palmgren said that he was critical of the newspaper's coverage of individual cases, most recently a series of articles about the discussion in the municipality. He also criticized the fact that negative news is given more space and prominence than positive news.

- I can give one example in today's newspaper, where on page 4, at the bottom, there is an article about the Headmaster of the Year. Couldn't it have been on the front page?

This was an escalation of what became known as the Norra Skåne scandal. Hässleholm is in beautiful countryside near the Göinge forests in northern Skåne, a medium-sized municipality with just over 50,000 inhabitants. It is a true centrist municipality, where the Center Party has dominated politics for decades. It was also a municipal councillor from the Center Party who started the battle over the town's newspaper, Norra Skåne, which is controlled by the local party organization. The leading conservative politicians in Hässleholm were not happy. Among other things, the paper had investigated and questioned a real estate deal that could be suspected of being a disguised loan to a company. In this small community, everyone knows everyone else. Center Party councilor Lars-Göran Wiberg complained to his party colleague Håkan Mattsson, who was chairman of the newspaper's board. On March 1, 2014, councilor Wiberg started the battle over the newspaper with a letter in Norra Skåne entitled "Where are the limits of good journalism? The conservative chairman of the council, Palmgren, followed suit a few weeks later. Both politicians felt that the newspaper was too controlling, and that the reporter Berit Önell was the worst of all. The complaints led the chairman of the newspaper's board to contact the editor-in-chief, Mimmi Karlsson-Bernfalk, and demand that reporter Berit Önell be fired.

Normally, a publisher is expected to defend her staff, but here it was the other way around. The editor-in-chief listened to the complaining politicians and bowed to pressure. Reporter Berit Önell was transferred and forced to quit her job as city reporter, a position she had held for many years. News director Anders Kauranen, on the other hand, stood up for his reporter and immediately resigned from his management position in protest.

- I can't be the head of a newspaper where the municipal councils decide who will report on the municipality, said the news director and became a reporter instead.

Many readers were outraged and canceled their subscriptions. The scandal attracted national attention, and both Norra

Skåne's management and the politicians responsible were severely criticized. The journalists' trade union at Norra Skåne and Skånska Dagbladet called for the editor-in-chief's resignation. National paper Dagens Nyheter wrote on its editorial page that "this is how you turn a municipality into a banana republic." The Swedish IRE (Investigative reporters and Editors)section organized a large seminar in Hässleholm in support of the newspaper's reporters, and readers demonstrated in the square. The municipality was awarded "Roller Blind of the Year" by IRE.

However, Lars Joel Eriksson, local chairman of the Center party, owner of Norra Skåne, defended the actions against the undesired reporter on the radio program *Medierna i P1:*

- We are a locally owned newspaper with 300 local owners who also live in our coverage area. They read our papers and react to what we write, and they need to feel that the local newspaper is on the side of the local community.

- But how do you know you are on the side of the readers, what does it mean to be on the side of the readers?

- To protect what might be the interests of ordinary citizens, so that the community can develop, so that it can attract businesses, people and tax revenue, and not end up in a vicious downward spiral where jobs disappear, the community's economy deteriorates, and municipal services deteriorate.

The local power holders won, the pushy politicians and the pliant editor-in-chief stayed. Reporter Berit Önell was forced to resign, but after negotiations with Journalists' Union, she received a severance package. With the money she received, she was able to start her own business. Since 2014, Berit Önell has been running a local news site about Hässleholm, Frilagt Hässleholm - *Independent local news and reviews,* which survives mainly with the help of crowd funding from supporting subscribers and some advertising. The site has daily news from the municipality and is supported by the local readers' network "The Independent Press Group ". It reaches over 9000 unique readers each week.

What happened in Skåne is not unique. Local political beliefs that the local press should be on the side of the local community are much more common than desirable. When you scratch the surface, it turns out that real news is not always what the small or big powers want. The pressure on local newsrooms and local reporters to pick and choose news that "favors" the small community is too great, and it is directed at many small newsrooms in Sweden and other countries.

This is not an unknown phenomenon, and it was vividly portrayed on stage by the Norwegian playwright Henrik Ibsen in his classic drama *An Enemy of the People.* The final lines of Ibsen's 1882 drama capture the terrible loneliness of the local truth teller. The main character, Dr. Stockman, reveals that the water in the small spa town's baths is contaminated, but what are the consequences of his reports? The spa is the "beating heart of the village," attracting guests from far and wide to the small Norwegian coastal community. But the bathers have mysteriously fallen ill with typhoid and stomach ailments. The first suspects are all "strangers" carrying the disease, but Dr. Stockman is not satisfied with rumors and vague assumptions. He wants proof, so he takes samples of the water and sends them to the university for analysis.

He proudly presents his findings to his family and the editor of the local newspaper, *Folkviljan* (The will of the people). Now that he has documented that the water is contaminated, it can be fixed. The waterworks can be rebuilt and the water pipes re-routed to save the bath. The editor of *Folkviljan* calls Dr. Stockman a hero and deems him worthy of being honored by society in a flag-raising ceremony.

But while the facility is being cleaned up, the baths must be closed and the renovation costs a lot of money. What will happen to the resort's reputation, and how will real estate prices be affected? The difficult question is also whether the bathers will want to come back. It is a small community. Dr. Stockman's own brother is the mayor, and his father-in-law owns the tannery upstream, a facility that turns out to be the source of the emissions. Now the town's power holders are beginning to take notice. Maybe the results are not credible? Does this really need to be published? The owner of the newspaper's printing plant becomes cautious.

The existence of the small town is at stake, but also the future and fortune of the entire Stockman family is endangered by Dr. Stockman's revelation. What is the price of truth? The "compact majority" of the small town soon turns against the righteous doctor. The newspaper refuses to print Dr. Stockman's revelation. He is no longer the hero of the people. He can lose his familys inheritance. Dr. Stockman is an *enemy of the people* who stands alone in the final scene of the play, when he says his closing words:

- The fact is, you see, that the strongest man in the world is the one who stands most alone.

A modern enemy of the people is local paper *Östersundsposten* reporter Linda Hedenljung. She ran afoul of the establishment in this northern town when she uncovered strange dealings between a construction company and the municipal housing company *Östersundshem*. It was an investigation that also involved the city's great soccer hero, who had led the small club ÖFK to acclaimed world success. Daniel Kindberg was both chairman of ÖFK and CEO of *Östersundshem* when *Östersundsposten* began a series of critical articles in the fall of 2014. Linda Hedenljung writes herself:

Basically, credibility is the only real capital a journalist has. But what happens to that capital when society's elite says, more or less unanimously, that you lie, exaggerate and know nothing about anything? What happens to a journalist whose neighbor in the village likes a Facebook post by soccer hero Daniel Kindberg that takes all the credit away from her and her husband? A neighbor whose child is best friends with your child?

Linda Hedenljung was persecuted and harassed for years, but she always had the support of her newspaper and publisher, even though the owners of the newspaper were obviously being courted by the authorities she criticized. The reporter was accused of writing "useless rubbish" who had never done anything for Östersund. The pressure was high. But later investigations by the Swedish Economic Crime Authority and a public trial showed that the paper was justified in its statements. Those responsible were sentenced to prison by the district court when it became clear that the municipal company had paid bills to support the football club. The reporter received several awards, including Sports Journalist of the Year in 2019 and the Publicist Club's Grand Prize in 2020. But the road to that point was painful for Linda Hedenljung, who was just trying to do her job. In doing so, she actually did more for Östersund than most people.

A strong and active local journalism is vital for democracy. The threat doesn't just come from local party bosses trying to control local newspapers, or soccer fans who don't like having their club's finances scrutinized. The challenge also comes from an eroding economy and local newspapers going out of business. When local news disappears, citizens become less likely to vote, less politically informed, and less likely to run for office. Local officials act with less integrity and efficiency, and local businesses escape scrutiny, according to a report by the PEN Club of America.

It is serious, then, that many communities lack local newsrooms. In 2023, there were 40 *white spots* in Sweden, municipalities without an editorial presence. This number has remained constant in recent years, after a decline in the 2010s. The Institute for Media Studies monitors the development in annual surveys. Municipalities without editorial staffs include some of the country's less populated municipalities, as well as municipalities on the outskirts of larger cities.

There is no lack of public funding, but most of it is spent on municipal information rather than independent journalism.

The think tank Timbro's online magazine *Smedjan* showed in a survey that the number of municipal communicators in 2020 will be around 3 billions. This is a huge army that costs billions and dwarfs the state's spending on press subsidies, which for all types of support is budgeted at around one billion kronor for 2021.

In 2020, there will be 253 municipal communicators in the city of Gothenburg alone. Stockholm will have about 200, Malmö 170 and Uppsala 8. In many cities there are more informers than independent journalists. This uneven distribution of resources is perhaps one of the most serious threats to journalism that does not take into account who or what benefits or suffers from a story. The municipal communicators, on the other hand, acts on behalf of municipality who ultimately wants to present its organization and management in an attractive light. The issue is not quite the same for a local reporter as it is for a community communicator.

The imbalance seems to be growing. The magazine Resumé presented statistics in April 2021 showing that there are 6.4 PR consultants for every journalist. It is often the municipalities that hire journalists who have lost their jobs at the local newspaper. This is a national trend that affects information and transparency throughout the country. It is also difficult for newspapers to compete on salary with what municipalities can offer their communicators.

But elected politicians must be careful not to let communicators take over. In some political parties, elected representatives are not allowed to write their own op-eds, even in their local newspaper, without approval from the communications department. Communicators must approve all interview requests and, preferably, write down appropriate responses to possible questions. Political discourse is dying. Political apparatchiks have taken over.

Professor Bo Rothstein and his political science colleagues call this growing group of political appointees "policy professionals".

At the local level, it may even be the case that municipal information providers in practice obstruct and delay information, if not actually mislead. The events in Arboga and Köping covered by the *Bärgslagsbladet / Arboga* are just one example. The newspaper has a long tradition of scrutinizing its municipalities, but with fewer and fewer reporters and more and more communicators. Municipal politicians express their satisfaction with all the "nice" articles on the municipality's website, but when the real journalists look for information, they are often told that everything must be published by the communicators first. Newspaper reporters have to wait.

For example, Arboga Municipality's big savings of millions in schools in the spring of 2020 was given a more positive slant on the municipality's website than it probably would have been in the newspaper:

> Arboga municipality invests more than 635 million
> in primary and pre-primary schools!

In the municipal version, a budget cut is turned into an investment. And in the municipality of Köping, the city council chairman denied her plans to resign when the newspaper asked, only to verify the information a few days later on the municipality's own platforms. In Köping, the number of municipal information officers has doubled from 2 to 4 in a decade.

Reporter Anders Brage of the *Bärgslagsbladet / Arboga newspaper* notes that his newspaper now has fewer journalists than there are communicators in all the municipalities it covers:

- Communicators post on Facebook and municipal websites about openings and construction projects. They don't write about disgruntled employees, disappointed users or procurement disputes.

But Anders Brage argues that these communicators are not the "enemy". They are just doing their job:

- No, the enemy is democratically elected local politicians who think their own "tame" writers are safer than wicked independent critics in the free press. Who cut off advertising in the local newspaper and cancel subscriptions, while at the same time allocating millions of crowns to their own communications staffs. [...]

It is not a big step from municipal communicators to a society where the independent press is eradicated, as it is today in Belarus, Hungary and several other countries. [Journalists are a scourge. We are a nuisance. But ask the people of any totalitarian state if they miss the free press and the scrutiny and transparency that is the foundation of democracy. Ask the people demonstrating in Minsk whether journalists or the arrogance of power is worse.

We are not in the shooting business!

It's not our job to shoot anybody. That's the first thing. We're not into shooting business. We're in the business of reporting. And if in the course of reporting, some big beast in the wilderness comes down, that's part of the process. Is it the objective to bring down big beasts in the wilderness? No, I don't think so.

In a few seconds, Watergate reporter Carl Bernstein sums up the whole idea of being a news reporter. We're here to report - not to try to trap twelve-taggers. It's not our job to shoot anyone. That's another way of putting the requirement for consequence neutrality.

Bob Woodward and Carl Bernstein, two young reporters at the Washington Post, came up with the revelations about the background to the break-in at the Democratic headquarters in the Watergate office complex, in the summer of 1972. It was a revelation that would eventually lead to the forced resignation of the U.S. President.

But what were these young reporters thinking?

Did they intend to bring down Richard Nixon?

Were they looking to take down a twelve-tagger?

You can't write a book about consequence neutrality and real news without addressing the Watergate revelations and what the reporters were thinking. Woodward and Bernstein are legendary figures in American and global journalism. Bob Woodward struck again ahead of the 2020 presidential election with his tell-all book *Rage* about Donald Trump and Carl Bernstein was on CNN almost every day commenting on the election.

On visits to the U.S. over the years, I tried to get in touch with both legends. Maybe I didn't try hard enough, I never got the message through. It would be a failure not to be able to talk directly to the reporters about how President Nixon was removed from office. Finally, in March 2015, Carl Bernstein came to Sweden to speak at the big media conference, MEG, in Gothenburg. I was finally able to get my interview.

Erik Fichtelius: Well, Carl Bernstein, what were the consequences of the revelations you did in the Watergate affair?

Carl Bernstein: I think there's a lot of mythology about what we did. Our stories were the beginning of a process that led to the resignation of the president of the United States because that president was a criminal and presided over a criminal presidency from the beginning of his term to the end of his term. And we were able to obtain certain pieces of information very soon after the Watergate break in in June of 1972, that began to make it clear that there were events put into action by the president of the United States that that eventually were shown to be criminal. But there's a mythology that we were responsible for the impeachment or the resignation of the president. Rather, what we did is that our stories were read by a judge who then put pressure on the burglars in Watergate to tell their secrets. Then there was a congressional hearing that was convened by the Senate of the United States at which great revelations came about. That hearing was convened partly because the senators had read our stories. But then what we really did was that we were part of the process of the American system, the press doing its job, the legislature doing its jobs, the judiciary doing its job, and the political system responding to the information and demanding that Richard Nixon leave office.

Erik Fichtelius: So, in your own words, apart from all the mythology, what would you say? What were the consequences of your work?

Carl Bernstein: I'm probably not the best judge of that. I think there was a lot of interest among young people, particularly in journalism, because the results of our stories had a certain effect. And I think that people were drawn to that, perhaps for some for the right reasons, some for the wrong reasons. But I'm not the best judge of that. I it's a complicated process and it continues. I mean, Watergate has a place in the American story that is somewhat unique. And at the same time, what's not unique about it is that it is part of the American system working at its best. And unfortunately, right now we're living in an era when the American system is not working. I'm not suggesting that we have a president, of the United States, or have had any others that should have been removed from office, but rather that our political system is in terrible trouble, particularly the legislative branch.

Erik Fichtelius: But is it fair to say that the end result of the reporting that you started was the resignation of the president?

Carl Bernstein: I do not think that's the end result of our reporting. No. The end result of the whole process. Yes.

Erik Fichtelius: It was the resignation of the most powerful man in the world.

Carl Bernstein: Yes. Of the whole process working. Our stories, the legislature, the judiciary, politicians in Congress who turned against Richard Nixon and said, hey, he's a criminal, he must leave office.

Erik Fichtelius: And to what extent were these consequences, something that you could envisage when you started the reporting.

Carl Bernstein: I think when we started, we could not. But very early on, there was a day, about three months after the Watergate break in, Bob Woodward and myself, every day we would go get coffee together in a little vending machine room off the newsroom floor. And we had just learned about a secret fund that had been controlled by the principal aides to Richard Nixon that he'd paid for the bugging at Watergate and other undercover illegal activities against Nixon's opponents. And I put a dime in the coffee machine, and I felt a chill go down my back. We were about to do this story about this secret fund and who controlled it. And I said to Woodward, I said, oh, my God, this president is going to be impeached. And Woodward said to me, oh, my God, you're right. And we can never use that word impeach around the newsroom of The Washington Post because we do not have an agenda. We're here only to find out the facts. And we don't want our bosses and editors to think we have an agenda.

Erik Fichtelius: But when you understood that what were your deliberations?

Carl Bernstein: It didn't affect our deliberations. Our deliberations were about getting the information, continuing to report the story. It was very incremental. If you look back at those stories, they're not big stories that say the president of the United States is a criminal, at no point did it say that. It was incremental about this event, that event. And within a few months we were able to say in a story, the Watergate break in was part of a vast conspiracy of political espionage and sabotage that was orchestrated by the men closest to the president of the United States.

Erik Fichtelius: You say it was important to for you and to other people to understand that you didn't have your own agenda. Why was that?

Carl Bernstein: Because the job of the journalist is to find the best obtainable version of the truth, wherever the facts lead. If the facts had led to exonerating Richard Nixon, we should have presented those facts just wherever our job was to find out what happened.

Erik Fichtelius: Regardless of the consequences?

Carl Bernstein: Sure. Journalism, reporting is not done I believe to bring about a certain result in the political system or by the voters of the country. It's done to get the information out there so people can make up their own minds about things.

Erik Fichtelius: Why is this distinction so important?

Carl Bernstein: Because we're not the judiciary. We're not the electors. We're reporters. Simple as that.

Erik Fichtelius: How hard is that in real life?

Carl Bernstein: It's very hard. Look at the reporting I keep giving this definition, is the reporting being the best obtainable version of the truth? What? It takes persistence. It takes having common sense. It takes a good deal of being a good listener. It takes, I believe, not having a preconceived notion of where the story is going to take you. But you go where the facts take you. It has to do with context.

Erik Fichtelius: Are there any boundaries to this ruthlessness of reporting?

Carl Bernstein: Sure. The law. It seems to me that reporters ought not be breaking the law, that we shouldn't be breaking into people's houses, we shouldn't be tapping their telephones as as the Murdoch press did, for instance. [1]

Erik Fichtelius: That's about the methods. But when it comes to discuss the consequences?

---

1. The British tabloid News of the World, owned by Robert Murdoch, was revealed in July 2011 to have illegally tapped a number of celebrities' mobile phones and their answering machines. The news led to the paper's closure. But Murdoch's power has endured.

Carl Bernstein: No, no, it's very important the methods. And if we begin to adapt to illegal methods ourselves, as happened with the Murdoch press in the hacking scandal in England, that's a terrible thing. And it will undermine what it is we're supposed to do. So those prohibitions seem to me to be very important.

Erik Fichtelius: When you report the best attainable version of the truth, are there any boundaries to what consequences this can lead to and then what considerations you should have as a reporter?

Carl Bernstein: I'm not sure I understand what you mean.

Erik Fichtelius: Well, for example, issues of national security are there an end?

Carl Bernstein: It seems to me that we need to be responsible in terms of national security issues. I'll give an example. Bob Woodward, myself, some other reporters knew during the Cold War that the United States had tapped into the undersea cable that enabled Soviet submarine communication. And from that tap into that cable under seas, we were able to get vast amounts of information. Operation Ivy Bells was the name of the intelligence gathering program. We knew all about it. Of course, we didn't put it in the newspaper. You don't act in ways that would be inimical to the security of your community. It's basic. So, of course, there's a self-imposed restraint. But it doesn't mean, though, that if a president or senator or anybody else says if you disclose that it's going to endanger national security and you don't print it or put it on online, you must then make a judgment. Well, will it endanger national security? And you have to do your own reporting and make your own judgment. But I think you have to be very careful about these things.

Erik Fichtelius: Were there any considerations about national security in the case of Watergate?

Carl Bernstein: No. Nixon tried to say there were, but we said no, there weren't.

Erik Fichtelius: Why did he try to use that card?

Carl Bernstein: He tried it more with the FBI than he did with us because he didn't want the FBI to investigate into areas that he knew would lead to the cover up that he led, of what his presidency had been doing.

Erik Fichtelius: There are examples in American political history, when powers have interfered with using, playing the card of national security, for example, the incident of the Bay of Pigs when Kennedy interfered with The New York Times. What is your view on this?

Carl Bernstein: My view is that the journalists have to be very careful about accepting without doing their own tests to see if the authorities claiming national security are legitimately claiming it. More often than not, my experience has been they have not been legitimate claims. But that doesn't mean there aren't instances where there are. And I could cite a good number of them where they have been legitimate interests. And also, there's a basic concept that you don't disclose means and sources of intelligence gathering that would compromise those means and sources of the government's abilities.

Erik Fichtelius: I have tried to coin the word consequence neutrality, which is basically about the same concept that you're talking about. This means that the reporters should report the relevant information and true information. But you should not let the consequence of the news influence your decisions to publish or not. What is your view on this?

Carl Bernstein: I believe that the purpose of reporting is to get the story and the information out there, not to bring about a desired political result. And it's simple as that. The most important thing that a reporter does, or a journalistic institution, is to decide what is news. And that decision ought not be based on electing this candidate or that or passing this law or that it ought to be in regard to the facts and context about this politician or this law or whatever it is. It is not about trying to bring about a preconceived result politically.

Erik Fichtelius: Because then you will be a politician yourself?

Carl Bernstein: I think you then abandon your ability to continue to report in a way that people will have faith in your reporting.

Erik Fichtelius: And this is also an ethical view, of course, on our profession. What would you say is happening to this notion in today's reporting?

Carl Bernstein: I think there's much less problem with the reporting today. I think there's great reporting all over the world, maybe more than we've ever seen, particularly because of what's going on. Often, we don't know about in in Africa, in Central America, in Latin America. Great reporting about all kinds of

conditions and oppressions we that we don't usually publicize
in the West in traditional media. Great reporting and I see a lot
of it. By judging different organizations prizes by the work of
organizations that work on behalf of free speech and a free press. So
I think there's a more important problem and that is the way that
our information when we do have the best obtainable version of
the truth is received by citizens. I think in the Western democracies
particularly and in the democracies of the former communist east,
that there has become an ideological moat that is separating left
and right in which each side has become so enveloped by the
belief in its own sacrosanct principles and ideology that too many
individuals, ordinary citizens and politicians are not interested
in the best obtainable version of truth. They're looking for
information online, in newspapers, on television, for information
that will support their already held point of view. I think we have
a much bigger citizen problem than we have journalism problem.
2

Erik Fichtelius: In Sweden we have an analogy from game
hunting when it comes to journalism and it's in some circles
considered heroic to shoot and kill a big elk with more than twelve
tags on his horns. What do you say to this?

Carl Bernstein: I'm not sure. You mean the reporters are going
after big targets without thinking?

---

2. The interview was conducted in March 2015, while Barack
   Obama was president, two years before Donald Trump's
   time.

Erik Fichtelius: If you force a minister or a big guy in business to resign then you have succeeded in the sense, they think.

Carl Bernstein: I think you succeed by doing good stories that serve the common good, whatever the reason. But not because it's a particular individual that you're writing about or a particular objective except to do the reporting. I don't know what else to say.

Erik Fichtelius: Is it journalistic heroism, to shoot and kill a big guy?

Carl Bernstein: I think these questions are a little too simple sometimes. It's not our job to shoot anybody. That's the first thing. We're not into shooting business. We're in the business of reporting. And if in the course of reporting, some big beast in the wilderness comes down, that's part of the process. Is it the objective to bring down big beasts in the wilderness? No, I don't think so.

Erik Fichtelius: I don't think so either. So there were some consequences for you and your colleague, Bob Woodward's. What were these? I mean, this affected your life for sure.

Carl Bernstein: Of course, we were 28 to 30 years old at the time. We were reporting for The Washington Post on Watergate. We then wrote All the President's Men. We wrote a subsequent book called The Final Days, about the last year in office of Richard Nixon, which really and in many ways gave the dimensions of this criminal presidency that I'm talking about in a way that the original reporting for the Post only hinted at, as well as the human story of Richard Nixon. It's an empathic book, actually, toward Richard Nixon and his own personal tragic aspects as well as his criminal impulses. But obviously, it defined our lives professionally and to some extent in the way we're perceived by others. And yet we we're still, I hope, the same people basically that we've always been. But we've had great opportunities as a result of this. And we've written other books. Bob has written 16 books. I've written six and we do commentary, we give speeches. We're here at conferences like this one in Sweden. So we've been blessed and hopefully we continue to do the work. And particularly also to meet with our colleagues and try to help them understand some of the things we believe.

The Dangerous Pursuit of Glory, Gold, and Prizes

The two Watergate-reporters are among the most award-winning and celebrated journalists in the world. Their subsequent lives have been shaped by what they did as young reporters in Washington. But rewards were not something they planned or sought. Still, the rewards of successful journalism are not to be despised. Journalism prizes are fundamentally positive and encourage good reporting, although there are there are risks and a downside.

I got a lot of inspiration in Las Vegas. We cried at both lunch and dinner. For all their pomposity, they were still wonderful, these happy Americans, we thought. At every meal at Caesars Palace there was an award ceremony. We were there, a small delegation from Swedish public service radio and television, to try to understand if and how computers could be used in newsrooms. The most effective way to find out was to book a week in Las Vegas.

Every year the American news directors hold their conference. This time, in 1983, the RTNDA - Radio and TV News Directors Associations - held their big conference at Caesars Palace, so we had to join them. We met 2,000 news directors from small and large radio and television stations all over the United States. We were able to play roulette in the casino and quickly find the radio and television stations in the country that had started using computers in some way. There were ten in all, and they were all there in Las Vegas, along with the few computer vendors that were there.

But what impressed us the most were the big lunches and dinners with all the awards:

Breaking News Coverage Excellence in Sound

Hard News

Investigative Reporting

Lifetime Achievement Award

First Amendment Defender

The Murrow Award

Anchor and Producer Leadership Award

Personal Finance Reporting Award...

And on and on in endless categories. Wonderful speaches, statues, money, honors and diplomas. Applause and cheers. Why don't we have that in the old country? Why this Nordic stingy approach to praise?

We came home with clear ideas about computers. We had imagined that we might find some kind of computer where you could write and store your manuscripts and then search for them based on the words that were in them. Incoming telegrams would go into the computer and be available to the entire newsroom not just a few producers who got them on printer strips from a printer attendant every 30 minutes The run down of the program could be done in the computer. SVT's technical director said it would be well into the 2000s before such computers existed. But he said, go and find out for yourself, and we got tickets for the study tour.

In turns out that in 1983 there was only one news station with a functioning system. Reporters and editors in a fledgling newsroom in the south, together with some computer geniuses in California, had developed a program on something called a PC. It was everything we had dreamed of. Incoming telegrams on screens for everyone, script and run downs in the computer.

This brand-new television station was housed in the basement of a beautiful Southern mansion, with the radio station in a closet. The idea was to broadcast news around the clock, and this could not be done without the new electronic devices. We arrived at CNN just a few months after opening. The news channel then grew quite quickly with the help of its computers. It took a few years, but then we managed to install the same system at Swedish Radio and Television. But it was also another idea I took home with me, the whole award thing. After my week in Las Vegas, I made it one of my missions to help set up as many awards for good journalism as possible. I raised money for the Grand Eko Prize when Ekot, the news show in national radio turned 50. Today all former managing editors still alive make up the jury, and we have a lavish dinner each year to discuss worthy winners.

Then I went on to investigative journalism. As a board member of the newly formed Swedish section of IRE, Investigative Reporters and Editors, I was able to initiate the *Golden Shovel* for excellent investigative journalism. That is now one of the most coveted awards in the industry.

I almost failed in introducing what would become the *Ikaros Prize*. After my trip to Las Vegas, I proposed to the Producers' Association at Swedish Radio and Television that we should award a prize for the best programs of the year. I was met with mostly sour faces and someone who suggested that it would be more fun to have a *lemon prize* for the worst stories of the year. But now I had the spectacular ceremonies at Caesar's Palace in mind and knew I had to fight against the Scandinavian tendency to ignore success. I managed to convince my colleagues when I found an artist who could make a beautiful award in multiple copies. The young, promising glass artist Bertil Vallien had just had an exhibit in Stockholm with the theme *angels in art*. Bertil had created a flying Ikaros that soared to the heavens.

He made a design for a glass award, Ikaros in search of the sun. It is always difficult to give instructions to a wayward artist, but I tried to protest when Bertil made his suggestion.

- Ikaros flew too close to the sun, the wax in the feathers melted and Ikaros crashed into the sea. What kind of symbolism is that? I wondered.

Bertil grumbled a bit, but he understood my objection. He melted the bird Phoenix into the body of Ikaros. You must dare to try to succeed, and even if you fall, you can get up again, he explained. The Producers' Association award was named Ikaros and was for a long time a highly coveted prize for radio and television producers. Bertil Vallien himself is now one of Sweden's most celebrated and expensive glass artists.

The possible competition between Bertil Vallien and his wife Ulrica Hydman-Vallien, also a celebrated glass artist, gave us another prize. Strengthened by the success of Ikaros, I applied again to the Producers' Association. Without good managers, I argued, there would be no good reporting. We should have an award for excellent journalistic management. Ikaros had a father who taught him to fly - Daidalos. This time I was completely voted down.

What kind of kowtowing to authority was this?

Nevertheless, I contacted Ulrica Hydman-Vallien and told her that we had a much better prize in mind than the Ikaros her husband had made. This would be a unique work of art, more beautiful and glorious than the Ikaros with the Phoenix in its body. Could she possibly...?

Ulrica thought it would be fun to try to outdo Bertil and soon created the amazing Daidalos Vase. Lots of gold, bright colors, thick, heavy glass. A prize to be coveted. I took Ulrica's prototype to the next annual meeting of the producers' association. Then everyone voted yes ...

But how does the idea of consequence neutrality fit into this gold rush? Reporters and editors striving for rewards must have some kind of intention regarding the consequences. They report to win honor and glory, recognition and prizes.

In many countries it has gone so far that major newsrooms are systematically working to produce timely features and reports that can be nominated for major awards. In Sweden, too, there is a growing awareness of this prize hunt. Here, both editors and reporters strive for a desired outcome - as many prizes as possible. Is this legitimate? It would be difficult to argue that these efforts are inappropriate. If the story is published on its own merits because it is true and relevant, then there must be a reasonable incentive for the reporter or editor to make the effort to win prizes.

But sometimes the chase for prizes has led to cheating and fabrication. In the quest for glory and praise, the temptation to cheat is too great for some reporters. There have been several major scandals in recent years. Claas Relotius, a reporter for the German news magazine Der Spiegel, is one of Germany's most award-winning journalists. He won the prize for the best story of the year in Germany four times, and in 2014 he was named CNN's Journalist of the Year. He had an amazing ability to tell and find the most gripping stories about refugees from Mexico to Arizona, about the American death penalty, or about a Syrian pediatrician in Aleppo during the war.

Years later, he was exposed by a colleague. Relotius had made things up from start to finish. He had fabricated interviews that never took place, described places he had never been to, invented events that never happened. At least 14 major fake stories had made it through Der Spiegel's supposedly rigorous fact-checking process. The chase for gold had blinded both the reporter and his newspaper. Several similar scandals involving fake stories have also been uncovered in the United States and Scandinavia. The chase has a flip side.132

Most newsrooms present news about their own nominees and price winners in an almost parodic way. If a paper has received a nomination, it is widely publicized in its own paper, but most others remain silent on the matter. The winners are the most visible in their own papers. If radio wins, it is on top of the news, but a prize for television is at best a short telegram. Suddenly normal news evaluation is out of the question, and the news of one's own successes is published as if the sun were only revolving around one's own newsroom. It becomes propagandistic reporting, far from the ideals we are talking about here.

Despite this biased reporting, and in spite of the dangers of the prize hunt, I believe that rewards are mostly a good thing. But global journalism still lacks a prize: the equivalent of the Nobel Prize. A major international award for a courageous journalist or newsroom team that has exposed wrongdoing in a way that benefits humanity. I have tried in vain to persuade the largest media owners in Sweden to create and fund a new major international journalism prize. That will probably take global donors. But it is never too late ...

The secret cave in the forest, underwear and repressive tolerance

- What the hell are you doing?

The sergeant of the patrol who arrived at the scene shouted at the soldier who was standing on the ground with a scalpel in his hand and two severed hands. Next to a third body was another severed hand.

The Australian special forces had conducted a major helicopter raid in the southern parts of Zabul province in Afghanistan on April 28, 2013, killing four Afghans known as EKIA (*Enemy*

Killed In Action). Now the soldiers were collecting the hands of the dead, as trophies of triumph, or as they claimed, to identify the dead. The systematic mutilation of killed 'enemies' was reported further up the military hierarchy and became part of the super-secret documentation of how Australian troops were actually behaving in Afghanistan.133 The secret reports were labeled AUESTEO - *Australian Eyes Only* - and they revealed a terrible culture among Australia's special forces in Afghanistan. They were waging their own secret and bloody war against 'insurgents' in the country. The Australian military leadership's internal investigation into what happened described "problems, an organized culture, a warrior culture" where officers turned a blind eye to the abuses.

The report listed over ten specific incidents where the Australian special forces killed unarmed children and civilians. On one occasion in 2013, a man and his six-year-old child were shot dead during a raid on a house. Another time, a prisoner was killed when he was alone with the Australian soldiers. The armed forces' own documents spoke of unlawful executions. The report contained gory details of how Australian troops cut off the hands of slain Taliban. The secret reports were revealed by Australia's public service in the summer of 2017. The Australian Broadcasting Corporation (ABC) had gained access to *The Afghan Files,* which documented abuses by Australian troops from 2009 to 2013.134 Australia's elite troops in Afghanistan had systematically executed civilians and then covered up their crimes.

Young soldiers were ordered to execute prisoners so that they could count in its first killings.135 It became a major scandal.

But the question is whether a country's journalists should be able to expose violations of international law by its own troops. In Australia, police and prosecutors raided the ABC newsroom to try to track down who leaked the shocking documents. After a fierce and heated debate, an Australian court ruled in February 2020 that the police were within their rights. Protests by the ABC and independent media in Australia against the police action and the ruling have been longstanding. This was a test of principles in a country that should function democratically, but it was not the free flow of news that won in the first round. But the last word was not said.

The ability of a free media to report on violations of international law and the laws of war by their own troops is about how freedom of the press and freedom of expression works, both in law and in practice. A people must be able to know the truth about what is happening. Even in war and crisis. There is no lack of planning, even in Sweden. For several years, defense policy proposals have been raining down on the parliament. The defense should be rearmed, new regiments created, more conscripts trained and everyone should get better equipment. New combat aircraft, submarines and missiles are needed. The corona pandemic has also shown the vulnerability of society and the entire total defense must be rebuilt. Sweden needs better emergency stocks, stronger protection against different types of crises, better coordination and more exercises. The Russian war of aggression against Ukraine has created a completely new security policy situation. Old doctrines are being overturned and Sweden is joining NATO.

Psychological defense also needs to be re-established and strengthened. In early summer 2020, the Psychological Defense Commission submitted its report to the government. The inquiry proposed a new authority to "protect the open and democratic society, the free formation of opinion and Sweden's freedom and independence". The inquiry wrote:

> Protecting these values is part of Sweden's security policy. Sweden is already exposed to attacks of various kinds, such as cyber attacks and attempts to unduly influence information directed at Swedish authorities, elected officials, organizations, companies, editorial offices, journalists, researchers, civil servants and debaters. The psychological defense should be seen as a natural part of the work to protect the open society, free speech and Sweden's freedom and independence. An important part of this should be the overall ability to identify and counteract undue information influence and other dissemination of misleading information aimed at Sweden. This must be done with respect for the constitutionally protected freedom of the press and freedom of expression.

The establishment of the new defense authority has been a difficult balancing act. A strong authority is needed, for example, to protect Sweden from foreign influence campaigns and Russian troll factories. At the same time, a free media is the best protection against propaganda and influence campaigns. The primary task of the new authority will be to defend freedom of expression and opinion, even in times of war and crisis. But there has always been an area of conflict between state defense measures and independent newspapers, radio and television.

Since the fall of the Berlin Wall, Swedish society has been too unprotected against the various threats to the country. Perhaps the dismantling of military and civil defense after the collapse of the Soviet Union was far too rapid. If the psychological defense is rearmed, it is against a dark background of state control of the media, with little gray notes from the State Information Board to editors-in-chief during World War II and secret registration of political opinions long after the war. The old psychological defense's cooperation with media leaders was sharply questioned in the 1970s.

After the Russian invasion of Ukraine, it became clear that Sweden needed a stronger information defense, and the new authority was established in the fall of 2021, at a time when it was most needed. Like almost all men of my generation, I did my military service. When I enlisted in 1969, I tried in vain to get a journalistic military assignment, but it didn't exist at the time. Instead, I was drafted as a human resources assistant and officer in the reserves.

In the early summer of 1970, I reported to the air defense regiment Lv3 in Norrtälje, north of Stockholm. I belonged to a special platoon, with future doctors, pharmacists, priests, and HR specialists. I was to be discharged after totally15 months with the rank of sergeant. But first there was three months of basic military training. Then I had to wait until I graduated from the university to serve somewhere in the country. It was the same for the other young conscripts in my platoon. The future medical doctors would be most useful after graduation.

That summer at the regiment we had a small problem as recruits. For some reason we were given only one pair of underwear a week. That wasn't enough, so we had to use our civilian underwear, which we couldn't wash at the regiment. We tried to express our need of more frequent laundry changes to the officers and HR-department. But this request was first met with silence, then with a brief, unjustified refusal.

In the spring before my military service, I had started as a freelance reporter at the newly established local radio station Radio Uppland. I thought the story about the complaints of filthy underwear at the regiment was news. Now I borrowed a tape recorder from the radio station, took it to the regiment and interviewed my friends on the hatch. The medical students were credible witnesses.

"Prospective doctors sound the alarm about the filth on Lv 3" was the headline of the news report on the regional radio. The medical recruits began by explaining what a hotbed of bacteria a pair of underwear could become in just a few days.

I sent the tape with my interviews by bus from Norrtälje
to Uppsala, where the station manager received and edited the
material. Radio Uppland followed up with an interview with the
regiment's chief of staff. His answer about the lack of resources in
the defense was not very convincing. But now the honor of the
regiment was at stake.

The day after the radio report, the entire regiment was
called to a meeting in the auditorium. The colonel, the
regimental commander, was furious. Enemy forces had dragged
the regimental flag through the mud. Disloyal soldiers had openly
criticized Lv3 in the media. This was nothing short of a scandal.
Who did we think we were? I sat pale in the back of the room.
What reprisals could I expect? But the colonel did not seem to
understand that the traitorous scandal reporter was within his own
ranks. The colonel and the chief of staff were furious with those
who had complained, but I managed to escape the blame. The
meeting in the auditorium ended with the angry colonel briefly
announcing new procedures for changing clothes. Suddenly we
had three pairs of underwear a week. I had received very tangible
evidence of the power of the media. A single item on local radio
from a fresh reporter was all it took to get a whole regiment
new underwear. I had a clear vested interest in the story and was
reporting on my own behalf, completely unaware of the concept
of consequence neutrality.

The young recruits' request for a reasonable amount of
underwear per week was not a dissenting voice. No one was out
to undermine the armed forces, smear the regiment, or start a

revolution. It was just about underwear. But the bigger question, of course, was how to deal with these kinds of small complaints and criticisms without threatening the system. In the early seventies, it was a political idea of many small communist groups to take a small discontent and turn it into systemic criticism and eventually revolution. Small radical groups of soldiers began publishing underground stencil magazines in the regiments, magazines that mixed underwear criticism with revolutionary propaganda.

The top brass was concerned. The commander-in-chief at the time, Stig Synnergren, felt that the armed forces needed to take control. There was a need to channel information and criticism of misconduct, abuses and shortcomings in an orderly manner without overturning the entire system. The solution was the newspaper *Värnpliktsnytt*, (Conscription News) founded in 1971. *Värnpliktsnytt* would be editorially independent of the government and military, with a civilian editor-in-chief as independent publisher. The paper would be a voice for conscripts, produced by conscript journalists and freely distributed to all enlisted soldiers.

Värnpliktsnytt was published as a tough tabloid paper and was quickly a success. It became a school for young journalists, and I asked to be transferred to *Värnpliktsnytt* when it was time to be called up again. By then I had combined my studies with work as a freelance for several years for the radio, television and the evening newspaper Aftonbladet in Paris, and was reasonably well qualified. I started at Värnpliktsnytt in the late summer of 1974. The newspaper was liked by the conscripts, but hated by shouting sergeants and harsh captains who tormented their soldiers. But the generals and the minister of defense were satisfied, the conscripts had a channel for criticism and complaints without having to rely on communist stencil magazines. The commander-in-chief Stig Synnergren was personally involved in the work and mission of the paper. He visited the newsroom several times and even attended a late-night party with the newsroom staff.

Many career journalists learned the basics at *Värnpliktsnytt*, and the editors liked to cultivate the myth of the magazine as a true elite school for reporters. The magazine was discontinued in 2010 when conscription in Sweden was abolished.

At the newspaper I learned a lot about tabloid journalism and got to visit almost every regiment in Sweden. Among other things, I wrote about the low daily allowance, injustices in the military punishment system, and the conditions for using the military at political demonstrations. But others saw the paper as a threat to the system and came to the defense of the outraged sergeants and captains. Many lower officers saw *Värnpliktsnytt* as a kind of communist subversive newspaper. The conservative member of parliament Mr. Wachtmeister (M) submitted a motion to the parliament in 1975 demanding the closure of the newspaper:

"The fact that the military leadership turns a
blind eye to the plethora of seditious publications
distributed in our military barracks seems strange,
to say the least. The compatibility of the so-called
soldiers' newspapers with the freedom of the press

should be reasonably debatable. However, the
difference between what seditious organs of the
extreme left can get away with and what can be
read in a publication such as *Värnpliktsnytt*, which,
according to the Minister of Defense, aims to be a
forum for the exchange of opinions and information,
should be enormous. Unfortunately, the opposite
is true; articles in *Värnpliktsnytt* could just as easily
have appeared in a communist pamphlet. There
is reason to question the rationality of allocating
appropriation to a body that has taken on the
task - as all the commanding corps on regiments
1 10/ Fo 43 formulated it in a joint letter to the
Minister of Defense - of "creating and maintaining
an antagonistic relationship between officers and
conscripts". The aforementioned cooperation is
certainly not facilitated by such a newspaper; on
the contrary, it is openly sabotaged. It is almost
inconceivable that such a thing can happen with
state funds, even within the highest leadership of the
Defense Ministry. There is therefore no reason to
continue publishing *Värnpliktsnytt*."

The motion was rejected by the majority of the Defense
Committee in parliament, which referred the matter to the
Minister of Defense, who argued that it was important for the

newspaper to have a journalistic position independent of the Ministry of Defense.

The whole structure of *Värnpliktsnytt* brings to mind the German Marxist philosopher Herbert Marcuse, whose 1965 book on "Repressive Tolerance" (A Critique of Pure Tolerance) influenced a generation of left-wing activists and academics. The tolerance of opposition and criticism by those in power in a bourgeois liberal society was not true tolerance, Marcuse argued, but only served to preserve the hegemony of power. Oppression was maintained under the guise of tolerance. "One makes tolerance an instrument for the perpetuation of slavery," Marcuse wrote.

The overarching goal of the small regimental communist newspapers was to fuel the demand for social upheaval and revolution. Behind a facade of critical journalism, the goal was to overthrow the system. *Värnpliktsnytt*, on the other hand, had the overarching goal of channeling criticism and opposition within the system. Marcuse could perhaps have used *Värnpliktsnytt* as an example of what he meant. But he would certainly have had more difficulty with the general ideas behind the Swedish defense, namely, to defend and maintain democracy and everyone's freedom of opinion and expression. Marcuse wanted to abolish it; he was a revolutionary and wanted to overthrow the system. Therefore, tolerance should only go in one direction, to the left. The right, the conservative forces, the power, should not be tolerated. According to Herbert Marcuse, it was justified to restrict the freedom of expression and opinion of the opponents of the revolution:

"The exercise of political rights (such as voting, writing letters to newspapers, senators, etc., protest demonstrations where violence is not met with violence) in a totally administered society only serves to strengthen this administration by testifying to the existence of democratic freedoms - which have in fact taken on new content and lost their effectiveness. In such a situation, freedom (of opinion, assembly, expression) becomes an instrument for approving unfreedom."

Herbert Marcuse's arguments were fundamentally undemocratic and would ultimately lead to the overthrow of democratic institutions if they became reality. *Värnpliktsnytt* would probably get the boot. But not only *Värnpliktsnytt*, Marcuse's reasoning generally leads to oppression and censorship. The Swedish total defense system is designed and planned to defend democracy. According to these plans, Swedish Radio and SVT should be a strong part of the total defense and be able to continue to provide free and independent news coverage even in times of war. What applies is regulated in the broadcasting license for radio and television:

"SR/SVT is therefore obliged to continue its activities in case of war. If Sweden is in a state of high alert, SR/SVT is, according to the broadcasting license, an independent organization with national defense tasks and is directly subordinate to the government. At the same time, SR/SVT shall, as far as possible, maintain the peacetime structures in a state of high alert, and the provisions on programming activities shall also guide it in a crisis or in a state of high alert."

How does this work in practice? What does history teach us, and what will it really be like when war comes? When I was appointed head of news in national radio in 1987, it dawned upon me:

- Now you are the boss in the secret cave too! I was told. You will oversee the news departments war organization!

The job of leading Ekot included leading Ekot during war. In times of trouble, Ekot, along with the parliament, the government, the newspapers, and the television news, would move to different secret shelters in mountain caves in the "inner zone". Before I could accept this responsibility, I had to understand how it would work in practice. Would Ekot become part of a propaganda machine? The answers I got from the defense planners were very well thought out constitutionally. We have a defense to protect our democratic system of government. Of course, borders and territory must be defended, but what we really must fight for, I was told, is democracy. It is the right of the people to elect representatives in municipalities, county councils, parliament and government and have independent courts. And not least protect our right to free speech and free, independent media.

I remained skeptical; this is very solemn words. Answers were needed to the questions of who should be responsible for news broadcasts, staffing of the news organization, and to the risks of censorship.

The principle of civil responsibility permeates the whole idea of Swedish national defense. Whoever is responsible in peace must also be responsible in war. The civilian manager must also be the manager in a state of war. This includes the responsibility of the publisher. It is a sole responsibility, which means that it is the publisher alone and no one else who decides at any moment what is to be published or not. There is no censorship in Sweden, not even during war; this was a deliberate decision when the current press freedom legislation was adopted.

The main point about the civilian manager being responsible even in war is that it is the democratic structure that we are defending. It is not only the manager who must intervene in a crisis situation, but he or she must involve all of his or her civilian staff in the operation as much as possible. This is the structure of the Swedish national defense, and civilian officers should perform their duties in war as well, if possible and necessary, subject to the requirements of conscription, military requirements, and reserve officer placement. There may be a conflict here.

Planning applies to all news media. Television must be able to broadcast, newspapers must be able to print, and there are TV and radio studios, printing presses, and newsrooms in various mountains. The special printing ink for use in war has even been tested on the UNT's newspaper presses.

Ekot has its own secret cavern in "the zone". It will have housing, studios, broadcasting and editing equipment, communication facilities, and contact with other mountains in the inner zone, where the government, parliament, and military leadership are located. Ekot would also have its own staff in these other mountains. But there was one acute problem. The spy Stig Bergling had sold all the mountains and their functions to the Russians. Therefore everyone needed new caves, including Ekot. In practice there was no place to move, but it had to be arranged...

What about staffing? Well, that also turned out to be a problem when I took over. The only people who were actually placed in the Ekot organization were me as the managing editor and two odd employees. There was some kind of war planning, but the staffing obviously needed to be reviewed. Perhaps not everything was as it seemed or as it was written in the plans. There was no program schedule, and thus no staffing plan, and thus no idea of how many journalists were needed. The whole proud national defense planning turned out to be a Potemkin backdrop. No cave, no reporters, no schedule. Did the Russians know?

I decided to take it seriously. I made sure to take the relevant national defense courses myself, and appointed Lisa Söderberg, then producer in the newsroom, as my "general". This was long before Lisa Söderberg became Director General of Swedish Radio. She also took the defense courses, drew a schedule, and made a staffing plan. Reporters and producers were deployed to war assignments in the newsroom after proper security checks. No one had to pass a security check for their regular jobs, but to get into the war organization, something else was required.

Building Ekot's war organization in the late 1980s was not an easy task, and it took several years. We got installed in a new mountain and got a functioning organization, at least on paper. By the time we were done, the Berlin Wall fell in 1989 and no one longer cared about a functioning defense. The threats were gone and defense scaled down. I myself never participated in a live exercise with the entire Ekot organization, although other exercises were conducted by the Psychological Defense, in which Ekot employees also participated. But in the mid-nineties most exercises were halted. Everyone expected peace.

Swedish society was naive after the fall of the Wall. Today, many people believe that we should not have disarmed the way we did. The cost of withdrawal is high. Perhaps I was also naive about all the constitutional promises? It may look good on paper, but what would it have been like in practice? The traces from the Second World War are frightening. Despite the oldest freedom of the press law in the world, the state managed to control the dissemination of information, ban the transport of dangerous newspapers and harass critical journalists.

There is a powerful scene in Jan Troell's 2012 film *Judgement of a Dead Man* about Torgny Segerstedt, the Gothenburg liberal who stood up to Hitler with his writings in the morning newspaper *Göteborgs Handels- och Sjöfartstidning*. The editor-in-chief is summoned to a private audience with King

Gustaf V. The king lights a cigar and turns to Segerstedt in a stern manner:

- You're harming Sweden's interests with your writings, the king says. This can no longer be tolerated. Besides, the country could not defend itself for more than ten days. And I have no desire to wander around in the woods while they shoot at us, as they did to my relative king Haakon of Norway.

Segerstedt listens quietly and hesitantly, but finally answers:

- Of course, I don't want a war either, but your people could suffer worse. To lose their freedom.

- You are blinded by your hatred of the Germans, replies an indignant Gustaf V.

- I don't hate the Germans, I hate the Nazis.

- We still don't understand why you write the way you do.

- As if it helps to write against my conscience.

- I think we know why you help the Jews. By the way, we should tell you that, given the choice between Germany and Russia, we would rather become Germans than Russians.

- With Your Majesty's permission, I, for my part, prefer to remain Swedish.

- The audience is over, says the King and stands up. As Segerstedt stood in the doorway, the King said:

- Remember, if there is a war, it's your fault!

The lines in the movie are based on notes and conversations by writer Kenne Fant with Torgny Segerstedt's son Torgny T. Segerstedt, as well as the account in his daughter Ingrid Segerstedt Wiberg's book about her father.

The author Vilhelm Moberg was among those who resisted fascism, and after the war he complains about self-censorship during the Second World War:

> "And what could you say on the radio during those years? There was certainly not much. In any case, dissenting opinions about our foreign policy were not allowed on the radio. The deviations of the coalition government from the line of neutrality could not be mentioned. No one would have thought it possible that Torgny Segerstedt, the harshest critics of our government on this point, would be allowed to express his opinion on the radio. During the Second World War our radio was practically an organ of the Swedish government. And TT's news broadcasts were sometimes censored in deference to foreign powers."

This says a lot about how far the culture of silence went. The author and journalist Kurt Lindal, in a book on the role and attitude of Swedish radio during the Second World War, examined Moberg's claim. By checking the radio's register of participants, he shows that Segerstedt was never heard on Swedish radio during the war years.

There are mechanisms that go beyond the formal, there are invisible rules. The problem during the Second World War was not only state control and censorship, but also the voluntary submission of the media. When one's country is threatened, when the nation is fighting for its survival, it becomes more difficult to maintain independence and impartiality.

When I agreed to run Ekot even in wartime and asked about my role, I was told in no uncertain terms that statements about violations of international law by Swedish soldiers were news that should be published if I, as the publisher, judged them to be true and relevant. Anything else would be tantamount to propaganda. The freedom we defend is also freedom of the press and freedom of speech. Planning for this defense involves both military and civilian preparations. The whole point of these preparations is that the media should function as close as possible to the peacetime situation, even in war and twilight situations. Swedish reporters are not under military command in peacetime, nor should they be in wartime.

There are, of course, legitimate military secrets. Operational military information must be kept secret for purely practical reasons. As head of Ekots war organization, I had access to many secrets, such as where the mountain was located, how it was equipped and who was stationed there. It is quite reasonable that this information should be kept secret.

But the consequence of national defense planning is that Swedish reporters, stationed in wartime newsrooms equipped and protected by the Swedish military, must be able to expose violations of international law by the very soldiers who provide that protection. This is ultimately the difficult meaning of the concept of consequence neutrality in news reporting, and it is in war and twilight situations that the principles of democracy are tested. Would it work in practice? The principle of consequence neutrality applies, but still, there is a nagging concern that I may have been and am naive.

Will self-censorship and regulation, visible and invisible, turn news broadcasts into propaganda when the chips are down? The reactions to the Australian public broadcaster's revelations about the progress of its own troops in Afghanistan are a chilling modern example. But the story had a different ending than first feared. A kind of justice eventually prevailed. In mid-November 2020, after four years of investigation, Australian military leaders released a comprehensive report admitting serious abuses. 3,000 Afghans had been murdered and a warrior culture in elite units had gotten out of control, the report said. Children, farmers, and other civilians had been unlawfully killed, and the elite unit in question had been disbanded. 19 soldiers should be investigated for their crimes. The report recommended that the Australian government pay compensation to the families of the victims. The commander-in-chief, General Angus Campbell, was unsparing in his self-criticism, saying that the armed forces must now answer for their serious mistakes. He apologized "unreservedly" to the Afghan people:

- Some patrols took the law into their own hands, breaking the rules, making up stories, lying and killing prisoners, while those who tried to talk were discouraged, intimidated and discredited.

Before the report's release, Australian Prime Minister Scott Morrison called his Afghan counterpart to express his "great sadness" at the troops' behavior. Australia's public service was not wrong to expose the war crimes of its own troops. The month before the military's self-critical report was published, the prosecution of the journalists was dropped. Although the Attorney-General's Department believed it could prove that the journalists had committed a crime by receiving classified documents, he did not consider it in the public interest to prosecute. The significance "to Australia's democracy of public interest journalism" was one of the justifications.

Perhaps the system works. Still, I'm not entirely confident. Consider how the entire American press willingly acquiesced to the CIA's and the president's interpretation of national security for the Bay of Pigs attack in Cuba. Think of the raids of journalistic institutions in Australia in modern times, and think of how it worked in Sweden during World War II. How Torgny Segerstedt was never heard on the radio. What happens when the Russians come? Can we report impartially?

The vague wording in the current regulations that radio and television should be "subordinate to the government" during war is cause of concerns. In a state of war, the list of crimes under the Press Law is also expanded to include punishment for those who "spread false rumors or other untrue statements among soldiers that are likely to provoke disloyalty or discouragement". Could exposing war crimes committed by Swedish soldiers be said to cause "discouragement" among Swedish troops? I might be able to publish the information, but then I might be found guilty of treason and dismissed as the responsible publisher. All these elastic formulations, combined with nationalistic self-censorship make me really unsure about what would really happen in an emergency. The promised freedom has not been tested. Perhaps my whole commitment to building an independent news service even in war is based on false hopes? We do not know what it will look like in war or crisis. I know how I want it to work. Whether it will work in practice remains to be seen.

The Best Available Version of the Truth

What happens when there is juice in a tennis match? How long can juice last before it becomes a set or match point? How many balls does the winner have to hit? Suddenly I am unsure, even though I grew up playing tennis with my father. I am in the Roland Garros tennis stadium in Paris, early summer 1974, when I have established myself as a freelancer in the city, working for both Aftonbladet and Swedish Radio. And, on this particular day, also for Swedish Television sport news. The editors in Stockholm had called and asked me to do a report on a young Swedish tennis player who seemed to be doing well. I, who basically know nothing about sports suddenly became a sports reporter.

The first problem was how to get a TV crew in Paris. I've worked for radio and newspapers. But I called an acquaintance, a Swedish woman who was the photo editor of Elle magazine. I asked her where I could find a TV crew.

She had no idea, but she looked out the window and saw a TV crew that happened to be filming outside her office. It's a freelance TV company and she runs down to them so I can get in touch with the photographer. We meet the next day in front of Roland Garros. The rising tennis star Björn Borg is playing the Round of 16 final on one of the courts far away from Center Court. There are almost no spectators. A few girls sit in the front, a lone man high up in the stands, the TV crew and me.

It sounds like *juice* in French when it says 40-40, although I am not sure what the rules are for *deuce*, as the proper term is in tennis. The lone gentleman looks a bit Swedish, so I interrupt him. He does speak Swedish but seems very confused when I ask him about the rules for "juice".

- Where are you from?

He is no less skeptical when he hears that I am from the TV sports in Stockholm. A sports reporter who doesn't know anything about tennis?! But I obviously have a film crew with me ... The friendly gentleman relents and takes pity on me. I get an excellent guide to the game. He explains Borg's tactics and strategy. The man turns out to be Björn Borg's famous coach, Lennart Bergelin. When the match is over and Bjorn Borg has won, Bergelin approves an interview with the future star. This year, 1974, Björn Borg will win the French Open for the first time. But now it was only the round of sixteen, in front of a more than ignorant "sports reporter".

We continue filming the next day, during the quarterfinals on Center Court. It's hot and sweaty in the sun, and a rich old lady protest when we try to film from her front box. But I've got the interview and my footage, and I head to Charles de Gaulle airport to find an SAS flight home to Stockholm. I give the pilot the unprocessed film in a tin can. This was the way Swedish television used to send films home, through an agreement with Scandinavian Airlines. For the semi-final the following day, TV Sport sent a real reporter with his own film crew to Paris. Now Björn Borg has started his journey to stardom.

A news reporter shall report reality, what he sees or hears, to the best of his ability. News must be accurate, true and interesting. But what if the reporter has no knowledge and doesn't even understand what is going on? Then it is not possible to describe the events accurately. My experience in Paris on those early summer days in 1974 is common for a general assignment reporter. The reporter is sent out to cover something new about which he knows virtually nothing. A reporter often knows a little about a lot. We must recognize and admit our limitations. It is important to have the courage to ask for help. You can find out what you don't know. That is one of the exciting things about being a reporter. There's always someone around to help a struggling journalist, as long as he or she is willing to reach out. The reporter must be humble in his search for the truth. Then there will always be a Lennart Bergelin around.

In early November 2020, like so many others, I'm fascinated, zapping between CNN, Fox News, the New York Times and the Washington Post. What will happen in the presidential election between Donald Trump and Joe Biden? What a nail-biter! I learn all about the socio-economic conditions in Wayne County and manage to catch CNN just as they announce their prediction that

Biden has won the election with more than 270 electoral votes. What a relief. The truth wins in the end!

But the nail-biting doesn't stop there.

- I won the election! proclaims Donald Trump and wants to stop counting the votes.

But what is truth? Aristotle, one of the most important thinkers in Western philosophy, gave us his definition:

> "To say of what is that it is not, or of what is not that
> it is, is false, while to say of what is that it is, and of
> what is not that it is not, is true."

News editors should choose to publish news that is true and relevant, not because it favors or disfavors anyone. The concepts are interrelated and interdependent: relevance is related to the concept of news, which is discussed in a separate chapter; truth requires its own chapter, which can take its starting point in the developments in the United States after the 2020 presidential election. Yale history professor Timothy Snyder calls Trump's lie about a stolen election The Big Lie:

> "The claim that cheating and fraud robbed Trump
> of victory is a big lie not just because it defies
> logic, misrepresents the facts, and requires belief in
> a conspiracy. It is fundamentally a big lie because
> it reverses the poles of the moral field of American
> politics and turns the basic structure of American

history upside down [...] Post-truth is pre-fascism, and Trump is the post-truth president. When we abandon truth, we hand over power to those who use wealth and charisma to stage spectacles that take its place. If citizens do not agree on certain basic facts, they cannot create the civil society that would allow them to resist. When we lose the institutions that produce relevant facts, we tend to wallow instead in attractive abstractions and fictions. Truth is particularly difficult to assert when there is little of it. And Trumpism, like Putinism in Russia, is characterized by the decline of local news reporting. Social media is no substitute. It recharges the mental engines that drive us in search of emotional stimulation and comfort, blurring the distinction between what feels true and what is actually true."

The lies began when Trump was sworn in as president on January 20, 2017. At first, his lies and actions seemed more ridiculous than dangerous. The president said it was sunny when it was raining, and he claimed that there had never been a presidential inauguration with such a large crowd, even though the National Mall was empty compared to previous years.

Press Secretary Sean Spicer backed up the blatant lie, which was challenged in an interview on NBC's Meet the Press. That's when presidential adviser Kellyanne Conway coined the term "alternative facts." This would open the floodgates to more than 15 presidential lies or misleading statements a day over the course of the administration. The Washington Post has counted all of Trump's false or misleading claims since taking office in its daily updated Facts Checker database.

There are no alternative facts. There are only facts. Trump's inauguration in 2017 inspired me and author Martin Widmark to write a series of adventure books, *Scoopet*, for 9-12 year olds about some young people who start an online news site. Our idea was to inspire youngsters to seek out facts and distinguish news from news.

The lies surrounding the 2017 presidential installation angered philosophy professor Åsa Wikforss at the University of Stockholm:

- This blatant attempt to reject facts made me angry, she wrote. I thought it was time for a philosopher to make a contribution.

The result was a book that is, among other things, a long wrestling match with Donald Trump and his relationship with the truth. Those who want to delve deeper into the concept of truth should read *Alternative facts* where Åsa Wikforss writes that knowledge plays a role in a democratic society:

Authoritarian leaders always start by shooting at the truth. After all, the best way to influence people is not to force us to do things, but to trick us. Today's disinformation campaigns are particularly dangerous because they don't look like disinformation. It is not about bombarding people with clear political messages, as in the Soviet era, but about creating fake news and distorted narratives designed to exploit our fears and anxieties and get us to spread the disinformation ourselves.

The journalist Carl Bernstein has a beautiful phrase to describe the mission of the news reporter. He speaks of *the best available version of the truth*. There is a wonderful humility in that phrase, that we to the best of our ability is looking for the right now best correct version of what happened. Tomorrow the story may be different, or at least more nuanced, complicated, and complete. A reporter is certainly not an expert, does not know everything, rushes from topic to topic. But what journalists are good at is finding out about things they do not know or understand and then summarize it quickly.

An academic researcher can spend years working on a thesis, tweaking wording and checking sources. A news reporter works under different conditions. I find it fascinating how accurate news reporting is, given the circumstances. Real news reporting is a process of verification, with editing in an established editorial order.

American journalists and authors Bill Kovach and Tom Rosenstiel emphasize in their book The Elements of Journalism that "the essence of journalism is a discipline of verification":

> "In the end, the discipline of verification is
> what separates journalism from entertainment,
> propaganda, fiction, or art. Entertainment - or its
> cousin, "infotainment" - focuses on what is most
> diverting. Propaganda selects facts or invents them to

serve the real purpose: persuasion and manipulation.
Fiction invents scenarios to get a more personal
impression of what it calls truth. Journalism alone
is focused on the process employed to get what
happened down right."

Verifying facts is the central function of journalism. How to
do this was, of course, formulated by the ancient Greeks. The
Athenian Thucydides was writing about the Trojan Wars in 500
BC, and he wanted to make them credible and factual. He took on
the task knowing that bad memories, different perspectives, and
politics could cloud his vision:

> "As for my actual reporting of the events ... I
> have made it a principle not to write down the
> first version I happen to come across, nor to be
> guided by my first impressions. Either I was present
> at the events I describe, or I heard about them
> from eyewitnesses whom I could verify as closely as
> possible. Nevertheless, it was not easy to find out the
> truth. Different eyewitnesses gave different accounts
> of the same events when they told their stories out of
> bias for one side or the other, or out of incomplete
> memories."

Philosophy professor Åsa Wikforss emphasizes that knowledge
requires that (at least) three conditions are met:

- You should have a belief, a psychological state with a specific cognitive thought content (that it is raining, that the earth is round, that 18 people are drinking coffee in the office).

- The belief must be true. The content of the thought must in some way correspond to the world: It is raining, the earth is round, 18 people are having coffee in the office.

- The belief must be based on some form of good reason or evidence. One who merely guesses correctly does not have knowledge.

Knowledge must be true. It actually rained when Donald Trump was inaugurated in 2017. Joe Biden won the 2020 election. This is not a matter of taste. Knowledge is not only in our heads, it is also in the world, in reality. The truth I am convinced of must be based on good reasons. There must be evidence. The need for evidence also has a bearing on the concept of objectivity. Åsa Wikforss writes:

> "It is also important not to confuse the claim that there are objective truths with the claim that we as individuals are objective. To be objective means to base your beliefs on evidence - to carefully consider and weigh all the available evidence. Anyone who lets their emotions get the better of them, or who ignores

some of the evidence and just picks and chooses what
suits them, is not objective in this sense."

The Swedish scientist, debater, cabinet minister, and Nobel
laureate Gunnar Myrdal struggled with the question of objectivity
throughout his life. He himself was both a scientist and a
politician. Could one be both - in an objective way? In 1968
he published *The Problem of Objectivity in Social Research.* His
arguments and questions have a clear connection to journalism. It
is quite possible to substitute the journalist for the researcher in his
argument:

> "The most fundamental methodological problem of
> the social scientist, then, is this: What is objectivity?
> And how does he achieve objectivity when he seeks to
> establish facts and causal relationships between facts?
> How can he avoid bias? [...]."

Then there is another problem: how can the researcher be
objective and practical at the same time? What is the relationship
between the desire to understand and the desire to change society?
How can the search for truth be reconciled with moral and
political aspirations? How can truth be linked to ideals?

These are the big and difficult questions journalists face.
Questions that lead many to say that it is not possible to be
objective; we are all stuck with the beliefs and legacies that
Myrdal lists. But the fact that it is difficult should not discourage

anyone from trying to achieve or strive for that goal. It is a reasonable demand that reporters refrain from pursuing their own political agendas. In other contexts, society demands objectivity, or impartiality and objectivity, as a formal requirement for government authorities and officials. Indeed, it is a cornerstone of our legal system that judges, doctors, and other public officials do not allow personal interests or opinions to guide them in the exercise of their profession or office. No one wants the judge to judge based on who he is related to or who he knows, likes, or agrees with. A surgeon should not operate on his family or friends first. The director of social services should not get a Corona vaccine for himself or his relatives before the old people in the nursing home have had their shots. Independence, integrity, and objectivity may be difficult to live up to, but they are reasonable requirements. They apply to many functions in society and must apply to journalism.

What happens in today's polarized political climate is that perspectives are distorted, war becomes peace and white becomes black. The nationalist right is particularly active in various online forums, spreading hate and propaganda that tries to emulate traditional journalism. Its writers like to scold the established media for spreading fake news, when in fact it is they themselves who spread fake news by imitating the form of real news. Åsa Wikforss uses the counterfeiting of bank notes as a metaphor in her book *Därför demokrati (Therefore democracy)*:

Let us return to the concept of fake news. The term should not be used as a collective term for all kinds of disinformation. But for a very specific kind of disinformation: totally or partially fabricated information presented in the form of a news item. It is "false" in the sense of fake, as in the case of counterfeit banknotes. A fake news item pretends to be news: it looks like a news article or a news broadcast, just as a fake banknote looks like a real banknote. The attempt to imitate the shape and style of real news is made for the same reason that fake banknotes are made to look like real banknotes - it gives the impression that what we have in front of us has the right origin and is therefore valuable. In the case of news, it is about giving the impression that the information is the result of a journalistic process, with its professional standards and peer review mechanisms, and is therefore credible. Since we are accustomed to receiving information about our contemporary world precisely in the form of news, fake news is a type of disinformation with high political explosiveness.

To defend the possibility of a well-informed democratic debate, impartiality and objectivity in news reporting are necessary. Although many argue that objectivity is a utopia because everything is subjective, I believe that impartiality and objectivity are reasonable requirements for a news reporter. Objectivity is an ideal that can be achieved, even if it is difficult. It is important to separate the different parts of the concept. Åsa Wikforss reminds us that we, as human beings, find it difficult to be objective:

- But this does not mean that there are no objective truths. Even if all people were always hopelessly subjective in how they formed their beliefs, some of our assertions would still be objectively true or false. Thus, what characterizes objective truths is that they are independent of anyone's beliefs about the matter.

The inevitable values lie in the selection. What the scientist chooses to research or what the journalist chooses to report is ultimately a matter of values, not an objectively obvious choice. There is a subjective and evaluative dimension to choosing to research the quickest way to kill piglets rather than the possible harmfulness of cadaver feed. It is an evaluative choice to devote an entire newspaper on a given day to climate change, even if each article is based on evidence and facts.

Cultural and national conventions determine what the media should report about flying saucers, Icelandic trolls, or Indian ghosts. It is a propagandistic decision to report only on crimes committed by "Arabs". It is the twists and turns of the zeitgeist when a newsroom has many labor and crime reporters and fewer stock market analysts. This can be managed both in the moment and over time by a deliberately balanced news reporting. No matter how the selection is made, every story, every feature can be presented with impartiality and objectivity. It is also important for any news organization to beware of false balance, i.e. allowing a completely unreasonable and fabricated position to be balanced by a fact-based one. It is not balanced to allow a Holocaust denier to "debate" on equal terms with a concentration camp survivor. The Holocaust really took place; it is not a debate between different positions.

Objective means unbiased and factual. This is not just an ideal or a utopia, but a legal requirement that characterizes Swedish legislation and the entire state administration. The Swedish constitution states that "courts and administrative authorities and other persons performing public administrative tasks shall in their activities take into account the equality of all before the law and observe objectivity and impartiality". The constitution stipulates that "the authority shall be objective and impartial in its activities".171 This is not negotiable. It is not a matter of taste. In fact, it is the foundation of our society. Political science professor Olof Petersson sums it up as follows:

> "Journalistic media that report and investigate are a prerequisite for the free formation of opinion, which, according to the constitution's portal charter, is a prerequisite for the Swedish national government. The judiciary and the administration are responsible for ensuring that public power is exercised in accordance with the law and that the equality of people is respected. Freedom of research is now constitutionally protected and means that research problems can be freely chosen, research methods can be freely developed and research results can be freely published. Objectivity and impartiality are prerequisites for media, administration and research, and thus for the open society of democracy."

This is also reflected in the formal requirements for the public service broadcasters. The broadcasting licenses for SVT, UR and SR state that the right to broadcast must be exercised impartially and objectively, "taking into account the fact that there must be broad freedom of expression and information in radio and television. Before broadcasting a program, [broadcasters] shall verify the factual information contained in the program as accurately as circumstances permit. The choice of subject matter and its presentation shall focus on what is relevant and essential".

A special oversight board with independent members, appointed by the government, oversees how the public service fulfills these requirements. I have been one of these members since 2020. The Review Board carries out various reviews of practice and finds that the "impartiality provision aims to prevent the broadcasters with the largest number of viewers and listeners from using their strong position to promote their own opinions on political or other controversial issues. The impartiality requirement applies to anchors, reporters and others who, by virtue of their position in a program, may be perceived as representatives of the broadcaster. The provision means that an anchor or reporter may not make evaluative statements or take a position on controversial issues."

These are demands and ideas with roots in ancient Greece, with threads to European philosophy and history, and with links across the Atlantic. The requirements and rules that follow are very much alive for public service radio and television, but also for the press, even if it does not have the same formal requirements as public service. But there is an interesting exception to this impartiality. It concerns the very foundations of democracy, and is stated in Chapter 5, Section 1 of the Radio and Television Act:

> "Anyone who broadcasts radio with a license from the Government shall ensure that the program activities as a whole are characterized by the basic ideas of the democratic system and the principle of the equality of all people and the freedom and dignity of the individual."

This is important, says Jesper Strömbäck, professor of journalism and communication at the University of Gothenburg:

> "Public service radio and television should not be impartial when it comes to democracy. They should not be impartial when it comes to the equality of all people. It should not be impartial when it comes to the equal right of all people to freedom and dignity. Given this, the news media should also not be impartial when it comes to, for example, racism, Islamophobia, misogyny, or funkophobia. Since all of this contradicts both the basic ideas of the democratic state and the principle of the equal value of all human beings, the news media have a moral and the broadcast media a legal obligation to take

a stand against racism, Islamophobia, misogyny and funkophobia."

This is important to remember at a time when the authoritarian right is making progress and keeping the current government in line, when the normalization of far-right ideas has already gone far, and when people are increasingly divided into "us and them". In such a situation, the broadcast media, including the public service, should not be impartial to the ideas and policies of the (right wing party Sweden Democrats) SD and, increasingly, of the government: to undermine democratic rights and freedoms, to differentiate between people on the basis of origin, and to discriminate against people on the basis of skin color, national and ethnic origin, linguistic or religious affiliation, and sexual orientation.

From this perspective, the problem is not that the media in general and the public service in particular are biased. Perhaps the problem is that they are not sufficiently biased in favor of the basic ideas of the democratic state and the principle of the equal value of all people.

The provisions of the democracy clause have not been reviewed by the Review Board very often. However, SVT has been condemned for not distancing itself quickly and clearly enough from undemocratic statements made by the Sweden Democrats. For example, it is contrary to the democracy clause to claim that "Muslims are not human beings," as a speaker at the SD party congress in 2017 claimed from the podium during the live broadcast of SVT Forum, without SVT's commentators on the scene distancing themselves until the next day. The review board ruled:

> "The politician's statement that Muslims are not fully human was clearly offensive to people of the Muslim faith. The statement was made in a speech at a party conference, which SVT broadcast and continuously commented on. As SVT did not, with the support of the democracy provision, address and respond to the statement in or in close connection with the broadcast, the program violated the provision on the special impact requirements of television."

Therefore, it is not possible to remain neutral in the face of threats to democracy and the equality of all people. The meaning of the Radio and Television Act will certainly have to be tested more often and more thoroughly. The issue of objectivity, impartiality and impartiality in the media is a long and complicated one, as political scientist Olof Petersson shows. He has written a fascinating and detailed biography of another political scientist, Jörgen Westerståhl, who came to dominate the debate on objectivity in the media in the 1960s and 1970s.

- As a citizen in a democracy, I want to be able to make up my own mind. I react strongly when the newscaster tries to impose his perspectives on me, Westerståhl wrote.

The debate about Swedish Radio was also fierce in the 1960s, and the conservative party chairman at the time, Yngve Holmberg, claimed that he had lost the 1968 election because the Social Democrats had been supported by the media, and that radio and television had one-sidedly favored the government. And during the Vietnam war, Swedish Radio was accused by both sides of the debate of presenting a biased and unfair picture.

In an attempt to respond to the criticism, then-director general Olof Rydbeck decided to commission a study to measure objectivity. The task went to Professor Jörgen Westerståhl in Gothenburg. It became an extensive and, over time, increasingly controversial project. Westerståhl examined not only the election campaign and Vietnam coverage, but also the coverage of the mining strike in Kiruna/Malmberget, a hostage drama, the revolution in Portugal and the Norwegian debate on Europe.

Westerståhl soon found himself on a collision course with several radio and television journalists, the radio director general and many academics. To assess the Vietnam coverage on Swedish Radio and Television, Westerståhl compared it to the coverage in the daily press, not to what actually happened in the war. Westerståhl's study became the basis for an acquittal by the then Rewiev Board on the grounds that the coverage on radio and television showed "largely good conformity with the average assessment in the eleven newspapers". This raised several questions and objections:

But what about the truth?

Was it not objective to report on the Song My massacre?

Is objectivity the same as an average of what is written in some major Swedish newspapers?

The measurements became discredited. In 1975, when Westerståhl attacked an individual journalist for reporting on the revolution in Portugal "with a bias in favor of the Communist Party and the revolutionary popular committees," Westerståhl was transformed into an actor rather than a researcher. The next radio director general, Otto Nordenskiöld, reacted strongly in the news departments defense and commissioned new investigations.

Westerståhl was scolded for being "too objective," his methods were rejected, and he was accused of ignoring facts and truth in favor of an artificial balance. Lars Furhoff, rector of the then Journalism Institute, which later became the School of Journalism, wrote that the goal of objectivity was "an unreasonable, even dangerous illusion. Instead, he wrote, journalism should be "an extra-parliamentary power factor" capable of presenting events and "creating new opinions" independently of the values of those in power. Westerståhl replied that "Furhoff's Marxist friends usually never report news that is unfavorable to their own side or the regime". Now Westerståhl was becoming more of a polemicist than a researcher and was also opposed by several philosophers at Stockholm University, who criticized him for ignoring the question of truth and being content to reduce objectivity to "non-partisanship".

The essential thing must surely be what is said, not how it is said, the critics argued, and mocked Westerståhl's content measurements. His basic claim of the right to make up one's own mind and not have someone else's perspective imposed on one, is both reasonable and sympathetic. But when he tried to quantify this in his measurements, his ambitions to achieve a generally useful objective analysis failed. Westerståhl's grand plans to measure not only the media but also educational materials and textbooks came to nothing.

The struggle over the concept of objectivity has continued for decades. The Institute for Media Studies describes this in one of its reports:

> "Journalism must be true. Otherwise, strictly
> speaking, it is not journalism. But how true
> should it be? And above all, who decides? In
> recent years, the accusations against the media of
> misrepresenting reality have increased in intensity.
> Is professionalized journalism, which strives for
> objectivity and impartiality, for truth and relevance,
> being rejected in favor of subjective narratives? Are
> we no longer convinced that it is possible to find a
> story about what has happened?"

The authors point out that "objective" is a term that many, especially younger journalists, now prefer to avoid:

> "The professional, impartial - or, if you like, objective
> - journalistic ideal is challenged here, because in
> the media where young people hang out, there is a

subjective ideal with strong feelings and opinions.
In many other circles, the idea of an independent,
truth-seeking newsroom is also being challenged."

Professor Bengt Johansson of media studies in Gothenburg
provides a thorough research overview in the anthology Media
Studies and notes that objectivity is elusive:

> "The question of journalistic objectivity is in many
> ways a perennial one. Even if the ideal of objectivity
> can be questioned, it will not disappear. The
> relationship of news to the social conditions that
> journalism claims to report on is central, both from
> a democratic and a power perspective. Journalism is
> not an invention; it pretends to report on something
> that has actually happened. But the fact that more
> and more people are realizing that journalism cannot
> reflect reality completely objectively does not mean
> that the question of news objectivity is obsolete. The
> effort to find out what actually happened and to try
> to give a full picture of events are still ideals worth
> striving for."

Objectivity and truth are elusive concepts. But the fact that
they are being challenged, not least by younger journalists, and
eroded in a polarized media climate on social media, makes it all
the more urgent, especially from the audience's perspective, to

make demands on news reporting. Evidence-based and verifiable descriptions of what happened, what are the facts, and the best available version of the truth are necessary for a democratic, public conversation to function.

The Royal Swedish Academy and Conspiratorial Power Projections

"If the women want to call themselves furies, goddesses of vengeance, most of them are megaras: the envious ... So cleverly manipulated by the major daily newspaper, which seems to have hatred for the Royal Academy, the ultimate target of the attack, in its DNA. Which openly boasts of its disgust for 'high culture'; for concepts such as difference and quality. Who here has seen the opportunity to reach through me, and especially through you, into the high assembly to break it up; perhaps to gain insight and power over it in the end. And is it now the long and unimaginative search of *Dagens Nyheter* for the phantom "man of culture" reach its goal? Will the man finally be singled out and hanged?!"

This is how former member of the Royal Swedish Academy Katarina Frostenson describes the events at the Academy in 2018. According to this reasoning, the newspaper *Dagens Nyheter* should not have exposed the poet Katarina Frostenson's husband (the "you" in the quote) as a sex offender because he is one, but to take revenge and damage the Academy. The reporters have a purpose, they are jealous and have an agenda. They are "megaras", "angry and nasty women" according to the Academy's own glossary. The author in her rallying cry, clearly articulates her thoughts about what has happened. She is not alone. Her colleague in the Academy author Horace Engdahl has the same idea:

> "What has happened is that a kind of pseudo-opinion
> has been whipped up by people in culture
> news department who compete with the Swedish
> Academy in terms of influence and prestige. They
> want to hurt us. Publicity is war, and we made a
> classic mistake. We were popular for a long time.
> We had it too good, and all experience shows that
> this is dangerous. You lose your readiness. You don't
> see the signs in the sky. You don't listen to the
> murmurs in the back. When the attack came, we were
> unprepared."

The notion of a conspiracy of hostile forces is elegantly conveyed by both veteran writers. Dagens Nyheters reporter Matilda

Gustavsson, who wrote the revealing article and then an acclaimed book about the whole affair, is a vengeful megara. The criticized academy members join a long line of historical power holders who have reacted to descriptions of their actions and interpreted them as mean-spirited attacks by hostile forces.

It is not about what happened, what is right or wrong, true or false, but about the supposed agenda of the messenger. It is all a conspiracy. We can call it the conspiratorial projection of power. Anyone who is subjected to scrutiny and criticism is unwittingly subjected to a hostile drive. The drive consists of a collection of malicious conspirators who are out to hurt and kill. What you have done becomes secondary. The fault here is the "hunting drive".

This is a fundamental mechanism of the power holder under scrutiny. Not even the highest-level military leadership, who should be trained to counteract hostile attacks, real attacks, is spared. In the early 2000s, a group of reporters from the Swedish newspaper Svenska Dagbladet investigated how the top military brass dealt with representation, overtime pay, taxis and travel between work and home. The Commander-in-Chief's wife had accompanied him on several trips, and senior generals did not follow their own approval rules and regulations for representation, travel and compensation. The criticism eventually came from the Defense Ministry's own internal audit. But while the audit was underway, the generals perceived the whole thing as an attack by some kind of foreign power. I recall several angry conversations I had with senior officers who saw themselves as victims of a hostile attack. The reporters were seen as having an agenda to get at the defense leadership. It was not the generals' own actions that were at fault, but the malicious reporters who were out to do harm.

The pattern repeats itself. As soon as the information doesn't fit, the messenger is accused of being on a personal or hostile mission. Consider the Indian prime minister's reaction to Ekot's revelation about Bofors: Rajiv Gandhi claimed that Ekot was "part of a conspiracy and had spread false allegations on behalf of the CIA to destabilize the Indian system and damage the regime".

During the 1976 election campaign in Sweden, I was a general assignment reporter at Ekot and had to add some more unusual features to the election coverage. The unpopular legal expert Carl Lidbom was Minister of Trade and was going to Dalarna on a campaign tour. I was asked to accompany him. We took a bumpy train to Ludvika, and during the trip Carl Lidbom tried to play down his importance in the campaign. He was just one of many campaigners, he said. When we finally arrived, not many social democrats in Dalarna knew who the distinguished guest was. In the evening there was a dinner with the local party committee in Ludvika, and I was invited. I placed the microphone on the middle of the table when Carl Lidbom ordered pâté with Cumberland sauce as a starter. The room echoes as a dozen steady workers repeat:

- Paté, paté with Cumberland sauce.

Carl Lidbom wonders if the lamb chops will be good, but then he sees another dish on the menu and wonders:

- Sole? Certainly not in lake Siljan ...

Everyone at the table orders fish like the trade minister. It must be sole, even if it was not caught in Siljan.

The next day, the journey takes them to the stubborn leather workers in Malung. Lidbom is asked a lot of worried questions about exports and competition, but no one dares to ask why the visitor is wearing a big, fancy French leather coat, instead of the ones produced in Malung. My radio report from Carl Lidbom's tour of Dalarna is not an immediate success for the top politician. But it makes good radio. An everyday report in the election campaign that captures the gap between an intellectual social democratic establishment in Stockholm and a down-to-earth voter base unaccustomed to expensive French leather coats and Cumberland sauce.

The Social Democrats lost their long hold on power in the election of 1976. This probably had little to do with my sound report from Carl Lidbom's campaigning in Dalarna. At least it did not dominate the political analysis of the historic election result. But Carl Lidbom himself was convinced that the piece had played a role. The following year we met in a completely different context, and a grumpy Carl Lidbom approached me and reminded me that we had met during his trip to Dalarna.

- I guess you got what you wanted, we lost the election!

I don't remember if I produced an answer. But I do remember how astonished I was that the former Minister of Trade could read such intentions into my report. He was also angry that I had "hidden a microphone in the flowers" during the dinner of sole and pâté. That's how he interpreted my open recording. And what did his clothing brands have to do with it?

During the 1994 elections, 20 years later, I was a political reporter and commentator for Aktuellt, the 9-o'clock TV news. A story about the formation of political factions in my old hometown of Uppsala fascinated me. *The Word of Life Church* had grown strong in and around Uppsala, and this rather extreme religious sect also had explicit political ambitions. Pastor Ulf Ekman traveled around the country praying to God for a miracle in the elections. "God will help the Christian Democrats to victory, and the Kingdom of Heaven will come closer," he proclaimed. Photographer Paolo Rodriguez and I filmed an election rally with prayer for party chairman Alf Svensson in Oskarshamn. There was something new and unusual about this request for direct divine intervention in a Swedish election. However, Alf Svensson's success in the general election was not based on prayers in the Pentecostal Church and other congregations, but on the party's defense of common human values based on "Judeo-Christian ethics". Opposition to abortion and prayers were downplayed in the official rhetoric. Alf Svensson presented himself as generally decent and not speaking in tongues. This *Word of life* connection was troublesome, but it still won votes.

In the spring of 1994, a few weeks before the nomination meetings for Parliament, County Council and Municipality, the Christian Democratic branch in Uppsala suddenly received several hundred new members from the community of Storvreta and the neighborhood around the Word of Life Church in eastern

Uppsala. In practice, it was a well-organized coup. On the eve of an important meeting, the local branch of a small party suddenly gained many times its previous membership. This was a unique and powerful influx of members. Now the balance of power in the previously small KD branch in Uppsala changed. New party members from the Word of Life church won a majority. How would they act at the nomination meeting?

Word of Life organized "strike-off meetings" in the church after services. The pastors went through the nomination lists and explained to the parishioners, who had now become party members, who to vote for and who to cross off. Most important was to vote for parishioner Mikael Oscarsson, chairman of the national organization *Yes to Life*, a militant anti-abortion organization.

The Word of Life is like a partisan faction within the KD. Using coup-like methods, they had seized power over a local branch and were now able to control the nominations. The church had provided leadership. The nomination meetings of political parties have always been open in Swedish politics, but the majority of the Uppsala branch decided when the crucial meeting started that the media should not be present. Paolo Rodriguez and I were forced to pack up our cameras and microphones. Pastor Ekman's candidates were seated during the closed meeting. Mikael Oscarsson was placed at the top of the parliamentary list and remained an MP for decades.

But during the factional fighting in Uppsala, party chairman Alf Svensson chose to remain silent about Word of Life. There may have been 25,000 votes at stake nationally. Then maybe you have to compromise a little with party discipline. The party leader even accepted that a popular and successful county councilor who was not part of the Word of Life was removed from power. Her protests went unheeded as the religious faction took control of the local government. But the party leadership's inaction was a choice, a conscious decision not to lose votes. I reported on the conflict, the strangulation, the coup and the transfer of power. The party leadership did not appreciate it.

On election night in 1994, I walked around the parliament building. The conservative government under prime minister Carl Bildt had lost power. Alf Svensson would have to give up his position as cabinet minister for development aid, and Inger Davidsson, the first deputy chairman of the Christian Democratic Party, had lost her position as minister for civil affairs. She was sitting on a sofa in the party's parliamentary office when I walked by. She looked at me angrily and, as I recall, used the same phrase that Carl Lidbom had used almost twenty years earlier:

- I guess you got what you wanted, we lost the election! she hissed. The same turn of phrase, similar wording. At the same time, a perfectly understandable human reaction to defeat. It is much easier to blame hostile external forces than your own actions.

Failure. The media are enemies.

But they can also be seen as friends when things are going well. Not even the Speaker of Parliament can always see clearly her own constitutional role and that of the media. Ingegerd Troedsson of the Conservative Party was Speaker from 1991 to 1994. Like many speakers before and since, she waged a fruitless battle against "unnecessary petitions" in the Riksdag. During the general petition period, MPs can propose just about anything. Many lesser-known MPs take the opportunity to introduce petitions, not to make a real difference, but to attract attention, if only at home in the local press. Thousands of parliamentary petitions are therefore submitted every year about things that Parliament should not decide, or has already decided, or which are generally not even real proposals.

It casts a shadow over the work of the parliament and leads to a lot of unnecessary bureaucracy and paperwork. I did a feature on this in Aktuellt and also interviewed the speaker. She was excited about the question and was happy to oblige. When the interview was over and I was leaving her lounge in the speaker's corridor, she suddenly hugged me and thanked me for "helping her in the fight against unnecessary petitions". Somewhat embarrassed, I tried to wriggle out of her grip and explain that I was not there to help her. I mumbled something about how I found the issue of all the weird petitions interesting in and of itself, regardless of who was fighting them.

The media does not have to be there to help or hinder. They can still report. In 1995 the candidate to become social democratic party chairman and thus prime minister, Mona Sahlin, was subjected to a "hunting drive". She had bought some Toblerone chocolate and was forced out of power, it was said. She became a media fixture for decades, with increasingly disturbing revelations about unpaid bills, piles of parking tickets, forged certificates, broken finances and a chaotic personal life. But wait a minute. Was Mona Sahlin ousted by the media? Was it really Toblerone that brought her down? A lot can be said about Mona Sahlin and the so-called Toblerone affair, but unlike many other political leaders, Mona Sahlin has not succumbed to the usual power projection of the media's mistakes and intentions. Mona Sahlin even rejects the whole hunting metaphor.

The truth is that Mona Sahlin had long abused the use of the government credit card and used it for private expenses for travel, car rentals, foreign vacations, food and clothing amounting to tens of thousands of kronor. The Ministry of Justice forced her to surrender the credit card, cut it up and demanded a refund. But the rhetorically skilled Mona Sahlin has managed to coin it the *Toblerone affair*. At a press conference, dressed in white, she herself "revealed" that she had found receipts for diapers and Toblerone, "even two Toblerone," which she had mistakenly paid for with the government's credit card. For this, she is now being hounded by the media and forced out of office.

What was a gross misuse of the government credit card turned into a trivial chocolate purchase in the blink of an eye. Very clever. But there was no hunting drive. Many people in power like to use this term to describe the work of journalists. Former Prime Minister Ingvar Carlsson, for example, often returns to the drive metaphor when describing his frustration with the media in his memoirs.

But what is a game hunting drive?

Wikipedia says:

The **game drive system** is a hunting strategy in which game are herded into confined or dangerous places where they can be more easily killed.

The Swedish National Encyclopedia's definition is clear:

There are two methods of hunting. One consists of a driving dog following the animal until the animal comes within range of the posted shooters. The other method involves drovers walking in a line (drive chain) and driving the animal toward a shooting chain.

Thus, whether dogs or drovers are used, it is a coordinated effort to kill wildlife. Hunting in this sense would be a clear violation of the principle of consequence neutrality. Moreover, such coordination between competing news organizations is not even possible. Would there be a secret editorial board in some basement planning the hunt and deciding which politicians to kill? The game drive metaphor is particularly misplaced in journalism.

Mona Sahlin herself has never claimed to have been subjected to a hunt. Instead, she uses the metaphor of being run over by a hundred small steamrollers all rolling down the same hill. Small rolling steamrollers are difficult to control or coordinate.

- I have always maintained that the reason I had to resign was primarily because of what I had done, what my own party thought, but also because of the media coverage, says Mona Sahlin. There is a big difference between saying that the media fired me. If you take up an issue and pursue it with the intention of changing, dismissing, pushing a certain position among politicians, I don't think journalism should do that in a democracy. And especially not when so many other institutions of democracy in Sweden today are being questioned in such a way. Who do people trust today, who do they believe in? If the public starts to doubt that what we hear and read in news journalism are not truths and facts, but opinions, and if they start to lose faith in the media, then that is very dangerous.

Mona Sahlin did not use the hunting metaphor, but instead used what is perhaps the most common trick of those in power to deal with criticism, the "pity me method". We were all made to feel sorry for the woman who had only bought two Toblerone. The media were mean, even if they weren't after her like hounds. This trick was also used by County Governor Sigvard Marjasin when he was caught cutting and pasting his expenditure receipts. It was used by financier Refaat El-Sayed when his false doctor's hat blew off and was introduced by former U.S. President Richard Nixon in the early 1950s.

Senator Richard Nixon was President Dwight Eisenhower's running mate in the 1952 election. But during the campaign, Richard Nixon was accused of receiving large illegal campaign contributions, and he was in deep trouble in the debate. Richard Nixon responded by giving one of the first live televised speeches in political history. It would come to be known as the "Checker

Speech". Nearly tearful, Nixon looked earnestly into the camera and promised to give a full account of his personal finances. He talked about the houses he owned and what they were mortgaged for. His wife Pat had to make do with a "respectable Republican cloth coat" and no mink coat. No, Nixon was unfairly attacked by communists, vicious liberals, and mean reporters. They had even accused him of accepting Checker, the little black-and-white cocker spaniel the children loved, given to them by a sympathizer. "But no matter what they say about it, we're goanna keep him," declared Nixon, the dog-loving father.

Fortunately for him, the checker method was born and Nixon became Vice President.

Some commentators during the Sahlin scandal pointed out the rhetorical similarity between Nixon's checker trick and Mona Sahlin's Toblerone number. But Sahlin was not immune. Now she was even more pitied. The nasty journalists were worse than ever, comparing her to one of the worst U.S. presidents ever.

- Did I bomb Hanoi? I heard Sahlin hiss back.

In the game hunting metaphor and the Checker methodology, journalists are made enemies of the criticized ruler. Even if the journalists themselves did not want or try to become enemies or actors with their own agendas, they are made so by the cunning politician. By accusing journalists of intending to kill or harm fact-based criticism is disarmed.

This may have been the strategy of former US President Donald Trump. By portraying the traditional media with increasing ferocity as the enemy of the people, Donald Trump managed to turn them at least into enemies of the president, and thus into actors, activists who do not deserve to be taken seriously or trusted. It's a diabolical plan that has partially succeeded. As more and more Americans lost faith in real news outlets, one of the foundations of social discourse was shattered. The hateful tone of Fox News reinforced a spiral in which media outlets built on a tradition of impartiality and objectivity became actors rather than reporters. CNN and MSNBC, as well as the New York Times and Washington Post, could be portrayed as Trump's opponents in their coverage, losing some of their credibility in the process.

"They're saying what they're saying not because it's true, but to get at Trump" became the narrative the alt-right could use. This was despite the fact that the two major newspapers, in particular, went to great lengths to defend their independence and the press tradition in which they were founded. According to this narrative, the New York Times revealed that Trump had evaded taxes not because it was news, but because it was out to get him. CNN, the Washington Post, and the New York Times are fake news outlets that lie because they have an agenda. All the accusations of collusion with Putin and Russia, all the criticism of abuse of power, lies and sexual assault did not bite Trump because they came from enemies of the people, not truth-seeking reporters.

When the media then correctly pointed out that the president was lying, he made them look like debaters again. It was precisely to avoid becoming actors, journalists avoided the word "lie" for several months after Trump's inauguration. It was considered too partisan. But as it became increasingly clear that what the president was saying was simply not true, that it did not correspond to reality, only then did news reporters switch to using the word lie. The Washington Post began its lie count, and the president's falsehoods were noted in the ongoing coverage. As the presidential election approached, Twitter and Facebook began raising red flags about the president's lies, and several television networks simply went off the air when Trump or his lawyers began lying about the election. Many of the president's statements were demonstrably untrue, inaccurate, exaggerated - outright lies. The press was no longer afraid to call a spade a spade, but it also made the media vulnerable to being portrayed as biased.

Then comes the next question. Should the media report and disseminate lies at all? Even when they come from the White House? This reinforces and spreads the lie. On the other hand, it is true that the president said what he said, and it would be difficult not to report what the head of state actually said. But if the media then corrects the president and points out that what he said is a lie, it gives him more room to portray the media as enemies out to get him. Basically, it becomes a no-win situation with a president who has abandoned all norms of political discourse in a functioning democracy. This is why it becomes so dangerous when the media lose their position as those who strive to present real news, verifiable facts, or the best available version of the truth.

Media that are allegedly driven by their own agenda risk losing credibility and thus becoming harmless to power. Megaras do not deserve to be taken seriously.

The cat who cost millions but saved billions

Andy Black is 23 years old in early 2007 when he begins to feel so ill and weak that he moves in with his mother in Plymouth. He lives in the attic of his childhood home, a small house by the sea. He is forced to give up his job as a broadcaster on the small Talk Sports radio station in Waterloo, London. He was a lively young man who loved nice clothes, Italian shoes, good music and a pleasant night out at the pub. Now he seems almost demented and increasingly forgetful. His mother, Christine Lord, is worried. Her beloved son has trouble keeping his balance and is losing weight. When he tries to walk across the floor, he staggers and collapses like a drunk. His body aches. "Mom," he says, "something is wrong. But I don't know what."

The doctor prescribes pills for depression, but Andy, or Andrew Lord, as he goes by without a stage name, is getting worse. He would rather stay home with his mother than go out to the pub. One evening in the spring of 2007, his mother watches a TV documentary about the mad cow disease. Confused, emaciated cows falling over and seeming to have lost their spark. Christine

Lord thinks Andrew is behaving like the mad cows. She demands new tests at the hospital. The doctors do a lumbar puncture and an MRI. The hospital in Southampton hospital keeps Andrew. He is absolutely terrified: "Mom, Mom, why am I here? Why can't I move? What's happening?"

In July 2007, Andrew Lord is diagnosed at Southampton Hospital. He has contracted the human variant of mad cow disease, variant Creutzfeldt-Jakob disease (CJD). Andrew faces a terrible and inevitable death. Doctors give him six months. He was not alone. As early as the mid-1990s, several British teenagers and young adults began experiencing personality changes, becoming aggressive, making terrible noises, and twisting their arms and legs. Doctors began to investigate and found that the young people were suffering from a form of senile dementia. More and more children and teenagers became ill and died. Suspicion grew that mad cow disease, or BSE, could be transmitted from animals to humans. Autopsies showed that the brains of the dead had the same damage as the mad cows.

But the authorities and the government continued to deny any link between BSE and humans. Only after the deaths of ten young people was the government forced to back down. On March 20, 1996, long after the first outbreak of mad cow disease, the British Minister of Health finally admitted to Parliament that the disease could be transmitted from animals to humans and that this was the likely explanation for the deaths of the young people. British meat was banned worldwide. But then it was time. The incubation period can be very long. Andrew Lord found this out another ten years later.

He is in his room in his mother's house. She tries to feed him, but soon he can't eat properly. He cannot walk, can barely move his arms and legs. He needs 24-hour care and is getting thinner and thinner. Mother Christina Lord watches over his bedside and borrows a video camera from the BBC to record his death struggle. The prions destroy his brain tissue, the brain dissolves from within. Andrew begins to regress into childhood, soon remembering only the nursery rhymes his mother sings to him. He loses more and more weight. The disease takes over part of his body. Soon he can't speak, can't even close his eyelids to sleep, and needs round-the-clock care. His stomach couldn't digest food, and Andrew wasted away. He died on the evening of December 16, 2007.

At least 226 people have died from the human variant of mad cow disease. Mostly in England, but also in France, Spain, Portugal, the Netherlands, Japan, Canada and the USA. Most of those who died had visited Britain at some point in the years 1980 -96, where they had eaten cheap sausages, plain burgers and meat pies made from the by-products of Britain's abattoirs and the grayish sludge known as mechanically recovered meat pulp, the scraps of slaughterhouse waste. In the UK, many children had ingested the dangerous meat products in fast food outlets, school lunches or baby food jars.

Mad cow disease is caused by diseased body parts from cattle, horses, fallen stock and slaughterhouse waste. Nerve or brain tissue from cows with BSE (bovine spongiform encephalopathy) can transmit the infection to humans. Those affected by the fatal human variant of Creutzfeldt-Jakob disease were on average 27 years old.

But before the suspicions about the disease were scientifically documented, agriculture, the food industry, and politicians did everything they could to deny the problem. Mad cow disease began to ravage the United Kingdom in 1990, and concern spread throughout the country. Television and newspapers were filled with images of emaciated, aggressive cows staggering and falling over. The price of meat plummeted and questions and concerns were directed at the government. British Agriculture Minister John Gummer called a press conference in a burger restaurant to reassure the public. Posing for the cameras, he ordered a burger for himself and one for his four-year-old daughter, Cordelia. Smiling, they ate their burgers in front of movie cameras and photo flashes. "There is no cause for concern, and I can honestly say that I will continue to eat meat, and my children will as well, because there is absolutely no cause for concern," said the agriculture minister 1990.

The Swedish radio-documentary *Mad Cow Disease* gives a shocking account of the course of events. The whole world was affected by mad cow disease. Except Sweden, because my cat, Bits, licked all the hair off her tail. When Bits became ill in the fall of 1985, Swedish Radio had just started Konsumentekot, (Consumer News) where I was producer and presenter. Bits got her name because she loved to step on the keyboard of my brand-new computer. But now she had started scratching and licking her tail, which was getting thinner and more snake-like. When the cat's stripped tail started to look really bad, I went to the vet. It was a small basement clinic in cramped quarters in the center of Stockholm, with a vet who was doing research at Ultuna, the agricultural University in Uppsala. He examined Bits carefully but had difficulty making a diagnosis.

- There's something wrong with the food, he muttered, explaining that he and his colleagues at Ultuna had long suspected that there was something harmful in industrially produced dog and cat food.

They had tried to investigate and test whether, for example, precipitation from the aluminum cans was getting into the food. But the scientists had never found any scientific evidence to support their suspicions. The vet's advice was that Bits should avoid industrial cat food and eat homemade food instead. Anyone who has a cat knows how difficult that is with these stubborn creatures of habit.

At the same time, Konsumentekot had begun to show that consumer issues were real news, about crooked banks, false marketing, deceived consumers, and bad food. Even consumer news could be on top of the news agenda. The new Konsumentekot editorial staff naturally read the trade press, including *Tidningen Supermarket*, a very well-informed and attractive magazine for the food trade. The magazine ran a big story about how Sweden was "maturing as a pet food country". Industrially produced dog and cat food accounted for 25-30% of what animals ate, and it was the fastest growing profit generator in grocery stores.

The industry hoped to double the levels to those in the U.S. or the U.K., where more than half of pets ate factory-produced food. The magazine reported on a large store where the shelves were converted to be filled with dog and cat food instead of diapers. The profit margin was over 30 percent, and total sales of pet food exceeded one billion Swedish crowns. It was this profitable food that the vet in the basement suspected had made Bits sick.

Here was the link between the cat food and my cat. It was written in tiny letters on the cans of cat food: feed fat and meat meal. This had to be investigated! With the help of freelance journalist Per Gulbrandsen, we began an investigation into animal meal. It quickly turned out that there was a lot of material on the subject at the University of Agriculture and in Uppsala. At Ultuna, we were advised to contact the local Agricultural Board in Uppsala. There was the real but long anonymous hero of the story, the agricultural adviser Anders Larsson. For years he had suspected that the "protein-enriched" feed (meat meal and feed fat) for cattle, horses and pigs was actually making the animals sick.

For a long time, Anders Larsson waged a lonely battle against cattle feed containing ground up carcasses. He informed the farmers in the region of Uppland, courted managers, scientist and the farmers' cooperative companies, but he found it difficult to get a hearing. He collected boxes of material and tried to warn the feed producers and get more research done. The critical agricultural consultant began to become dangerous as he challenged powerful forces in a profitable industry. PhD student Lena Molin has written a well-documented and fascinating dissertation on Anders Larsson as a dissident. She describes, for example, how the national farmers' union LRF tried to get its branches in Uppland to sign a petition against Anders Larsson and have him dismissed. This failed because he had the support of both his managers and individual farmers in Uppland. Lena Molin shows how the farmer-owned slaughter industry, authorities and ministries ignored the warnings for many years and silenced all suspicions about the harmfulness of the feed, long before Konsumentekot's revelations.

As late as 1982, the Agricultural Board in Uppsala wrote to the National Board of Agriculture requesting that it urgently investigate the risks of using animal raw materials as animal feed. The Board of Agriculture responded by commissioning the Swedish University of Agricultural Sciences (SLU) to study the raw materials from the Uppsala region.

In 1984, a research group of several leading professors and veterinarians at the Agricultural University SLU applied for research funding for this purpose. However, the application was rejected by the Swedish Agricultural Fund, where representatives of LRF had great influence. In practice, the owners of the carcass mills succeeded in stopping research into the possible harmfulness of the feed the year before the scandal broke. Until then, there had only been *suspicions* about the feed and problems with the actual handling of the carcasses. There were reports of problems with farmers dumping rotten cow carcasses in front of the plants and the "raw material" being shoveled into the carcass mills. Anders Larsson, who had long warned to deaf ears, was delighted when Konsumentekot contacted him in the fall of 1985. At first he wanted to remain anonymous, burned by the resistance of the farmers' cooperative. He gave us a heavy box with documentation on feed fat, meat meal and carcasses. The large box contained most of what was worth knowing, including reports of dogs and cats being discarded in the carcass mills. When we also heard about a circus elephant, our interest grew.

At the same time, several members of the editorial staff were skeptical that it could be so bad that dogs and cats were also being ground up. It was hard to believe it was possible, given what all the dog and cat owners would say. The result was that pets were unknowingly eating their fellow species. The reporters also wondered how the carcass mills could get their hands on these dogs and cats. It seemed unreasonable that a master or mistress would voluntarily take their pet to a cadaver mill, whose existence was also kept in the dark. However, if the carcass mills were receiving dogs and cats, they could conceivably be coming from a large animal hospital. The veterinarians might have to get rid of dogs and cats that did not survive and whose owners could not bury them in their yards.

Konsumentekot listed all the animal hospitals in the country, and the entire editorial staff started calling around. In the end, we found Halland Animal Hospital. Chief veterinarian Lars Gustafsson told us openly that his hospital was sending 5-10 dogs and cats a week to one of the carcass mills. The scandal was real.

Anders Larsson had warned the editors that the Slaughterhouse Association would try to hide what they were doing. Several reporters made simultaneous and surprising visits to some of the abattoirs. I myself went to the "conversion plant" in Stenstorp outside Skara. It was located in a nondescript old brick factory building with tall chimneys and signs indicating where the carcasses could be unloaded. As I stood in the parking lot preparing the recorder, a large truck rumbled into the area.

- I am coming with cadavers, the driver said into my microphone.

I knocked on the door and was greeted by a happy site manager, Tore Sund. He was not ashamed to show me, a curious observer, what was going on. It banged and rumbled as he showed me around and let me record what would be broadcast on Konsumentekot on December 3, 1985:

- Here we have the crusher. It crushes them completely. It's like ... it's in there, by the way, what's being crushed.

- A sticky mass then.

- Yeah.

- Does it smell bad in here?

- Well, that's because intestines and stuff like that don't smell so good, and there's a lot of dung in there. It contains some intestines and so on.

- But can this really be a good raw material for...?

- Apparently it is. There are many such mills in Sweden that do the same thing.

- What is the meat meal used for?

- Yes, it is used to feed animals on the farm. Both the fat and the meal.

- So that means the other animals, they eat the dead animals?

- Yes, that's right!

The report first broadcast on morning news broadcasts attracted enormous attention and anger. The big story was that dogs and cats were also ground down in the carcass grinders. Several listeners told us that they vomited while listening to the radio that morning. Others wondered what they had given their pets. A poor pensioner from the north called our telephone hotline and wondered what she herself had eaten. But the CEO of the slaughterhouse industry lied totally cheeky in the program and denied the very existence and function of the carcass grinders before he was forced to admit the facts.

The then Minister of Agriculture, Svante Lundkvist, was sitting in a government limousine on the way to Arlanda airport that morning. After hearing the news on the radio, he asked the driver to turn around and to go back to Stockholm and call a crisis meeting. That same afternoon, the Minister promised a ban on the operation. The feed producers immediately stopped adding the carcass meal to its products. With extraordinary speed, a new law banning cadaver meal was enacted in time for January 1, 1986. It was from now on forbidden to use material from self-dead or killed but not slaughtered animals in feed for anything other than fur animals or zoo animals. The ban also applied to processed products such as meat and bone meal and fats.

This quick ban created huge problems for the farming, slaughter and pet food industries. Dog and cat food manufacturers had to drive to the shops with trucks to bring back cans and packages that nobody wanted to buy anymore. Buried carcasses were destroying the groundwater on the island of Gotland. For Christmas, many people were reluctant to buy pork, and after New Year's Eve, unsold Christmas hams were thrown away for a pittance.

The whole cadaver ban, the change in farming practices, the change in the production of "enhanced feed" for cows and pigs, new raw materials for the dog and cat food industry and the huge loss of goodwill for the whole farming sector cost enormous amounts. Farmers now had to start paying for the destruction of dead animals. Costs skyrocketed for trade, farms, feed manufacturers and meat producers. It is difficult to calculate this, but it is not unreasonable to assume that the conversion amounted to hundreds of millions of kronor. The industry's anger towards me and my cat was great. For a while it felt as some angry big farmers and industry top brass would have preferred to see both me and my cat in some of the efficient cadaver mills.

The carcass ban caused problems a few years later when Sweden began negotiations for EU membership in the early 1990s. Sweden wanted to keep several national exemptions from what applied to other EU countries. It was perfectly understandable for the EU negotiators that Sweden demanded exemptions for snuff and the liquor monopoly, but they could not understand the cadaver issue. EU representatives questioned the Swedish ban on carcass handling and demanded scientific evidence. The Swedish argument was that Swedes thought that carcasses in animal food were "disgusting". The reference was a radio program a few years ago, but that was not a strong argument in a membership negotiation.

A national ban is still a ban and the Swedish negotiators stood their ground. Against all odds, Sweden got to keep the strange and unscientific cadaver ban when the country joined the EU. It had been a difficult negotiation and Sweden was initially granted only a three-year derogation. By December 31, 1997, Sweden must be able to scientifically demonstrate the harmfulness of cadaver feed.

But Sweden never had to provide evidence. Instead, they came from Great Britain after BSE broke out there in the early 1990s. The cows' nervous systems collapsed, the animals were unable to walk and fell in agony under their own weight. At the time, there was no scientific evidence that the disease could spread from animals to humans, as it would later do to Andrew Lord and hundreds of other young people. But by 1997 the world had been convinced, and in 2001 meat-and-bone meal from cadavers was banned throughout the EU, 15 years after the Swedish ban. The human and economic cost was enormous. The disaster was global and terrible, and not just human. Agriculture suffered enormously. In Britain alone, over 4 million cows were culled and destroyed. British meat was banned throughout Europe. "There is no disease that has generated such a massive regulatory framework, such incredibly high costs for surveillance, for abattoirs, for sampling, and for trade barriers between countries," said Professor Marianne Elvander many years later.

I have never found a proper calculation of the costs, but globally
it must be many billions in extraordinary costs to agriculture,
the meat and feed industries, trade and restaurants in countries
throughout Europe and the world affected by mad cow disease.
None of these consequences even occurred to Konsumentekot
when the report aired. For us the story was interesting enough, as
real news. That the various parts of the farming industry, mostly
owned by the farmers themselves through their cooperatives, grind
up dead cows and pigs, dogs and cats, and mix them into feed for
farm animals and pets is simply put, great news.

Britain could have avoided all this if the BBC had a more modern
switchboard. After the great attention in Sweden in December
1985, Ekot asked its London correspondent Kerstin Persdotter
to investigate the carcass mills in England. Were British dogs
and cats also being ground up? Kerstin contacted the BBC's
distinguished agricultural correspondent, who politely explained
that it was probably the same in Britain as in Sweden. The British
Isles also had large processing plants for slaughterhouse waste. But
the knowledgeable BBC correspondent explained that he could
not possibly be responsible for broadcasting such news. After
all, the English loved their dogs and cats, and they would be
outraged by a story about their pets being ground up in large
mills. Listeners would call the BBC switchboard, which could not
handle such pressure. It was an old telephone exchange and the
BBC's agricultural correspondent did not want to contribute to its
collapse. British dog and cat owners were not told, so only Sweden
escaped in horror.

My cat Bits had to start eating home-cooked cod and porridge, and Konsumentekot published its own recipe book for dog and cat food, with the listeners' own vet-checked tips on what to feed the animals. However, Bits never really recovered and died a few years later.

The farming industry finally realized that Sweden had benefited from the carcass ban, and Hans Jonsson, who was chairman of the National Farmers' Union in 1995-2001, invited me to a fancy lunch at his office to "thank me on behalf of the Swedish farmers". The wealthy farmers in south of Sweden gave me the award "The rose of Skånes farmers" in 2001.

In the spring of 2020, the Royal Swedish Academy of Agriculture and Forestry issued a study to remind us of what happened. With its booklet, the Academy wanted to "prevent collective forgetfulness from taking over and causing fatal mistakes to be repeated. Academy president Eva Pettersson wrote that when BSE was at its worst, it caused death and horror around the world:

The fact that society's collective memory is short when it comes to crises and disease outbreaks became particularly clear in the spring of 2020, when the coronavirus paralyzed large parts of the world and hospitals were on their knees. In Sweden, the health system was initially unprepared for the onslaught of patients needing intensive care, and our emergency stocks had long since been depleted. [...] Historically, after every major media event in the case of a communicable disease, there has been a noticeable silence in the press and social media. Society has all too quickly forgotten what we should have remembered - that there is always a risk of new disease outbreaks!

About the author

Erik Fichtelius is one of Sweden's most experienced and well renewed journalists. He has worked as a news reporter and publicist since the 1970s, mainly for the three public broadcasting companies. First as a reporter, producer and managing editor in national radio. He then moved to Swedish Television as a political correspondent and commentator on the news program Aktuellt. He initiated and ran SVT 24 Direkt, a Swedish version of C-SPAN. From 2009 to 2015, Erik Fichtelius was Director General of Swedish Educational Broadcasting, UR.

As an author, Fichtelius has written several non-fiction books, and the crime novel Venture Capital as well as a book about Historical Cats. He has published several text-books about journalism, i.e ,*What is News? and News journalism – ten golden rules* ,that has been translated to many languages like Russian, Arabic and Vietnamese. His acclaimed TV documentary about the Swedish Prime Minister Göran Persson (Chairman Persson) was broadcast in 2007 and the book Aldrig ensam - alltid ensam (Never alone – always alone) about the PM:s ten year in power, was published the same year.

Together with author Martin Widmark, he has written Scoopet, a series of adventure book about politics and journalism for 9-12-year-olds.

Erik Fichtelius has twice been awarded the Stora Journalistpriset,(Sweden's equivalent of the Pulitzer Price) in 1986 and 2007 as well as several other awards. In 1996 -97 he was visiting professor of journalism at Stockholm University, and in 2009 he received an honorary doctorate in media and communication studies at Mid Sweden University.

In 2015-201, Erik Fichtelius led the work to develop a new national library strategy on behalf of the Swedish Royal Library.

He has also served as chairman of the Publishers' Association and on the board of the Publicist Club, the Swedish section of Investigative Reporters and Editors, the Association of Parliamentary Journalists, the Swedish Radio Producers' Association, the TV Academy Club 100, and the Swedish Institute of International Affairs.

Today, Erik Fichtelius is an author and lecturer, and a member of the Oversight Board of Radio and Television.

Erik is married to journalist Ulrika Beck-Friis, director of the Swedish Media Institute. They have two daughters and live in Stockholm.

Notes

Introduction

- Erik Fichtelius, *What is news and 100 other very important questions*, Stockholm: Bokförlaget Langenskiöld, 2016.

- Erik Fichtelius, *Nyhetsjournalistik - Tio gyllene regler*, Stockholm: Utbildningsradion, 1yy7 and 2008.

- Yuval Noah Harari, *Sapiens - A Brief History of Humanity*, Stockholm: Natur & Kultur, 2015, pp. 30-32.

- Frances Williams, *Dangerous Estate - The Anatomy of Newspapers*, London: Readers Union, Longman, Green and Co, 1958, p. 8-9.

- Philip N. Howard, *Lie Machines: How to Save Democracy from Troll Armies, Deceitful Robots, Junk News Operations, and Political Operatives*, May 2020, Yale University Press.

- Ingrid Carlberg's book '*The Puppets*' captures the history

of lies, propaganda and manipulation, tracing the threads
from the Russian Revolution to the present day.
Norstedts 2023

- Erik Fichtelius, *Dagens Eko - nyheter i radio under 50 år*,
  Sveriges Radios förlag 1987

- Erik Fichtelius, "Behovet av den hänsynslöse och
  trolöse journalisten" in *Hålla huvudet kallt*, Bokförlaget
  Daidalos, 2023.

Mom, dinner and bribes

- Ingvar Carlsson, *Så tänkte jag - Politik & dramatik*,
  Stockholm: Hjalmarsson & Högberg Bokförlag, 2003.

- Jan Mosander, "Vapenhandlaren" in *Bland spioner,
  kommunister och vapenhandlare*, Stockholm: Fischer &
  Co, 2012, pp. 262-307.

- *Dagens Nyheter*, 1990-08-11; TT-AFP, 1990-08-10.

- *Fichtelius' name must no longer appear in the magazine!*

- *Upsala Nya Tidning*, 19969-10-16.

- Mikael Bergling, "IB hade informatörer på DN",
  Journalisten, 2003-01-14,

- "Troligt med fler informatörer", *Journalisten*,

2003-01-21,
journalisten.se/nyheter/troligt-med-fler-informatorer;
"TV-chefen skulle bli ny chef för IB", *Journalisten*,
2003-01-21, https://www.journalisten.
se/nyheter/tv-chefen-skulle-bli-ny-chef-ib; "Minst fyra
Säpo-agenter på SR", *Journalisten*, 2003-01-21,
fyra-sapo-agenter-pa-sr.

- Erik Fichtelius, *Apfällan - så använder jag min PC*,
  Stockholm: Carlsson Bokförlag, 1985.

- Martin Gelin and Karin Pettersson, *Internet är trasigt -
  Silicon Valley och demokratins kris*, Stockholm: Natur och
  Kultur, 2018.

- Fred Turner, *From Counterculture to Cyberculture*:
  Stewart Brand, the Whole Earth Network, and the Rise of
  Digital Utopianism, Chicago: The University of Chicago
  Press, 2006.

- Ingmar Karlsson, *Ett utrikes liv*, Lund: Historiska Media,
  2021

Do not help the dark forces

- Lasse Granestrand, I Sveriges väntrum - om pressade
  politiker, flyktingar och ett land i förvandling,
  Stockholm: Norstedts, 2007, p. 137.

- Ingvar Carlsson, DN Debatt, *Dagens Nyheter* 1yy6-01-16.

- *Dagens Nyheter*, 2000-04-06.

- *Dagens Nyheter*, 2003-03-31.

- Ola Nilsson interviewed in the TV series *Ten Golden Rules*, UR 1997.

- Review Board, decision SB 461/96 1996-11-25 Dnr: 32/96-20 et al, decision SB 462/96 1996-11-25 Dnr:33/96-30, decision SB 463/96 1996-11-25 Dnr: 37/96-24, 47/96-24, 77/96-24, 82/96-24, 86/96-24, 67/96-24, decision SB 480/96 1996-12-0y Dnr: 251/96-21 and 255/96-21.

- Kerstin Vinterhed, *Dagens Nyheter*, 1996-19-12.

- Johan Rosquist, *Morality in court. Investigations of honor-related violence in Sweden 1997-2017*, Gothenburg: University of Gothenburg, 2020.

The bitch got what she deserved

- BRÅ, Kriminalstatistik 2019 - Konstaterade fall av dödligt våld, Stockholm: Brottsförebyggande rådet, 2020.

- Linus Bylund, *Expressen,* 2020-04-16.

- Jan Scherman, "Straffa journalister som är bias", *Fokus,* 2020-02-27.

- Kersti Forsberg, "Hur hamnade vi här?", *Det nya normala - ett hot mot demokratin*, Kalmar: Medieinstitutet Fojo, 2021, https://fojo.se/ detnyanormala/.

- Carl Heath, "Näthat och falska påståenden ett allvarligt hot mot svensk demokrati", *Det nya normale - ett hot mot demokratin*, Kalmar: Medieinstitutet Fojo, 2021, https://fojo.se/detnyanormala/.

- Antje Jackelén, Twitter, 2021-04-05.

- Erik Fichtelius, 'What Homer has to teach us about migration policy', *Fokus,* 2019-08-29.

The art of burning a marijuana plant

- *Kamraterna*, April 1980.

Celebrities, facts, relevance and news

- Economic Museum, "Calculating the value of money", https://ekonomiska-museet.se/rakna-ut-penningvardet/.

- Johan Galtung and Mari Holmboe Ruge, 'The Structure of Foreign News: The Presentation of *the* Congo, Cuba and Cyprus Crises in Four Norwegian Newspapers',

Journal of Peace Research vol 2, no

* Håkan Hvitfelt, *På första sidan - En studie i
nyhetsvärdering,* Stockholm: Beredskapsnämnden för
Psykologiskt Försvar, 1985.

* Erik Fichtelius, *Nyhetsjournalistik - Tio gyllene regler,*
Stockholm: Utbildningsradion, 1997 and 2008.

* Erik Fichtelius, *What is news and 100 other
very important questions,* Stockholm: Bokförlaget
Langenskiöld, 2016.

* Alain Chanel, *Penser la formation des journalistes,*
Strasbourg, page 72: Université Robert Schuman, 1966.

Sham marriages and smuggling

* Eugeniusz Smolar, "The circle of hope: Samizdat,
Tamizdat and radio", *New Eastern Europe,* no 3-4, 2019,
https://neweasterneurope.
eu/2019/05/02/the-circle-of-hope-samizdat-tamizdat-
and-radio/.

* Polish Communist Party (PUWP), 'Polish Workers and
Party Leaders: A Confrontation (Transcript of Meeting
in Szczecin Shipyard 23 Jan. 1971)', *New Left Review,*
1/1y72: https://newleRreview.org/issues/
i72/articles/polish-communist-party-puwp-polish-

workers-and-party-leaders-a-confrontation-transcript-
of-meeting-in-szczecin-shipyard-23- jan-1971.pdf.

- Erik Fichtelius and Göran Skånsberg, "Szczecin in
  January 1971", Sveriges Radio P1, 1972-01-07.

- Ewa Wacowska, *Rewolta szczecińska i jej znaczenie*
  (The Szczecin Revolt and its Meaning), Paris: Institut
  Litteraire, 1971.

- Leslie Woodhead and Boleslaw Sulik, 'Three Days in
  Szczecin', Granada Television, 1976.

- Stig Fredrikson, *Alexanders kurir - Ett journalistliv
  i skuggan av det kalla kriget*, Stockholm: Carlsson
  Bokförlag, 2011.

Censorship - the antithesis of consequence neutrality

- Jane LeRwich Curry, *The Black Book of Polish Censorship*,
  New York: Random House, 1984, p. 67.

- Digital Public Library of America (dp.la).

- Robert Darnton, *Censors at Work*, New York: W.W.
  Norton & Company, 2014.

- BBC, "Jozsef Szajer: Hungary MEP quits allegedly fleeing
  gay orgy", 2020-12-01,

- Teresa Küchler, 'In Hungary, nobody knows about the politician's sex party', *Svenska Dagbladet*, 2020-12-04.

State-tv?

- Kerstin Brunnberg and Göran Elgemyr, *Dagens Eko - Nyheter i radio under 50 år*, Stockholm: Sveriges Radios förlag, 1987.

- Kurt Lindal, *Självcensur i stövelns skugga*, Stockholm: Carlsson Bokförlag, 1998.

- Eino Tubin, *Förfäras ej - 50 år med det psykologiska försvaret*, Stockholm: Styrelsen för psykologiskt försvar, 2003, p. 13.

- Olof Rydbeck, *I maktens närhet*, Stockholm: Bonniers, 1990.

- Oloph Hansson, Intresset ljuger aldrig - Striden om makten i och över Sveriges Radio, Stockholm: Ekerlids Förlag, 1998.

- Sveriges Radio, "Belarus bidrag stoppas från Eurovision Song Contest", Kulturnytt, 2021-03-11, https://sverigesradio.se/artikel/belarus-stoppas-fran-eurovision.

- press release, "EBU Executive Board agrees to suspension

of Belarus Member BTRC", 2021-05-28.

- Monika Djerf-Pierre and Lennart Weibull, *Spegla, granska, tolka*, Bokförlaget Prisma, Stockholm, 2001.

- Jörgen Cederberg and Roland Hjelte, *Tala till och tala med*, Bokförlaget Legenda, Stockholm, 1y84.

- Stig Hadenius, Kampen om monopolet - Sveriges radio och tv under 1900-talet, Bokförlaget Prisma, 1998.

Republican or Royalist?
- *Svenska Dagbladet*, 2020-08-05.

- *Svenska Dagbladet*, 2020-08-02 and -05; *Dagens Nyheter*, 2020-07-18 and -09.

- *Dagens Nyheter*, 2020-12-20.

- Omar Magnegård and Elisabeth Tarras-Wahlberg, *Mitt liv med Prins Bertil - Prinsessan Lilian berättar*, Stockholm: Ekerlids Förlag, 2000, p. 40.

- Jan Mosander, "Om prinsens hemliga väninna och Toivos tårar", *Bland spioner, kommunister och vapehandlare*, u.o.: Fischer & Co, 2012, p. 155ff.

- Erik Fichtelius, "Vad vore Almedalen idag utan direktsända parti-ledartal?", *Almedalen - Makt, magi och möten*, Lena Lid Falkman (ed.), Stockholm School of Economics Institute for Research, IR, 2018.

Shoot the journalist!

- National Assembly of the Socialist Republic of Vietnam Independence - Freedom - Happiness, Law No. 103/2016/QH13 Press Law.

A perfect double failure

- Arthur M. Schlesinger, *A Thousand Days - John F. Kennedy in the White House*, Greenwich: Fawcett Publications, 1965. p. 260.

- Peter Wyden, *Bay of Pigs - The Untold Story*, New York: Simon and Schuster, 1979, pp. 26-27.

- Karl E. Meyer and Tad Szulc, *The Cuban invasion - The chronicle of a disaster*, New York: Frederick A Praeger, 1962, p. 77.

- Victor Bernstein and Jesse Gordon:, *The Press and the Bay of Pigs*, The Columbia University Forum, 1967.

- David Halberstam, *The Powers That Be*, London: Chatto & Windus, 1969, pp. 446-448.

- Richard Reeves, *President Kennedy - Profile of Power*,

New York: Simon & Schuster, 1993, p. 83.

- Clifton Daniel, "Excerpts from Speech on Coverage of Bay of nigs Buildup", *New York Times,* 1966-06-02, p. 14: https://www.nytimes. com/1966/06/02/archives/excerpts-from-speech-on- coverage-of-bay-of- pigs-buildup.html.

- John F Kennedy Library, "Address: 'The president and the press,' Bureau of Advertising, American Newspaper publishers Association", 1961-04-29.

- Peter Kornbluh, *The Nation,* 2017-03-23.

- Howard Jones, *The Bay of Pigs*, Oxford University Press, 2008. Andrew Tully, *CIA, the Inside Story*, New York: William Morrow, 1962.

- Trumbull Higgins, The perfect failure: Kennedy, Eisenhower, and the CIA at the Bay of nigs, New York: Norton, 1986.

- John Stacks, Scotty, James B. Reston and The Rise and Fall of American Journalism, Little, New York: Brown and Company, 2003.

The local newspaper should have nice news and help its community

- Filip Struwe, "Nyhetschefen hoppade av i protest", SVT, 2014-04-29

- Sveriges Radio P4 Kristianstad, "Tidningen 'destruktiv enligt kommunalråd", 2014-03-26, https://sverigesradio.se/artikel/7821766.

- Dagens Nyheter, 2014-07-13.

- Sveriges Radio, "Midsommarspecial: Hela historien om konflikt på Norra Skåne", *Medierna*, 2014-06-22, https://sverigesradio.se/ avsnitt/386126.

- The Independent Press Group, https://gruppenforoberoendepress. wordpress.com/.

- Henrik Ibsen, *Nutidsdramer 1877-99*, Oslo: Gyldendal Norsk Forlag, 1992, p. 216.

- Linda Hedenljung, "Att granska ortens storhet", *Det nya normale*, Medieinstitutet Fojo, 2021, https://fojo.se/detnyanormala/.

- Linda Hedenljung: *Bluff, mygel och korruption. Så skapades det jämtländska fotbollsundret*, Modernista, 2022.

- America, "Losing the News", 2019-11-20, .

- Adam Danieli, "Så många är de kommunala

kommunikatörerna", *Smedjan*, 2020-08-16,
https://timbro.se/smedjan/sa-manga-ar-de-kommunala-kommunikatorerna/.

- Swedish Press, Radio and Television Authority, *Annual Report 2020*.

- Gunnar Nygren, "Bättre för det lokal - men ökad osäkerhet på sikt", *Mediestudiers årsbok* 2019/2020, p. 12,
https://mediestudier.se/publikationer/mediestudiers-arsbok-3/.

- Anders Brage and Helena Tell, "politiker tar makten över informationsflödet", *Bärgslagsbladet/Arboga Tidning*, 2020-10-09.

- Anders Brage, 'Maktens röst gör demokratin skenbar', *Bärgslagsbladet/Arboga Tidning*, 2020-10-09.

We are not in the shooting business

- Bob Woodward, *Rage*, New York: Simon & Schuster, 2020; Bob Woodward and Carl Bernstein, The *Secret Man - The Story of Watergate's Deep Throat*, Bonnier fakta, 2007;

- Bob Woodward and Carl Bernstein, *The Final Days*, Simon & Schuster, New York 1996;

- Carl Bernstein, *Chasing History - A kid in the newsroom*, Henry Holt and Company, New York 2022.

- *The quest for glory, gold and prizes*

- Spiegel legt Betrugsfall im eigenen Haus offen", *Der Spiegel*, 2018-12-19.

- *The secret cave in the forest, underwear and repressive tolerance*

- Dan Oaks and Sam Clark, "'What the f*** are you doing': Chaos over severed hands", les-shed-light-on-notorious-severed-hands-case/84y6674.

- ABC News, "The Afghan 7iles", 2016-06-11, news/2016-06-11/killings-of-unarmed-afghans-by-australian-special-forces/.

- Yan Zhuang and Thomas Sibbons-Neff, "Blood Lust and Demigods: Behind an Australian 7orce's Slaughter of Helpless Afghans", *New York Times*, November 18, 2020.

- SOU 2020:29.

- Uno Tubin, *Fear not - 50 years of psychological defense.* Stockholm: Board of Psychological Defense, 2003.

- Ulrika Häggroth, Sanningens soldater - en minnesbok om

Värnpliktsnytt 1971-2010, Stockholm: Värnpliktsnytt, 2011.

- Herbert Marcuse, "Repressive Tolerance", 1967: https://sites.evergreen. edu/arunchandra/wp-content/uploads/sites/397/2018/ 07/tolerance.pdf; Herbert Marcuse, *Critique of Pure Tolerance*, Brandeis University, 1967,9

- Jan Troell, *Judgment over dead man*, 2012.

- Kenne Fant, *Torgny Segerstedt - en levnadsskildring*, Stockholm: Bokförlaget Atlantis, 2006

- Vilhelm Moberg, *Morgon-Bladet*, 1977-02-23.

- Kurt Lindal, *Självcensur i stövelns skugga*, Stockholm: Carlsson Bokförlag, 1998, p.9-10.

- Erik Fichtelius, Article in the *Geneva Conventions 50 years*, Stockholm: Försvarsdepartementet, 1999

- *New York Times*, 2020-11-18.

- ABC News, "ABC journalist Dan Oakes will not be prosecuted over Afghan Files leak", 2020-10-17, dan-oakes-afghan-files-prosecution-decision/12661304.

- Sveriges Rikes lag (2018:1801)

The best available version of the truth

- Aristotle, "Metaphysics", quoted in Christer Sturmark and Douglas Hofstadter, *Konsten att tänka klar*, Stockholm: Fri Tanke, 2022.

- Timothy Snyder, 'The American abyss', *Dagens Nyheter*, 2021-01-13.

- NBC News, "Kellyanne Conway: Press Secretary Sean Spicer Save 'Alternative Facts'", *Meet the Press*, 2016-01-22, https://www.youtube.com/watch?v=VSr77DQg7c8.

- *Washington Post*, "Facts checker", politics/trump-claims-database/

- Åsa Wikforss, *Alternativa fakta - om kunskapen och dess fiender*, Stockholm: Fri Tanke, 2020

- Åsa Wikforss, Stockholm University, "170 sekunder om kunskapsresistens", 2019-02-22, der-om-kunskapsresistens-1.427896.

- Mats Ekström, "Vad är sanning i journalistiken?", *Sanning, förbannad lögn och journalistik*, Stockholm: Institute for Media Studies, 2020

- Bill Kovach and Tom Rosenstiel, *The Elements of*

Journalism, New York: Three Rivers Press, 2014, p. 98.

- Gunnar Myrdal, The *Objectivity Problem in Social Research.*Stockholm: Rabén & Sjögren, 1968, p. 11.

- Olof Petersson, 'Objectivity in media, administration and research: a political science perspective', *Ord och rätt - Festskrifl till Hans-Gunnar Axberger*, Visby: 2010,

- Ministry of Culture, "Tillstånd för Sveriges Television AB att sända TV och sökbar text-tv", Lu2019-02006, 2019-12-07, regeringen.se/4abd2c/contentassets/8c24422cf3ce4184 8af8d36a8y83638a/tillstand-for-sveriges-television-ab-at t-sanda-tv-och-sokbar-text-tv.pdf.

- SVT's broadcasting license § 13.

- Myndigheten för press, radio och tv, *Granskat och klar* - Granskningsnämndens *praxissamling*, Stockholm: Granskningsnämnden för radio och tv, 2013.

- Jesper Strömbäck: Medier måste vara partiska ibland, Borås tidning 23-09-11

- Olof Petersson, Statsvetaren: Jörgen Westerståhl och demokratins århundrade, Stockholm: SNS 7örlag, 2011.

- Jörgen Westerståhl, *Objektiv nyhetsförmedling*, Göteborg: Akademiförlaget, 1962, p.162f.

- Elin Gardeström and Lars Truedsson (eds.), *Sanning, förbannad lögn och journalistik*, Stockholm: Institute for Media Studies, 2020

- Bengt Johansson, "Den svårfångade objektiviteten - journalistiken, partiskheten och sakligheten", *Sanning, förbannad lögn och journalistik* Institute for Media Studies, 2020, p. 141ff.

The Royal Swedish Academy and conspiratorial projections of power

- Katarina Frostenson, *K*, Stockholm: Bokförlaget Polaris, 2019.

- Matilda Gustavsson, *Klubben*, Stockholm: Albert Bonniers Förlag, 2019, p. 187.

- Ingvar Carlsson, *Så tänkte jag - Politik & dramatik*, Stockholm: Hjalmarsson & Högberg Bokförlag, 2003.

- Mona Sahlin interviewed in the radio series *News journalism - ten golden rules* UR 1996:

- Richard Nixon, "Checkers Speech", Richard Nixon Foundation, 1972-09-23,

The cat that cost millions but saved billions

- Eva Pettersson, *Mad cow disease - Meat dung and cannibalism.* Stockholm: Kungliga Skogs- och lantbruksakademiens tidskrift, no 3/2020,

- Hugo Lavett, Galna Kosjukan P3 Dokumentär, 2019-03-31.

- Erik Fichtelius, *Historiska katter*, Stockholm: Bokförlaget Langenskiöld, 2018,

- Lena Molin, *Nyttiga bakterier och sjuka djur*, Stockholm University, Department of Economic History, 2007, pp. 230-232

- Lantbruksstyrelsens författningssamling, 1987:37.

- Stig Widell, "*Meat* and bone meal in the epicenter of the BS7 crisis", and Kajsa Hakulin, "The BS7 crisis 1996-2001 and how the European Union's TS7 legislation came about", *Mad cow disease Meat* meal and *cannibalism*, Stockholm: Kungliga Skogs- och lantbruksakademiens tidskrift nr 3, 2020.

- Hund och katt-kokboken, receptsamling från Konsumentekot, Stockholm: Sveriges Radios Förlag, 1986.

Thank You

- How exciting and important. We want this book. And we want it now! Christer Sturmark, CEO and publisher of *Fri Tanke* was enthusiastic from the start. This is exactly how every author wants to be treated when presenting an idea to a publisher. The journey from our first meeting to the finished book with an innovative publisher has been unusually enjoyable. It's been an exciting dialogue, not only with Christer, but also with Martina Stenström, Fri Tanke's publishing manager, about everything from individual changes to the meaning of each chapter and the color of the cover. Emanuel Holm, the editor, has handled my manuscript with both pleasure and surgical precision.

It was even more fun for me as an author when the publisher decided to publish the book in paperback. This gave the material a second chance, and I shortened, corrected, updated, and added. And now I hope a shortened and translated version can reach the world.

This book summarizes the experiences of a long professional life, and many friends, colleagues and professional contacts have given me strength and knowledge along the way.

My TV-colleague Elisabeth Stanczyk helped me to understand Poland with sharpness and drastic humor. My old student friend, the Polish democracy activist Gienek Smolar, has also provided invaluable, comprehensive and knowledgeable feedback. The once hopeless but later successful interpreter Bengt Samuelson has also guided and helped me. My radio colleague Jan Mosander double-checked what I wrote about Bofors and his adventures with the royals. Reporter Anders Thunberg had time to read and comment on the story of his report on the Assyrians in Södertälje before he died.

Professor Åsa Wikforss took the time to help me verify the truth, even though she was in the middle of finishing her own related new book, together with her brother Mårten, Therefore Democracy.

Kerstin Brunnberg, Hans Dahlgren, Linda Hedenljung, Allan Larsson, Kjell Lindström, Veronika Menjoun, Göran Persson, Annika Ström Melin, Staffan Sillén, Håkan Syrén, Ewa Thorslund and Berit Önell have also inspired, read and commented on important parts. The office of the Broadcasting Review Board has helped me to find relevant decisions.

Political science professor Olof Petersson has been an invaluable support, inspiration and teacher from beginning to end. Research methodology, headline writing, objectivity and psychological defense - nothing was foreign to Olof when he read my drafts.

Author Martin Widmark read, commented, and sat on my shoulder the whole time, yelling "think about design and drama!"

My best friend Claes Ljungh encouraged and growled as he read with his moral compass in his fist.

My wife Ulrika has tirelessly read and commented on draft after draft with skill and finesse, though she is probably tired of the Bay of Pigs. She has the ability to electrify my work and the text. Although it can be painful for me to hear that a text that is "perfectly clear" in my eyes still has "potential for improvement", there is a love in reading and improving.

The Swedish Media History Association is an important player in supporting research and study of the press and broadcast media, including the annual publication of the Media History Yearbook. The association has supported my work with one of their media history fellowships.

Many thanks to everyone who helped me get the hang of why we need journalism.

Erik

www.ingramcontent.com/pod-product-compliance
Lightning Source LLC
LaVergne TN
LVHW051058180726

843512LV00020B/1519